Advance Praise for

Green Restorations

Green Restorations is a truly excellent guide for anyone considering preserving and/or "greening" their existing home. It will be an invaluable resource to anyone involved in improving the long term viability of our nation's aging housing stock. Lubeck makes this potentially confusing subject straightforward and logical — an amazing accomplishment.

— Sarah Susanka, FAIA, architect
and author of *The Not So Big House* series and *The Not So Big Life*

Green Restorations should be on the bookshelves of at least four groups: owners of historic homes; contractors who work on historic homes; preservationists who need to be better able to explain energy conservation options to owners of historic properties and architects who are willing to learn from someone who actually hangs doors and installs flooring.

— Donovan Rypkema, Principal, PlaceEconomics
And author of *The Economics of Historic Preservation*

Green Restorations is an incredibly useful tool for helping owners of older homes get the energy-efficiency they want without sacrificing the historic character they love. It's been said that the most important piece of "green" technology is a caulking gun — but Lubeck's refreshingly straightforward book demonstrates that common sense and a commitment to sensitive stewardship are mighty important, too.

— Dwight Young, National Trust for Historic Preservation
And author of *Alternatives to Sprawl, Road Trips Through History,
Saving America's Treasures,* and the bestselling *Dear Mr. President,*
and the "Back Page" feature in *Preservation* magazine.

Green Restorations comes as an important new resource just now for owners, builders, designers and preservation advocates. It serves as a much-needed reminder, at a time when experimental new green buildings are getting disproportionate attention, that the first goal of sustainability is to care for the sustainable treasures we already have.

— Michael Mehaffy, Chair, USA Chapter International Network for
Traditional Building, Architecture and Urbanism (INTBAU)

With *Green Restorations*, Aaron Lubeck has stepped forward to provide a significant and much needed resource for the advancement of stewardship of the built environment. In a clear and straightforward manner, he gets right to the heart of the important matters to dispel the myths, misunderstandings, and misperceptions that often accompany historic house rehabilitation. I highly recommend *Green Restorations* to all those involved in the practice and advocacy of building rehabilitation as a means to achieving sustainability and, especially, to those unfamiliar with or even dismissive of the idea.

— Robert A. Young, PE, FAPT, LEED-AP,
author of *Historic Preservation Technology*

Green Restorations is a book you'll want to read first with a pen in hand. It's practical, practical, practical. Author Aaron Lubeck takes less of an encyclopedic approach to all options, and instead provides the reader with realistic choices based on his experience and wisdom as a contractor who must balance for his clients the emotional goals of green preservation as a cultural and environmental imperative. If you are thinking about restoring a house, or improving the efficiency of the house for environmental and financial reasons, this book is a must read.

— Todd Ballenger, CLA, NIFEd author of *Borrow Smart Retire Rich*

Truly a first of its kind, *Green Restorations* is a straightforward guide for anyone interested in historic homes with the green design choice in mind. Author Aaron Lubeck shares his firsthand experience while providing the compelling environmental argument for preservation. Our homes can be inspired and energy efficient, with renewable materials and smart energy use achieving a living example of sustainability in action.

— Quayle Hodek, CEO and Founder, Renewable Choice Energy

Lubeck is a matchmaker. The preservation and green movements should be kissing cousins not feuding Hatfields and McCoys. Clearly and concisely Aaron lays out a solid foundation for their relationship, mutual values, shared interests and physical attributes, then shows us how the world of design would benefit from their marriage.

— Gwyn Ronsick, Gwyn Ronsick Designs

Until Aaron Lubeck combined his extensive knowledge of and experience with historic and sustainable construction to produce *Green Restorations*, sustainable historic restoration was scary new territory and mostly "learn as you do". With Aaron's insightful, detail by detail, guidance within this encouraging/confidence building source book, everyone now becomes "experienced" and formidable projects become clear, step by step, and manageable. With *Green Restorations* help our efforts toward heritage preservation for a sustainable life style can now touch anyone's home.

— Eddie Belk, AIA/LEED AP, preservation architect / speaker

Aaron Lubeck has created a book that makes us smarter about how to preserve America's historic homes. *Green Restorations* demonstrates that green can (and should!) be a natural component of historic preservation. The detailed information contained in this book is invaluable in helping renovators make smart decisions that will ensure our historic homes will last for centuries longer, as the original architects and builders had hoped.

— Bob Kingery, Co-founder, Southern Energy Management

Green Restorations is the comprehensive guidebook for homeowners to make decisions about conserving energy and reducing their environmental impact. Aaron Lubeck draws on deeps stores of know how to help individuals improve aesthetics, save money and address today's pressing energy and climate challenges. The cleanest electron is the one never used at all.

— Kris Lotlikar, Co-founder, & Vice President Renewable Choice Energy

Never have two subjects been so compatible in their broad objectives of preserving what is beautiful in the world and making the most out of our valuable natural resources, but so hard to integrate in the particular. *Green Restorations* provides an excellent starting point for anyone wishing to bridge this woeful and unnecessary gap, and get started turning our most beloved architecture into our most sustainable.

— Stephen and Rebekah Hren, Authors of *The Carbon Free Home*

Aaron Lubeck sees 'the big picture.' Preservation of historic structures is vital for our collective memory and environmentally conscious construction techniques are vital for our planet. *Green Restorations* presents in very clear terms that these oft-conflicting positions are interdependent, and shows how for future generations we cannot have one without the other. This book for the first time puts it all together, marrying the theory and practices of both preservation and sustainability in a methodology that is technical enough to guide architects and contractors, and is easily accessible for the owner of a vintage home considering upgrades to whole house restorations. Finally!

— David Maurer, AIA, LEED-AP Maurer Architecture / TightLines Designs, Inc.

Green Restorations

SUSTAINABLE BUILDING AND HISTORIC HOMES

AARON LUBECK

NEW SOCIETY PUBLISHERS

Cataloging in Publication Data:

A catalog record for this publication is available from the National Library of Canada.

Cover design by Diane McIntosh.

Cover images: House: © iStock/Mark Tenniswood; Paintbrush: © iStock/Hugo Chang

Interior images: Photos © Aaron Lubeck or Trinity Design/Build by permission, except where noted
Illustrations © Aaron Lubeck or Trinity Design/Build by permission, except where noted

Printed in Canada.
First printing February 2010.

Paperback ISBN: 978-0-86571-640-7

Inquiries regarding requests to reprint all or part of *Green Restorations* should be addressed to New Society
Publishers at the address below.

To order directly from the publishers, please call toll-free (North America) 1-800-567-6772, or order online
at www.newsociety.com

Any other inquiries can be directed by mail to:

New Society Publishers
P.O. Box 189, Gabriola Island, BC V0R 1X0, Canada
(250) 247-9737

New Society Publishers' mission is to publish books that contribute in fundamental ways to building an
ecologically sustainable and just society, and to do so with the least possible impact on the environment,
in a manner that models this vision. We are committed to doing this not just through education, but
through action. This book is one step toward ending global deforestation and climate change. It is printed
on Forest Stewardship Council-certified acid-free paper that is **100% post-consumer recycled** (100% old
growth forest-free), processed chlorine free, and printed with vegetable-based, low-VOC inks, with covers
produced using FSC-certified stock. New Society also works to reduce its carbon footprint, and
purchases carbon offsets based on an annual audit to ensure a carbon neutral footprint. For further information, or to browse our full list of books and purchase securely, visit our website at: www.newsociety.com

NEW SOCIETY PUBLISHERS

FSC
Mixed Sources
www.fsc.org Cert no. SW-COC-000952
©1996 FSC

For Sally Lubeck, my mother,
who taught me that the trick in life is to figure out what you love to do,
then convince somebody to pay you to do it

Contents

Acknowledgments

My many thanks to all those past and present at Trinity Design/Build where I am grateful for all I have learned and am amazed at how much I continue to learn every day: Naomi Lipke, Heather Wagner, Ali Shoenfelt, Bob Harris, Ben Humphrey, John Elliot and Todd Hershberger. The dedicated environmentalist commitment of Jon Rucker, Alan Spruyt and Brandie Sweany always raise the bar to the highest standard. Thanks to Andrew Sprouse, ever the devoted preservationist. Particular thanks to Sara Davis Lachenman, who has inspired many a house to be saved and further amplified my love for old homes. I'm indebted to all past clients who've believed in the values of sustainability and old homes — and believed in myself and the experts I've surrounded myself with to get the job done right. Thanks to Preservation Durham and Preservation NC for their tireless efforts to preserve our built environment, and to Todd Ballenger, Michael Chandler, Barry Spiegelglass, Bob Kingery, Blair Kendall, Logan Kendall, Joe Lemanski, Coby Linton, Leslie Mason, Paul Toma, Randy Lanou, Ellen Cassilly, Dan Jewell and Izzaldin Mateen for random bits of professional inspiration and guidance. Thanks to Gary Kueber, Paul Toma, Bob Kingery, Larry Tilley, Jim Harris, Trent Boutz, K Brown, Matt Thompson, Sharon Wevill and Julie Solo for their excellent editorial input into the content of the book. Most of the drawings were developed by the hands of Brandie Sweany and Sara Davis Lachenman, two phenomenal designers who I have been blessed to work with at Trinity. I could not have brought the project to fruition if not for Sage Rountree, Betsy Nuse, Bob Kemp and New Society for their belief in me and experience in publishing. Finally, thanks to my wife Silver and two beautiful children who patiently put up with the long night hours of writing.

Aaron Lubeck
Durham, North Carolina

Foreword

by Donovan Rypkema,
author of *The Economics of Historic Preservation.*

Donovan Rypkema is principal of PlaceEconomics, a Washington, D.C.-based real estate and economic development consulting firm. The firm specializes in services to public and non-profit sector clients who are dealing with downtown and neighborhood commercial district revitalization and the reuse of historic structures. He is the author of The Economics of Historic Preservation: A Community Leader's Guide *and teaches a graduate course in preservation economics at the University of Pennsylvania.*

First things first — *sustainability* and *green buildings* are not synonyms. And yet cities around North America are racing each other to see who can adopt sustainability ordinances the fastest. But rarely are they about sustainability at all. They are about mandating solar panels, waterless toilets and backdraft dampers. The more enlightened might even require a bike rack or two, but the greatest emphasis is on green gizmos.

Sustainable development has three components — environmental responsibility, economic responsibility and social/cultural responsibility. The checklist approach of organizations such as the US Green Building Council and their LEED (Leadership in Energy and Environmental Design) certifications are measures of green buildings, NOT of sustainable development. To think that green building is all there is to sustainable development is like thinking that going to the dentist is all there is to health care — an important element but far from the whole picture.

Furthermore the green building approach focuses almost entirely on the annual energy use of a building, when, in fact, the energy expended to build the structure is 15 to 30 times the annual energy use. This is called *embodied energy* and is defined as the total expenditure of energy involved in the creation of the building and its constituent materials. None of the measurements of annual operating costs account for this embodied energy.

Windows are a great example. Some building materials salesperson peddles aluminum storm windows based on how much energy (and therefore money) will be saved if you install them. What the seller doesn't mention is that 30% of all those *lifetime warranty* windows are replaced within ten years. Nor is it mentioned that it takes 126 times as much energy to manufacture an aluminum window than repairing an existing wood window. Nor is it mentioned that only 10% of heat loss is through windows; the vast majority is through the roof and walls. Nor does the seller mention that adding just 3½ inches of cheap fiberglass insulation in the attic has three times the R factor impact as moving from the least energy efficient single pane window with no storm window to the most energy efficient window. Mike Jackson, FAIA, of the Illinois Historic Preservation Office puts it succinctly — "If it says, 'maintenance free' it means it can't be fixed." And yet, millions of homeowners are spending billions of dollars, thinking they are being both frugal and environmentally sensitive, tearing out existing windows and replacing them with aluminum storm windows. In fact, they are being neither.

All of which means that those of us who care, not just about so-called green buildings, but about comprehensive sustainable development have a ways to go in telling our story.

But that is beginning to happen. A handful of architectural firms around the country are specializing in how to combine their expertise in historic preservation with energy saving rehabilitation, many of these architects being LEED certified. A handful of planners and urban designers — Michael Mehaffy of the firm Tectics immediately comes to mind — have been thinking, writing and speaking about sustainability on this larger scale. This has lead to the creation of the International Network for Traditional Building Architecture and Urbanism (INTBAU).

For half a century after World War II we in North America were told that technology had all the answers on how to build both buildings and cities, and that the 3,000 year history of how good cities and good buildings were built was now irrelevant. Instead we ended up with crappy buildings and crappy cities. And importantly in the context of this book, cities and buildings that were not remotely sustainable. So INTBAU and a new generation of architects, planners and preservationists are being humble enough to look for lessons of history rather than approaching the built environment with the excessive arrogance of technology.

Which is the real danger of the green gizmo approach not only to comprehensive sustainable development, but even to green buildings. I'm certainly no Luddite, and technology can certainly be part of the sustainable development equation — just not its entirety.

The major national environmental groups are still focused myopically on the environmental component of sustainable development, ignoring the economic and social/cultural aspects. The Nature

Conservancy recently tore down a 100-year-old warehouse building in Indianapolis in order to build a LEED certified, suburbanesque green gizmo building. But trickling up from the bottom there are some environmental journalists — Lloyd Alter of the online publication *Treehugger* and Knute Berger of Crosscut.com for example — who are clearly making the connection between historic preservation and sustainable development.

So, however small at the moment their numbers, we now have architects, planners and journalists (and even a few local politicians) who understand that sustainable development is much more than green buildings, and that the checklist approach to gizmo green does not sufficiently recognize the environmental contribution of existing buildings, particularly historic ones.

Now to this small but growing advocacy and practice group we can add Aaron Lubeck. This is a vitally important addition. There are those of us who think and write about these issues. There are architects and planners who specify what should be done. But with Aaron, we get a guy who is actually doing it — who is reinstalling claw foot bathtubs, who is repairing existing windows to make them energy efficient, who recognizes what are the important characteristics that need to be maintained in a historic home and which can be appropriately modified.

The architect Carl Elefante is the one who coined the phrase, "The greenest building is the one that isn't torn down and hauled to the landfill." And he's right, of course. But that doesn't mean that historic buildings cannot or should not be improved in their energy efficiency. That is where this book makes a major contribution.

Green Restorations should be on the bookshelves of at least four groups: owners of historic homes; contractors who work on historic homes; preservationists who need to be better able to explain energy conservation options to owners of historic properties; and architects who are willing to learn from someone who actually hangs doors and installs flooring.

Every fifth grader learns that to save the environment we need to reduce, reuse and recycle. What does historic preservation do? Rehabilitation of historic buildings reduces the demand for land and new materials; reuses energy embodied in the existing materials, the labor, skills and the urban design principles of past generations and recycles the whole building. In fact, historic preservation is the ultimate in recycling.

Aaron's book teaches us all how to do that.

The standard international definition of *sustainable development* is: the ability to meet our own needs without prejudicing the ability of future generations to meet their own needs. The rehabilitation of historic houses does just that. The demolition of historic buildings is the polar opposite of sustainable development; once they are razed they cannot possibly be available to meet the needs of future generations.

But that isn't the only germane definition. Architect and urban designer Steve

Mouzon, founder of *The Original Green,* has identified the characteristics of sustainable buildings: lovable, durable, flexible and frugal. Aaron Lubeck's work in *Green Restorations* focuses on buildings that nearly always meet the *lovable* test — historic homes. He then identifies the ways to make sure that they remain durable and become flexible, with a constant eye toward the pocketbook — the frugality element of Mouzon's equation.

So go and buy a solar panel and a waterless toilet if it makes you feel good. But if you really want to be part of sustainable development rehabilitate an historic home. Aaron Lubeck will tell you how to do that.

Donovan Rypkema, Principal
PlaceEconomics
Washington, DC

Introduction

Buildings, too, are children of Earth and Sun.

— Frank Lloyd Wright, architect

I *bought an old house. I want to restore it in a green way.*

As a restoration contractor with an overwhelmingly academic clientele, I hear that a lot. The historic districts of my hometown are chock-full of homeowners who want to restore their houses employing values that honour both preservation and green principles.

I wrote this book to offer practical suggestions to both homeowners and their contractors. Whereas the balance of green building books focus on seldom-used methods like straw bale and rammed earth construction and others are little more than encyclopedias of every single green option (practical or not), I aim to emphasize core techniques and address questions consistently seen in practice today:

- Is sealing my old crawl space a good idea?
- My heating bills are massive, what should I do?
- Should I replace or restore my windows?

These decisions must be looked at from the green side and the preservation side, addressing the cultural, environmental and financial implications of each. With windows, for example, the energy efficiency comparison of historic windows versus modern, Low-e, double pane alternatives must be weighed against the embodied energy of replacements and general rehabilitation cost benefit. Since windows are so crucial to the preservation equation, there are specific solutions where original single pane glass can be retained for its character and historic value while the greater window assembly is upgraded to meet modern efficiency expectations. Other home features don't have an historic value per se, but are justifiable expenses in an old home rehabilitation and open the door to use *historic* incentives for *green* technology.

- Did you know that a high-end $6,000 solar hot water system is a qualifying historic rehabilitation expense that can almost immediately pay for itself through the use

1

of tax credits, and the only stipulation is that the roof panels must be out of view from the streetscape façade?

With historic tax credits there are specific guidelines and incentives that encourage window rehabilitation. And there may be local historic district restrictions or protective covenants that specifically exclude certain techniques, such as window and siding replacement. I have framed these debates in layperson's terms so homeowners who are looking to add only a few green features to their homes can make educated decisions with respect to each. We'll cover issues room by room, system by system. Given such organization, the hope is that the book will be useful for those considering a total restoration, or those little by little upgrading a kitchen or electrical system.

Green Restorations

- is the first guide for historic homeowners looking to undertake sustainable restorations.

- explains the massive financial incentive of historic tax credits.

- explains how to use historic financial incentives to pay for cutting edge green building systems and finishes.

In green building today, there is an extraordinary movement towards the mainstream. Where ten years ago green building might have been reserved for off-the-grid earth houses, today even publicly owned builders are promoting green features.

Preservation is also moving towards the mainstream, partly because of the expansion of tax credits in 1987 (and state expansions that followed) and partly because of the synergy and snowball effect created by the rebirth of urban corridors. As people move into the cities and restore old houses, more people feel comfortable moving back to the city to restore more houses. The real estate version of the *tipping point*, which accelerated flight from US cities to the suburbs in the 1960s and 1970s, now runs in reverse. As the flood gates open, neighborhoods are going from rough to desirable in an exceptionally short period of time. And governments in the US are fueling this movement by expanding local, state and national incentives.

Unfortunately, sometimes green building and preservation prescriptions are in conflict with each other, and where such conflicting information exist this book is structured to help readers make these tough judgment calls. Preservationists tend to view new techniques with skepticism, and green building (in practice and print) is entirely dominated by new construction. Green builders focus on new, high quality windows; preservationists require that you restore existing windows. Green builders love foam insulation because of its air sealing qualities; preservationists are skeptical because of its permanence. There's a natural suspicion between the leaders of the two movements. The suspicion is largely superfluous, because at the end of the day both movements have the common goal: *conservation.*

The book targets, metaphorically, my past, current and future clients. The book was largely written because of publication gaps indicated by former clients (one actually did a Google search on "Green + Restorations" and noted depressingly few hits). Remarkably few building professionals have taken the effort to understand, simultaneously, the green/preservation concepts at hand. On a publishing scale, similarly, there are books on green building as there are books on preservation, but there are no books that address both in chorus. For those undertaking a green restoration, this book aims to fill that void.

PART I: MOVEMENTS

SUSTAINABILITY

It all comes down to this simple fact: We can't build our way out of the global warming crisis. We have to conserve our way out. That means we have to make better, wiser use of what we've already built.

— Richard Moe, President,
National Trust for Historic Preservation

Sustainability is the pursuit of longevity. It's an object's ability to maintain. Things that don't last are not sustainable, things that do last are. The term sustainability is mostly used in the context of ecology, the study of life in a natural environment and humans' negative effect on the earth through climate change, urban sprawl and pollution. Without discounting any of these criteria, sustainability is a much broader concept than the sustenance of the earth. There are specific objects and systems worth saving for cultural, environmental, economic, historical and artistic reasons, too.

Old homes meet all such criteria. The rehabilitation of historic homes is a sustainable process because it saves existing material, demands less new material, does not require further sprawl, makes urban corridors denser, reduces commuting miles and creates more jobs for local tradespeople. Further, handcrafted homes offer personality unmatched by production building. For the patriot, the preservation of an old home is a front-row first-class seat in our country's historical record.

An old home evokes a spirit of stewardship consistent with environmentalism. The owner of an historic home serves as its steward in the same way that an environmentalist identifies with being a steward of the earth. The home was there before you were and will be there long after you are gone. An old home's permanence supercedes us. Such attitudes, love of community and urban participation are a crucial element of sustainability, and all are present in historic districts.

Questions to Ask

- What is sustainable about my house?
- What materials have proven long lasting?
- What materials are at the end of their useful life?
- What green building features are feasible in my home?
- How can I design my house for sustainable living?
- What are the least energy-efficient parts of my home?
- How is air quality in my home?
- Are environmental hazards present and active?
- What can I do now that will allow for easy remodeling by others in the future?

Quantifying and qualifying *sustainable building* is an inexact science. What one considers sustainable, another may consider wasteful. Recirculating hot water systems waste less water, at the expense of higher energy costs. Often best practice is in conflict with itself, forcing us into difficult and complex cost-benefit decisions. To assist in such decisions, various organizations have developed detailed green building guidelines and scoring systems. Academics consider ways to quantify intangibles such as environmental and social concerns through what has become known as the triple bottom line. Of course you can build sustainably without referring to any of these standards; they merely help to frame the debate and guide better decisions.

Criteria

Each scoring system has its pros and cons. The dominant scoring systems are the US National Association of Home Builders' (NAHB) Green Building, Green Globes and LEED-H. They have large overlaps in criteria and weighting. Each emphasizes energy efficiency more than other categories. Some, such as LEED-H, allow for more flexibility, a necessity in a country with diverse regions and construction budgets.

Notably, none of the scoring systems are designed for remodeling, let alone of historic homes. Since a remodel can range from painting a room to a $1million restoration, it has thusfar proven impossible to design a feasible scoring system that can cover all remodels. It is possible to apply new construction scorecards to old homes, though this tends to feel like forcing a square peg into a round hole. Because all the guidelines emphasize energy efficiency and tight building skins (aka envelopes), the only way to get a historic house to qualify is often through a gut job and major insulation retrofits. Sometimes this isn't possible or desirable, in which case, no green building scoring system is currently attainable.

Four themes run throughout each system.

1 Energy Efficiency

Energy efficiency addresses energy the home uses. The average home in the US spends $1,600 a year on energy: 12,800 kWh a year for electricity and 69,000 cubic feet of natural gas. Historic homes, with uninsulated leaky envelopes, will far exceed these numbers. Improvements include envelope tightening and energy efficiency gains through better appliances, lightbulbs and use of the sun. Scientist Amory Lovins argues that the US needs more *negawatts*, negating the need for additional power stations by committing to large energy efficiency gains and savings.

- Problems — Incandescent bulbs waste most energy as heat. Inefficient appliances and mechanical equipment are expensive to run. Utility rates can fluctuate. Poor daylight demands more artificial light.
- Solutions — Use energy-efficient fixtures, renewable energy sources and the sun for heat and light.
- Core Guideline — The US Environmental Protection Agency has systems for Home Energy Rating Systems (HERS) and Energy Star certification.

2 Indoor Air Quality

Indoor air quality (IAQ) addresses allergies, respiratory ailments and off-gassing chemicals. Air inside our homes is 20-30 times more polluted than outside air, and this becomes more of an issue in a tightly sealed home. According to AFM Safecoat, a manufacturer of eco-friendly paint, chemicals in building materials and fabrics have increased 500% since 1989. A healthy home requires fresh air intake, mechanical balancing and filtration. For years IAQ was dismissed as a non-factor; now, after energy efficiency, IAQ is cited as the most important feature of green homes.

- Problems — Formaldehyde, volatile organic compounds (VOCs) and other environmental hazards are widely present in old homes and modern materials. Tight houses with no filtration, fresh air intake or ventilation are prone to moisture and air quality problems.
- Solutions — Use formaldehyde-free, no-VOC products. Encapsulate materials that contribute to low-quality air. Remediate other environmental hazards. Omit carpeting. Add ventilation and moisture controls.
- Core Guideline — The American Society of Heating, Refrigerating and Air Conditioning Engineers (ASHRAE) outlines steps to improve IAQ in its technical standard 62.2.

3 Life Cycle Analysis

Life cycle analysis (LCA) addresses a home's cradle-to-grave impact through raw material acquisitions, manufacturing, construction, maintenance and operation, demolition and retirement — through reuse, recycling or complete disposal. Because of the difficulty in quantifying such impacts, LCA is largely qualitative and theoretical. Analysts debate how to (and whether to) calculate *cradle-to-grave* costs or cradle-to-gate costs, which address the more quantifiable and predictable costs of getting a building to the end consumer. Architect William McDonough's Cradle to Cradle philosophy, and subsequent 2002 book, originated from such life cycle analysis. McDonough argued that the typical end-of-life disposal step should be a recycling step instead.[1]

- Problems — Poor material longevity, non-local products, materials that are harmful to manufacture, concepts difficult to quantify.
- Solutions — Buy materials that have a proven track record of durability, like wood flooring. Buy locally. Buy materials that are rapidly renewable (such as bamboo) and avoid materials that are not (such as plastics). Use LCA criteria for discussion with suppliers and subcontractors.
- Core Guideline — Cradle to Cradle (birth to rebirth) concept and book by architect William McDonough.

What is Embodied Energy?

Embodied energy places value on resources that have already been spent, including material, labor and transport. In the sustainable stewardship of the environment, we must compare the costs of demolishing a structure or building new. Each home has material capital, labor capital, intellectual capital and transport energy embodied within it. By preserving a home, its energy is continually used. By demolishing (or by letting it sit vacant), that energy is lost. The Advisory Council on Historic Preservation estimates embodied energy per square foot of construction, tallying approximately 4 billion Btus of energy are embodied in a typical 2,500-square-foot home, the equivalent of 32,000 gallons of gasoline — 30 years' worth of fill-ups for the average commuter. And, further, demolishing such a home creates 200 tons of waste.

Fig. 1.1-3: *Though it's best to keep a home where it is, moving a home is preferable to total demolition. This home was moved a few miles, set on a new foundation and put back into service. A home saved is embodied energy saved.*

4 Resource Efficiency and Recycling

Resource efficiency and recycling address material sourcing and use. Materials should be rapidly renewable, and only necessary material should be used. Avoid overbuilding, as it can be a waste of material. Job site waste should be managed. The average 2,320-square-foot home generates between 3.5 and six tons of waste during construction, and gut jobs will create far more, as I discuss later. Consider how such waste is handled, and see what can be recycled. Water should come from fresh sources and be conserved wherever possible. Average per-person indoor daily use is 64 gallons, which can be reduced 30% through conservation.

- Problems — Water waste, high flow fixtures, leaks, hot water lag and standby heat loss. A project that lacks engineering demands more framing or concrete than is actually necessary. Project waste is difficult to recycle.
- Solutions — Repair leaks, use low flow fixtures, install a high quality hot water heater and place it near frequently used fixtures.
- Core Guideline — The US EPA WaterSense label certifies efficient water fixtures.

Green Building Scoring Systems

Green Globes is a Canadian bench mark that is licensed by the Green Building Initiative in the United States. The system does have an existing buildings guideline for remodeling. It is still largely written for commercial projects and has limited use for residential remodeling.

The United States Green Building Council (USGBC)

USGBC is a nonprofit, nongovernmental organization that creates and coordinates a national effort of providing sustainable building tools and bench marks to the public. It is best known for its LEED (Leaders in Energy and Environmental Design) program and annual Greenbuild tradeshow. It aims to significantly alter the way buildings are designed, built, operated and maintained. Founded in 1993, USGBC now claims over 15,000 member organizations. As of 2009, there are over 14,000 LEED-certified projects worldwide, with many states in the US doubling their number of LEED projects every single year. LEED-H for residential housing is a rating system launched in 2008. After much debate and discussion LEED v3 was launched in 2009, for the first time including additional credits for historic rehabilitation.

Points	Category
11	Innovation and Design
10	Locations and Linkages
22	Sustainable Sites
15	Water Efficiency
38	Energy and Atmosphere
16	Materials and Resources
21	Indoor Environmental Quality
3	Awareness and Education
136	Total Possible

Fig. 1.4: *LEED-H Point System.*

LEED-H, aka LEED for Homes, is the USGBC's certification program for residential housing. LEED has dominated the commercial market, standing as the lone scoring system for commercial green building. LEED-H uses a 136 point scale covering eight categories: 45 points gets your house certified, 60 points equals silver status, 75 points equals gold status and 90 points equals platinum status.

Eight categories are evaluated.

- Innovation and Design integrates the construction team and tradespeople in the design process to address items such as durability and solar siting.
- Locations and Linkages requires a socially and environmentally sensitive construction site.
- Sustainable Sites requires the minimal environmental footprint during construction.
- Water Efficiency requires water conservation for indoor plumbing and outdoor landscaping.
- Energy and Atmosphere requires a tight envelope and high quality systems.
- Materials and Resources requires efficient use of materials and selection of environmentally superior products.
- Indoor Environmental Quality measures and documents HVAC systems and filtrations, installation methods and ductwork to ensure high quality indoor air.
- Awareness and Education requires that a homeowner's manual be drafted to cover operation and scheduled maintenance of the home.

Though USGBC's target cost for building a LEED-H home is less than $1,000, the documentation and third-party verification process has proven laborious and thus costly — sometimes exceeding $5,000 per house. Production builders get some slack. Custom builders do not, and by its very nature all remodeling is custom. High costs have forced LEED up-market where homeowners can afford certification. Currently, the program does not address remodels, and though it's bound to happen eventually. I know of no attempts to certify an historic home. Due to the USGBC's clout and the widespread knowledge of its commercial brand, most experts think that LEED-H will eventually shake out as the dominant residential certification program.

REGREEN is a remodeling program created by USGBC. It is an excellent resource with ten specific case studies, organized by room.[2]

NAHB's *Green Building Guidelines* are an excellent source of basic green building principles. It scores seven sections.

Point totals achieve bronze, silver or gold status. The scoring system is flawed for remodeling, but the information is presented in an extremely easy format to understand. As a great self-auditing exercise, you can score yourself without using third-party verification (though an unbiased third party would be required if you want to achieve actual certification). Many local NAHB chapters have altered the system for a localized designation, a practice the NAHB encourages.[3]

Energy Star is a certification that requires a home to meet strict guidelines set by the

Section	Description	Bronze	Silver	Gold
1	Lot Design, Preparation and Development	8	10	12
2	Resource Efficiency	44	60	77
3	Energy Efficiency	37	62	100
4	Water Efficiency	6	13	19
5	Indoor Environmental Quality	32	54	72
6	Operation, Maintenance and Homeowner Education	7	7	9
7	Global Impact (points incorporated in other sections)	3	5	6
	Additional Points from Sections of your Choice	100	100	100
	Total	**237**	**311**	**395**

Fig. 1.5:
NAHB Green Building Guidelines

US Environmental Protection Agency. An Energy Star home is typically 20-30% more efficient than the basic building code. Achieving Energy Star involves detailed computer analysis, identification of the most cost-effective ways to improve energy efficiency and third party verification of sustainable building construction. The analysis considers heating, cooling, water heating, lighting, appliances and on-site power generation. Many utilities have discount programs for Energy Star certified homes; Duke Energy offers 5% electricity discount, for example. The program is really designed for new construction, but can certainly be retrofitted to fit old homes during a gut job. Certification costs $600-1,000 - money well spent to ensure an efficient house.

A Home Energy Rating Score (HERS) is a 0 to 100 scale measuring energy efficiency, using the 2006 International Energy Code as a baseline. The lower the score the more energy-efficient the home is. A home built to the minimum standards outlined in the IEC scores 100, while a net zero energy home scores a 0. Each point deduction is equivalent to a 1% energy consumption reduction. A home with a HERS index of 70 is 30% more efficient than one built to a minimum building code. A HERS index rating of 80 or lower is required for Energy Star certification.

Alex Wilson of Building Green argued that US secondary mortgage buyers should include HERS ratings in their future underwriting criteria.

A performance-based focus could also apply to mortgage subsidies and loan guarantees — perhaps using the home-energy rating system (HERS). … If the secondary mortgage market required a HERS index of 25 for new homes and 50 for existing homes, we would see a dramatic ramping up of energy performance.[4]

No final mandate has come out of the suggestion, but if Fannie Mae and Freddie

Mac bought into such a system, it would effectively become mandatory to build and remodel energy-efficient homes. There would be an immediate nationwide impact in building efficiency. Boulder, Colorado's admirably strict approach to building now require that all new construction, additions and major remodels achieve minimum HERS ratings, including a sliding scale that forces larger homes to be more efficient than smaller ones. Other governments are sure to follow suit.

The Triple Bottom Line, and How American Homeowners Blew It

Have you ever told a contractor

- Price looks great, but how does this effect my environmental footprint?
- We'll do it, but will your work be relevant 100 years from now?
- Your costs are totally reasonable, but what will this project do for the community?

These are legitimate questions that we should be asking, so why do these statements seem so ridiculous? Americans have been so indoctrinated to look at monetary costs — and only monetary costs — that we rarely consider the other costs of our decisions. On a consumer scale, nowhere is this error more grave and consequential than in our homes.

Sustainable Forestry = Sustainable Wood

Residential housing is primarily made from wood. The average US house in 1950 was 983 square feet, and size rose steadily until 2007. 2008 was the first year on record in which average house size declined. To build the current average (2,424 square foot) US home it takes about 33,000 board feet of lumber (1 inch thick, 12x12 inches) — that's roughly 121 trees.

Lumber is used for framing, window and door construction, trim, cabinets, flooring and in old homes, plaster lath. Lumber is increasingly sourced from Canadian forests, while trim work is sourced locally and abroad. Many exotic woods used for flooring, trim and cabinetry come from South America. How wood is timbered is the focus of much environmental concern and subsequent certification.

FSC-certified products earn the Forest Stewardship Council's stamp of approval for sustainable timbering.

An FSC-certified product is the leading bench mark for green lumber. The production logging industry primarily certifies under the SFI (Sustainable Forest Initiative) label, which FSC advocates argue is a weak stamp created by the logging lobby. The Alliance for Credible Forest Certification argues that the FSC board is fully independent, unattached to the lumber industry. They argue FSC has more stringent environmental and community protection standards, better monitoring of chain-of-custody and a consistent link between a label's claim and certified forests. So while pro-SFI documentation exists, few argue that it is a superior certification to FSC products. You are more likely to find FSC-certified products at green building specialty supply stores and SFI products at big box chains and builder supply outlets.

The Triple Bottom Line (3BL) looks beyond traditional economic and financial analysis, requiring that decisions also address social and environmental criteria. It is sometimes referred to as *People, Planet, Profit*. Where these three forces intersect, we maximize the sustainability of our actions. The triple bottom line was originally created to analyze corporations' social responsibility. Why has it not been applied to individuals? Why has it not been applied to housing?

Housing is, by far, the number one expense most US citizens incur. Almost 70% of Americans are homeowners, and the country's housing is worth over $10 trillion. In 2006, over $176 billion was invested remodeling homes and over $600 billion building new ones. Both figures are record high numbers. Little attention has been given to the other costs that come with all this construction.

Nowhere do Americans affect the environment more than in their housing decisions. Nowhere do Americans affect their community more than in their housing decisions.

Economic Decisions (Profit)

The economic component of the triple bottom line deals with easily quantifiable money. In traditional accounting, there is a single bottom line. On a profit-and-loss statement the bottom line indicates income, and on a balance sheet that line indicates worth. Traditionally, homebuyers consider *only* the purchase price of their home. Sustainable economic considerations imply

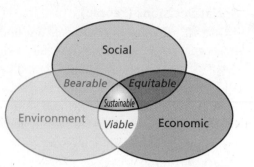

Fig. 1.6:
The Triple Bottom Line

we look at purchase costs and operating costs.

Owners (including landlords) fail to realize that a poorly designed or maintained home will yield higher utility expenses, higher maintenance expenses and additional deferred maintenance down the road. Call it the all-you-can-eat buffet syndrome: get as much as you can, pay as little as you can, with little acknowledgment of long-term costs. With this attitude immediacy triumphs over longevity.

Environmental Decisions (Planet)

There are certainly segments of the population that are starting to factor environmental concerns into their home. Still, nearly all green building is new construction, and new construction is almost always green-field development, on virgin land, with an emphasis on privacy over camaraderie. While these new homes may be beautiful engineering marvels, their rural locations separate occupants from the community, requiring roads and utility expansion, requiring new materials and transport. They fail to be equitable.

Social Decisions (People)

Social construction aims to create housing that allows for the interaction between families and businesses. Homes should be relatively close together, communities should be walkable, of mixed incomes and ethnicities. Neighborhoods that fail these criteria are private, unmixed, difficult to access and detached from society.

So we're left with an abundance of cheap homes that offer little emotional attachment to their owner. These are the kinds of structures people easily walk away from. Architects, builders, realtors and homeowners are all guilty of creating this problem. For too long, we've emphasized quantity over quality. We prefer huge new homes in sprawling suburbs rather than existing homes in established urban corridors. For the triple bottom line to succeed, this attitude has to be reversed.

What Can we Do?

First, we need to recognize that we are operating within a flawed system. We buy because the dollar-per-square foot equation looks right: 3,000 square feet at $100 per square foot sounds great! Who inquires about HVAC efficiency, third party energy testing or insulation? We should.

Ultimately, the triple bottom line has been adopted by individuals and will be carried out by individuals. Consumers can always shop locally or buy a hybrid car, but nowhere will they have such dramatic effect on their wallet, their community and the environment than with their home.

The easiest way to accomplish the triple bottom line is to rehabilitate an old home with these principles in mind. An old home is part of a community. It requires few additional materials, no further infrastructure expansion and contributes to a legacy of sustainability over consumerism. The mere purchase of a historic home often meets the criteria of the triple bottom line. We can further enhance these principles through the sustainable rehabilitation and operation of an old home, concepts explained in this book.

PRESERVATION

Historic buildings are the physical manifestation of memory — it is memory that makes places significant. The whole purpose of sustainable development is to keep that which is important, which is valuable, which is significant.

— Donovan Rypkema,
"Economics, Sustainability, and Historic Preservation"

Preservation is the movement that seeks to preserve, conserve and protect buildings, neighborhoods and/or other items of historic significance. The US movement, which is unique in many ways, has for two centuries saved many great buildings and encouraged rehabilitation and reuse of many others. But, as movements go, it's always been a bit of a red-headed stepchild, never becoming a household term, topic of conversation or embraced by the country as a whole. Preservation has never received the attention of the environmentalist movement, an effort with which it is inherently linked. Stewart Brand, in his excellent book *How Buildings Learn*, argued that the movement effectively grew up in the 1970s and 1980s to reverse all the bad development, demolition and ugly structures of the

1950s and 1960s. But he noted an important accolade preservation never achieved — recognition.

> Why wasn't it noticed in the media? … Preservation was one of the swiftest, most complete cultural revolutions ever, yet because it happened everywhere at once, without controversy or charismatic leadership, it never got the headlines of its younger sibling the environmental movement.[1]

In many ways, preservation is one of the US's greatest achievements that few know about, and its mass following is a fraction of the numbers who identify with sustainability and environmentalism. Dr. Robert E. Stipe, in his also excellent primer on preservation, *A Richer Heritage*, stated:

17

The problem now is to acknowledge that historic preservation is but one aspect of a much larger problem, basically an environmental one, of enhancing, or perhaps providing for the first time, a better quality of life for people. Basically [preservation] is the saving of people and lives and cities — not just buildings — that is important to all of us. We have before us an unparalleled opportunity, if we are determined, to contribute significantly to upgrading the quality of human existence.[2]

The link between saving buildings and saving the environment is not new. The idea that preservation is the *ultimate recycling* originated more than three decades ago. National Trust President Richard Moe reminded us that "as long ago as 1980, before the word 'sustainability' came into widespread use, the National Trust issued a Preservation Week poster that featured an old building in the shape of a gas can — a reminder that reusing an existing building, instead of demolishing it and replacing it with a new one, is one good way to conserve energy."[3]

Preservation is all about sustainability. In more ways than not, they're one and the same. Moreover, preservation offers cultural and economic benefits that environmentalism, by its nature, cannot. Culture and economics are associated with people, as is the built environment. The creation of a national park has many merits, but it cannot offer the cultural benefits of, say, rebuilding an abandoned tobacco mill into office space. Nor can the shutting of a coal plant have as positive an economic impact as a revitalized central business district. In each example the preservation achievement offers notable environmental gains. Adaptively reused mills demand less material and build on existing infrastructure. Revitalized cities and their work spaces require people to commute less and walk more. In these examples it is preservation driving environmentalism, not the other way around. What an often overlooked fact.

Why is Preservation Important?

Preservation is interconnected with national interests in five ways.

First, preservation has a fundamental link with sustainability. Merely choosing an old home over a new one is a huge step towards sustainable ends. The triple bottom line forces us to review social and environmental factors of our financial decisions. Through the rejuvenation of old cities and the lowering of material, waste and transport demands, the rehabilitation of an historic home is one of a select few commitments that positively affect all three bottom lines.

Second, preservation offers immense economic and national security benefits. Cities are efficient. And, as an added bonus, they already exist. Infrastructure is there, buildings are there, transport is there. Contrarily, our society is now dominated by suburban development built on the assumption of inexhaustible one-dollar-a-gallon gasoline. Economists have nearly universally concluded that such days are over. Dense development requires less gasoline and less dependence on unpredictable foreign sources of energy.

Third, preservation offers a vessel for education by protecting the built environment of the nation's history. The ability to see and touch such space helps children understand how their forebears lived and how they came to be. Old buildings serve as a physical link to bridge the gaps between the past, present and the future. Their evolution represents and encourages each generation to incorporate new ideas and technologies while honoring the traditions on which American society is built. The honoring of a building's past gives us a sense of place.

Fourth, preservation offers an unmatched quality of life. It embraces peculiarity and uniqueness in contrast to suburban monotony and uniformity. The culture and art of old houses is unmatched by new houses. Craftsmanship allows us to fall in love with a home. Where high society has always craved distinctiveness, now the middle class is fueling a wider preservation movement. And the movement has strong youth roots, too. Generations X and Y, lauded for their individuality and rebellion against their bland suburban upbringings, are the newest rehabbers.

Lastly, preservation honors value. Value allows us to appreciate the home as a place to live and raise a family, not strictly to make an investment. This is a newsworthy point, given the recent housing bubble that was driven by the failed overuse of homes as investment vehicles. In a rejection of today's throw-away consumerist culture, preservation values longevity. It's a classic case of cause and consequence: things that last are worth keeping. Things worth keeping, last.

Questions to Ask

- Is my home or neighborhood on the National Register of Historic Places?
- Who previously owned my home, and who occupied the home?
- What did the original structure look like, and why was it altered?
- What are the defining characteristics of my home?
- What can I do to the home that would enhance and honor its character?
- What local preservation resources can I draw from?

Preservation History

The preservation movement has a winding history that is useful to understand as a precursor to present-day practice.

Paradigm Shifts in Preservation

Over the years, preservation has evolved into a local, grass-roots movement.

1800–1970s
Philanthropists and the National Park Service rehabilitate museum homes.

1980s – present
The federal government financed developers to rehabilitate commercial buildings.

1990s – present
State governments finance residential rehabilitation through state tax credits to individuals rehabilitating homes.

The beginning of the preservation movement in the US is generally attributed to either the City of Philadelphia, for its preservation of Independence Hall starting in 1816, or to the women philanthropists who purchased George Washington's home at Mt. Vernon in 1858. Through most of its existence, the movement focused on saving museum pieces: properties that were valued for the owner or architect (John Hancock House, Falling Water) or the role they played in US history books (Empire State Building). Until recently, this kept the movement selective and elite.

For the last century, the preservation movement has been defined by government charters and policy shifts. In 1916 the US National Park Service (NPS) was founded, and in 1935 the federal government placed all its historic properties under their domain. In 1947 the private and nonprofit National Council on Historic Sites was founded, becoming the National Trust for Historic Preservation two years later. Today, this organization has the strongest influence on preservation policy in the US.

The 1960s and 1970s saw an expansion of the preservation movement through activism, particularly a growing rejection of federal urban renewal programs that destroyed so many historic buildings in the name of *progress*. In 1960 the US National Park Service launched the National Historic Landmark Program, the model for today's National Register of Historic Places. Columbia University's School of Architecture chartered the first preservation course in 1964, the first instance of historic preservation as an academic study in the US.

The single most important piece of preservation legislation in the US is the 1966 National Historic Preservation Act (NHPA), which expanded the National Register program and chartered a multi-layer infrastructure, including state and local historic agencies. It also authorized grants and incentives to states for promoting preservation. In 1967, the US Secretary of the Interior formally requested each state to form its own State Historic Preservation Office (SHPO, pronounced *sssh-POE*). Today, nearly all preservation work requiring government approval or tax credit review goes through a SHPO.

In 1973, the preservation movement spread from government to private interests. A few cities began deeding abandoned houses to individuals willing to rehabilitate (called *urban homesteading*), and *Old House Journal* began publication, catering to the dedicated patrons of the preservation movement. Five years later, Claremont, New Hampshire became the first entire neighborhood listed on the National Register, making individual listings redundant.

Thirty years later, there were over 12,000 National Register Historic Districts, 82,387 individually listed properties and 1,355,083 structures contributing to historic districts (an average of 112 per district).

Since the 1980s, tax policy has been the catalyst of the preservation movement in the private sector. Essentially, to increase the incentive for rehabilitating historic properties, federal and state governments have agreed to forgo tax revenue due from the private owner of a historic property. In 1981, Congress passed a 25% tax credit for the rehabilitation of historic buildings listed on the National Register. Within seven years, over $12 billion in rehabilitation activity was credited to this legislation. The program was so successful that some complained it was a tax haven for developers, and in 1986 Congress cut the credit to 20%, with some passive income limitations. A 10% credit was also allowed on all structures built before 1936, even if not on the National Register. This 20/10% federal tax credit policy is still in place today.

In the 1990s, several states mirrored federal programs by offering state credits for residential homeowners. Currently, 30 states have programs rebating between 10-50% of rehabilitation costs through tax credits. Each state differs in credit percentage, requirements and documentation, so projects need to be coordinated with SHPOs.[4] North Carolina, for example, has a 30% credit for non-income producing homes.

Today, the contemporary preservation movement is driven by market forces, government incentives and the sometimes

Rehabilitation Costs	$200,000
Tax Credit Rate (NC)	x 30%
Tax Credit	= $60,000

Fig 2.1: *North Carolina Rehabilitation Tax Credit — Non-Income Producing Property*

Herculean effort of determined individuals to save buildings. In coming years, preservation will see an expansion of local recognition, incentives and legal enforcement. State tax credits will continue to grow in popularity and value. Unfortunately, since residential tax credits generate rebates on state income tax, the mechanism is useless in states that do not tax income, such as Florida and New Hampshire. Such states' preservation efforts are at a comparative disadvantage to states with income taxes. There are now discussions to create a federal rehabilitation tax program, allowing for similar incentives in such states.

Preservation Standards

The sheer quantity of information on preservation programs and practices can be overwhelming. With its roots in high society and government policy, available preservation literature is sometimes overly academic, bureaucratic and poorly organized. However, this large and complex field of information can be distilled into a few core concepts: basic principles, the Secretary of the Interior Standard's for Rehabilitation (SISR) and local legislation.

Basic Principles

The most intimidating quandary facing rehabilitation-minded historic home owners is

Fig 2.2-3: *Detailing unique to historic homes. Preservation incentives and restrictions aim to protect such architectural character.*

K BROWN PHOTOGRAPHY

K BROWN PHOTOGRAPHY

twofold: *What can I do to my historic home?* and *What can't I do to my historic home?*

There are a few sets of principle guidelines available, generally featuring the same concepts organized in different ways. Most concerns can be addressed using three simple guidelines.

1. Preserve the windows by rehabilitating and restoring.
2. Preserve the streetscape façade including siding, roof, doors and porch railings as well as scale and massing.
3. Preserve the public living spaces by maintaining the integrity of the dining, living and entry rooms.

Architectural details, façades and public living spaces are the *holy trinity* of preservation. Alteration of these areas tends to violate the preservation ethic. Most tax credit problems originate from violation of one of these guidelines. Preservationists scowl at boxed-in front porches, vinyl siding and replacement windows. Proposals including such practices may disqualify an entire project from receiving tax credits.

The aforementioned trinity is an emotional issue for many preservationists, and for good reason. As craftsmanship is replaced, character is lost. Craftsmanship conveys itself, for example, in artisan windows. If discarded, the character of the home is destroyed. Trim detailing such as fireplace mantles, herringbone floors and door casings can be indicative of period styles. For these reasons, *repair over replace* is a general motif of preservation. After all, once something original is gone, it cannot be returned.

Standards for Rehabilitation

The US Secretary of the Interior Standards for Rehabilitation (SISR) is the guiding document for formal preservation decision making. You can think of it as the code book for the State Historic Preservation Office. Curious researchers may be pleased to find that a document with such a dreadful sounding bureaucratic title consists of merely ten brief points presented on a single page.

In short, whenever possible: (1) maintain the original use of the home, (2) and the character, (3) avoid changes that create a false sense of history, (4) respect changes that have been made to the home over time, (5) preserve craftsmanship, (6) repair rather than replace, and where replacement is necessary, replicate, (7) avoid methods that damage historic materials, (8) protect archeological resources, if any, (9) ensure new modifications are complementary but differentiated from the old, (10) and that these changes can be removed or reversed and the original structure kept intact.

Fig 2.4-5: *The addition to this 1920s bungalow was designed and constructed to complement the original house in style and massing, while differentiating with a roof break and window detail. The door connecting the old and new was purposely kept in place to preserve the original structure (consistent with SISR 10).*

Local Standards

While many of the preservation standards and goals originate with the National Park Service, most preservation work in the US happens at the state or local level.

States and cities offer additional preservation incentives, guidelines and restrictions. Local Historic Districts (figure 6), of which there are about 2,300 nationwide, often mirror National Historic Districts. They're

generally formed by local residents wanting to keep the cultural look and feel of their community. While national districts provide incentives for good preservation practice through tax credits, local districts are generally chartered for the physical protection of contributing structures through the regulation of rehabilitation work.

In this carrot and stick relationship, National Historic Districts offer financial incentives (the carrot), while Local Historic Districts implement legal and financial consequences for damaging privately owned historic buildings (the stick). An example of a damaged historic building is illustrated in figure 7.

The Secretary of the Interior's Standards for Rehabilitation

1. A property shall be used for its historic purpose or be placed in a new use that requires minimal change to the defining characteristics of the building and its site and environment.

2. The historic character of a property shall be retained and preserved. The removal of historic materials or alteration of features and spaces that characterize a property shall be avoided.

3. Each property shall be recognized as a physical record of its time, place and use. Changes that create a false sense of historical development, such as adding conjectural features or architectural elements from other buildings, shall not be undertaken.

4. Most properties change over time; those changes that have acquired historic significance in their own right shall be retained and preserved.

5. Distinctive features, finishes and construction techniques or examples of craftsmanship that characterize a property shall be preserved.

6. Deteriorated historic features shall be repaired rather than replaced. Where the severity of deterioration requires replacement of a distinctive feature, the new feature shall match the old in design, color, texture and other visual qualities and, where possible, materials. Replacement of missing features shall be substantiated by documentary, physical or pictorial evidence.

7. Chemical or physical treatments, such as sandblasting, that cause damage to historic materials shall not be used. The surface cleaning of structures, if appropriate, shall be undertaken using the gentlest means possible.

8. Significant archeological resources affected by a project shall be protected and preserved. If such resources must be disturbed, mitigation measures shall be undertaken.

9. New additions, exterior alterations, or related new construction shall not destroy historic materials that characterize the property. The new work shall be differentiated from the old and shall be compatible with the massing, size, scale and architectural features to protect the historic integrity of the property and its environment.

10. New additions and adjacent or related new construction shall be undertaken in such a manner that if removed in the future, the essential form and integrity of the historic property and its environment would be unimpaired.[5]

Local ordinances establish methods for reviewing proposed alterations or improvements to historic buildings, generally through a citizens' review board or an architectural planner. Local districts are mostly concerned with the exterior streetscape, so they rarely regulate or even review modifications to the interior of a building. Approval, through a certificate of appropriateness, is required prior to receiving building permits. The third party reviewer will work to preserve the streetscape and ensure the building's scale and character is in keeping with the neighborhood. In some cases, the reviewer may deny permits altogether for projects that do not meet these goals.

Preservation in Practice

There are many roles and professions in preservation practice.

- Preservation Societies, typically nonprofit organizations, that promote local preservation through recognition, education grants and sometimes acquisitions.

- Preservation Consultants, who guide homeowners through the design process,

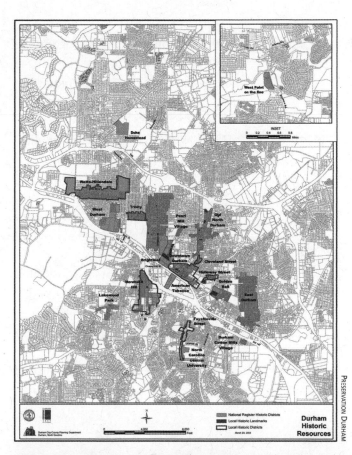

Fig 2.6: *Local Historic Districts generally follow National Historic Districts, like the Morehead Hill District in Durham, NC.*

Fig 2.7: *Preservation violations — a wraparound porch is finished in, negatively affecting this historic home's street façade. Botched* improvements *like these appear every month in* Old House Journal's *backpage "Remuddling" feature.*

complete tax credit applications, advise on preservation ethics and manage preservation regulatory burdens.

- Local officials, who pass and enforce legislation that generates good preservation work and regulates bad.
- SHPOs, who review tax credit applications, guide and archive rehabilitations and save homes through easements and acquisitions.
- Designers/Architects, who balance the forces of quality, preservation obligations and client means.
- Restoration Contractors, who follow instructions of other planners to rehabilitate the structure and advise on preservation issues as they arise in the field.

A few of these roles warrant further discussion.

Preservation Consultants

With respect to house rehabilitations, it's best to involve a preservation expert as early as possible. This may be an architect or designer trained in preservation, or it may be an independent preservation consultant. During a simple walk-through the expert can point out particularly interesting features of the home, what characteristics might be accentuated, what could be tastefully altered and most importantly, what you should *not* do. One particularly interesting skill of preservation consultants is their ability to find and analyze *ghostmarks*. Ghostmarks are evidence of something that existed before which has since been removed or altered. Often trim will show that a door is not original to the home, or patched round holes in wood illustrate where a kitchen once was. The discovery of ghostmarks often alters the design approach,

Official Terms

The National Park Service (NPS) offers guidance on different preservationist approaches, and their terminology is widely accepted by preservationists.

Restoration, as defined by the NPS, entails bringing back a property to it original state with original fixtures, finishes and sometimes even systems. It's rarely practiced in residential homes, and inconsistent with the content (and title) of this book. With respect to the NPS vocabulary, this book focuses on *preservation* and *rehabilitation*.

Preservation focuses on the maintenance and repair of existing historic materials and retention of a property's form as it has evolved over time. (Protection and Stabilization have now been consolidated under this treatment.)

Rehabilitation acknowledges the need to alter or add to a historic property to meet continuing or changing uses while retaining the property's historic character.

Restoration depicts a property at a particular period of time in its history, while removing evidence of other periods.

Reconstruction re-creates vanished or non-surviving portions of a property for interpretive purposes.[6]

either to accentuate or protect an original feature of the home.

With the nature of preservation, function (use/alterations) follows form (existing exterior/living spaces). For this reason, it is advisable to prioritize a preservation plan before beginning basic design work. The homeowner should start a project with a preservation consultant.

Preservation consultants are readily available in most medium to large cities. They can advise on tax credits, conduct house histories and help balance design and preservation desires. Consultants can also complete tax credit documentation and address local ordinance requirements.

Designers and Architects

Work with a designer who understands preservation principles. It is possible, and unfortunately not uncommon, for an uninformed architect to design a beautiful space that ruins a historic home. Fortunately, many design professionals based in old neighborhoods specialize in old homes. Participating in a historic home tour is a

Fig 2.8: *Top, an aluminum siding removal and siding restoration project reveals a keystone ghostmark, the outline of a trim detail that once was.*

Fig 2.9-10: *Center and bottom, a grand foyer staircase was split down the middle to partition a large home into two units.*
Exploratory demolition confirmed that the wall was not original, and suggested how to restore the original look.

Fig 2.11-12:
Experienced preservation contractors should have sample photos of their craftsmanship detailing things like exterior restoration, glasswork and flooring.

great way to meet designers and see their work. Designers love to meet-and-greet while their work is shown off. Today, more schools are offering degrees and concentrations in preservation, including preservation planning and preservation design. In addition to inquiring about a professional's field experience, ask for their educational background and professional designations.

Contractors

Good contractors can be hard to find, particularly those with preservation knowledge.

BASEMENT   1ST FLOOR

With the recent housing boom, many good contractors found endless work in new construction. But even good new construction contractors can be bad preservation contractors. The nature of repair, replication and restoration is dramatically different from installing new materials, and herein lies the primary difference between a general contractor and a restoration contractor. Where a general contractor aims to produce or replace, a restoration contractor aims to preserve. Since there is less art in home-building after 1950, the general contractor need not be concerned with preservation concepts. But for owners of old homes and their contractors, a higher standard exists.

Since many states do not require an architect to seal drawings on residential projects, homeowners may skip the design professional altogether and consult directly and only with a contractor. However this approach can yield some negative results. Clients confuse construction skill for design skill, and contractors can make judgment calls in the field that directly conflict with preservation principles. Be concerned if you hear: *Sure we can remove the wall between the dining room and kitchen, I'll just re-trim the door with newer trim, or I think you should replace those windows.* Ask for preservation contractor recommendations from your neighbors, local preservation societies and your SHPO. When you interview contractors, ask how many historic homes they've worked on. Most contractors have pictures on the internet or in a presentation binder, so be sure to ask to view past work.

DOLLARS AND SENSE

Historic preservation makes sense in large measure because historic preservation makes dollars and cents, but it also saves dollars and cents. Historic preservation is a rational and effective economic response to over consumption. To make a new brick today to build a building on site where there is already a building standing steals from two generations. It steals from the generation that built the brick originally by throwing away their asset before its work is done, and it steals from a future generation by using increasingly scarce natural resources today that should have been saved for tomorrow.

— Donovan Rypkema, *The Economics of Historic Preservation*

Questions to Ask

- What are the initial costs in purchasing the home?
- What will it cost to rehabilitate the home?
- Will my rehabilitation plan for the home qualify for historic tax credits?
- If so, how much will historic tax credits save me each month?
- What were the operating costs (second costs) over the past few years?
- How much will be spent, each month, on mortgage and operating costs?
- What can be done to lower operating costs?
- If I lower operating costs dramatically through energy efficiency gains, how much could it save me per month?
- Does the layout of my home and local zoning allow for the inclusion of a private rental space?

Finance can be a boring topic for many people so I apologize in advance for writing a chapter that deals with CPAs, tax implications, mortgage deductibility and the dollars and cents of homeownership. It has always amazed me that over 60% of Americans own a home, yet fundamental education about mortgages and taxes is completely absent from our formal education. One wonders if this failure in education contributed to the mortgage crisis of 2008-2009.

For nearly all of us, buying a home will be the largest investment we ever make. A home is the most expensive asset we will ever buy, and the mortgage will be the largest loan we ever take out. Still, while finances are a missing part of the average American's lexicon, there are large incentives to buy and help pay for homes in the US, and each mechanism is important to understand.

More significantly, historic homes offer interesting and specific benefits not available in suburban tract homes. Flexible zoning may allow for attached rentals, mixed use commercial/residential space or the ability to serve different needs at different times. Such elasticity is beneficial to the homeowner who might be able to start a business in a potential rental space one year and rent it residentially for income the next. Suburban neighborhoods, by contrast, come with restrictive zoning that forbids such flexibility making such opportunities unattainable for the suburban homeowner.

As Richard Florida argues in *The Rise of The Creative Class,* creativity is taking a growing role in our economy. Imaginative and inspired leaders are the catalyst driving the rehabilitation of urban neighborhoods. Uniquely, it is this group that is capitalizing on malleability of use. While creative individuals benefit from living close to the commercial corridors intrinsically linked

Fig. 3.1-2: *Rowhouse neighborhoods, mostly built between 1870s and 1930s … continue to provide homes to people of different incomes. One reason is because rowhouses are flexible; they can provide an owner-occupied home above and a rental apartment below or flats on different levels.*[1]

with historic districts, they also benefit from owning a home that can serve many different purposes from rental income, private home office or business expansion.

But the financial benefits of historic housing go beyond flexibility. I will discuss a few concepts essential to affording historic homes, including mortgage deductibility, historic tax credits and rental income. Not all are applicable to every homeowner. For others, options might not be desirable for other reasons. Some don't want to have an attached apartment in their home. Others don't want to deal with the regulatory burdens that come with historic tax credits. Still, for those that do take advantage of one or all three vehicles, the financial results can be astounding. Familiarity with and understanding of these concepts can help you save money, afford a larger home or conduct a better rehabilitation. The more options you are armed with, the easier it is to figure out the dollars and cents required for your project.

I will walk you through great secrets to affording historic homes, and show how many young couples, with real budgets and real lives, are affording landmark homes for the same (or less) than they might spend on a generic tract house in the suburbs.

First Costs — Purchase and Rehabilitation

The first cost of any asset is its purchase price. A home sale transaction is conducted by a willing buyer and seller agreeing on a price. In depressed markets historic homes can sell for $10 per square foot, while in sizzling markets they sell for up to $1,000 per square foot. Price is driven by design, location, safety, deferred maintenance, buyer and seller motivations and other market conditions.

Purchases involve transaction costs, otherwise known as closing costs. These include transfer or excise tax, insurance and property tax, attorney fees, surveys and flood certification, recordation fees, and real estate and loan broker fees, among others. Closing costs regularly tally 3–4% the cost of the home. In some cooler markets, it's common for a seller to pay closing costs, though this is less common in historic districts.

Banks will order an appraisal of your home, verifying its value. The appraiser will require a copy of the purchase contract, which will have the sale price on it. They will work to justify this price by comparing the subject property to similar homes that sold recently. Make sure you have an appraiser familiar with historic districts. Up until mid 2009, a broker could request a specific appraiser, which is a useful if not necessary request for valuing unique old houses. Unfortunately, due to the fraudulent activity surrounding the subprime crisis, this practice is no longer allowed.

A disproportionate amount of homes in historic districts trade hands without ever hitting a realtor's online multiple listing service (MLS), and lazy appraisers will only use the MLS for comparables. We've had more than one incompetent appraiser treat an historic structure as a production home, do a quick and inaccurate MLS comparable search and kill the transaction.

Loans originate through a bank or independent mortgage broker. The lender will review loan options with you, and there are a variety of products available. Traditionally, a 20% down payment is required, leaving 80% loan-to-value (LTV) to be financed. Other products allow for lower down payments, depending on the lendee's situation. Special products exist for vocational categories like veterans, teachers and state employees. Some traditional loans are available with rehabilitation budget allowances, such as an FHA 203k loan.

Construction-to-permanent loans allow the same loan to serve the rehabilitation and permanent financing once complete so there is no need to refinance. These specialized loans are ideal for major rehabilitation projects and are typically held by a local bank until construction is complete (at which time they are sold to the secondary market).

For major historic rehabilitations, a regional or local bank is the best lending source. Banks like to put lending opportunities into predefined program boxes, and large national banks tend to struggle to put historic rehabilitations into their boxes. Don't be surprised if you get some *you want to do what?* responses from your bank. Smart lenders treat major rehabilitations as new construction. On new construction loans there are land and construction. On historic rehabilitations, there are the preexisting property and rehabilitation costs. Though an historic home renovation is far from new construction, this traditional construction lending mechanism can get the job done.

Second Costs — Utilities

We are conditioned to think that the only costs that matter are the upfront costs of a home — that is the purchase price. In the

Getting a Loan

A bank will loan money based on four criteria, often called the *Four Cs*: Collateral, Capacity, Credit and Character. Those with all four will sail through the loan process without incident. Those with three, or even two, can get loans — but probably on less favorable terms. Those lacking all four will not be able to obtain traditional financing.

Collateral refers to your down payment, viewed by the bank as equity in the home. The more you have, the less risk you are, which makes you more attractive to a bank. Conversely, if you have nothing to put down, banks will be hesitant. Capacity refers to income, documented by pay stubs and/or tax returns. A two-year income history is commonly requested by banks. The more income, the larger the loan a bank will allow. Credit refers to your credit score (e.g. FICO), which indicates all the loans you've ever taken out and how well you've honored your commitment to pay them. Character refers to work history, largely how long you've been at your current job. Many banks will not lend to those with work histories shorter than two years, although some students are accepted.

Historic Tax Credits

State Historic Tax Credits are state-enabled financial incentives awarded for the approved rehabilitation of historic buildings. The credits are used to offset state tax liability. For the most part, they model the guidelines outlined in Section 47 of the US Internal Revenue Service tax code, the baseline for the federal income-producing (primarily commercial) tax credit. The purchase price of a building does not qualify; the cost to rehabilitate does.

How are tax credits used? In Virginia, for example, there is a 25% historic tax credit. So, a qualifying $200,000 rehabilitation would generate $50,000 in credits. If, for example, the owners of this home make $150,000 a year, they will owe Virginia $8,625 in income tax (5.75% rate). However, the historic tax credit will wipe out this liability entirely. The remaining $41,375 credit will also carry forward to the next tax year.

Each state has a slightly different program.[2] Most include five basic criteria.

1. What buildings qualify. Typically those on the National Register qualify, but some state or locally-listed historic properties will as well.
2. Detailed standards to follow in order to achieve a qualified rehabilitation; typically the Secretary for the Interior's Standards for Rehabilitation.
3. A minimum threshold of investment in qualifying expenditures must be satisfied.
4. A method for calculating the value of the credit, typically a percentage of costs spent within the original historic or preexisting structure.
5. An administrative body to manage the process; usually a state historic preservation office (SHPO) and/or a state department of revenue (DOR).[3]

Fig. 3.3: *28 states have state historic tax credits available to residential homeowners. Eight states do not tax income, and thus have no state-enabled way to offer incentives for such rehabilitation. There is currently no federal historic tax credit for owner-occupied property.*

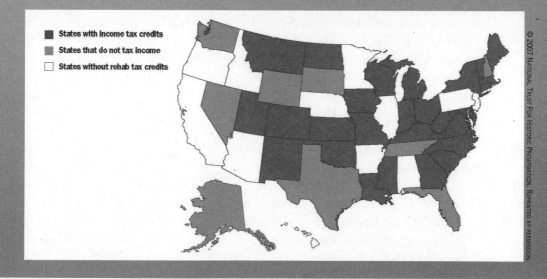

Legend:
- States with income tax credits
- States that do not tax income
- States without rehab tax credits

Qualifying Tax Credit Expenses

Some eligible items include

- Walls and partitions
- Floors
- Ceilings
- Permanent coverings, such as paneling, plaster, sheetrock and tiles
- Structural elements
- Repair of windows and doors
- HVAC
- Plumbing and plumbing fixtures
- Electrical wiring and lighting fixtures
- Chimneys
- Stairs
- Design and consultant fees
- Other components related to the operation or maintenance of the building

Ineligible items include

- Non-permanent cabinetry
- Carpeting (if tacked in place and not glued)
- Decks that are not part of original building
- Removal of a detached building
- New construction costs or enlargement costs (increase in total volume)
- Sitework, including fencing, landscaping, yard lighting, parking, paving, planters, retaining walls
- Feasibility studies and finance fees
- Personal property, including furniture, window treatments and appliances

process of buying a house, how rare is it to consider the long-term financial implications of home ownership, particularly operating costs?

Operating costs include all the costs to run the home. The most obvious operating cost, and the easiest to comprehend, is utility cost. Operational utilities include electricity, water and fuel — primarily energy costs. Luckily, utilities are also the easiest costs to minimize. At one extreme is a massive energy hog of a house with a leaky envelope or poorly installed systems. At 5,000 square feet, such a house might cost $2,000 a month or $24,000 per year to operate. That equals $4.80 per square foot in utility costs. We can expect comparable utility costs from leaky old homes with decaying systems. A tightened envelope and updated systems can cut operating costs by 1/3, in my experience, to about $1.56 per square foot, whereas a super tight, newly constructed house with high quality systems and passive solar design might have annual utility costs as low as $.60 per square foot.

The difference in historic house utility costs pre- and post-rehabilitation is huge. At $3.24 per square foot (averaging $4.80-$1.56), a properly rehabilitated 3,000-square-foot house could cost $9,720 less to run each year. If the savings are broken out over 12 months, the $810 saved per month is enough to afford an additional $150,000 in mortgage. Such savings allow

Tax Credit Lexicon

Carry back — The ability to apply current tax credits against state income taxes due in previous years.

Carry forward — The ability to apply current tax credits against taxes due in future years.

Certified local government (CLG) — A local government certified by the state historic preservation office with the capacity to administer historic preservation programs.

Disproportionate allocation — the disproportionate splitting of a tax credit's value through a partnership or corporations' members or shareholders.

Transferability — The ability to make an outright transfer or assignment of all or a portion of the tax credit to another person or entity.[4]

for a larger house, higher-end systems or better finishes.

Final Costs — Life Cycle Analysis

There's great debate on how to quantify life-cycle costs. Is more weight put on operating costs or disposal costs? How can we calculate transportation costs of materials that were installed eight decades ago? Still, historic homes offer a superior petri dish for such study. Old materials indicate life expectancies or half lives. A remodel might prove that wood floors are expected to last 200 years, while carpet should last ten. Or, that 100-year-old windows can be repaired, while 20-year-old replacement windows can only be replaced. The nature of life cycle analysis is theoretical, but when working in old homes it becomes very real.

Preservation economist Donovan Rypkema has noted

Real estate is an asset that typically has a long physical and economic life. It is certainly unfortunate, then, that all too often the standards of measurement for economic return on real estate investment are short-term criteria. Private-sector owners ought to measure life cycle costs; almost none do.[5]

How long will the home last? Is it repairable, or will it have to be entirely replaced when worn? How are original materials lasting? What is the estimated remaining life on elements of the home, ranging from flooring to systems? These are all important decisions made in the present, but with long-term implications.

It is prudent to consider two additional financial concepts: appreciation and declining market risk. *House appreciation* is the rise in an asset's value that the owner can realize through refinance or sale. Under current US tax code, sellers are allowed to realize a gain of up to $250,000 tax free ($500,000 for married couples) so long as they have lived in the house for a minimum of two years. Historic homes generally appreciate faster than suburban alternatives and are subject to less price fluctuation because homeowners tend to drop anchor and stay for the long haul. As downtown commercial districts are revitalized, surrounding residential districts can appreciate at incredible rates. It is not uncommon for historic residential districts to appreciate at two to four times the rate of surrounding non-historic districts.

Leverage is the practice of acquiring a large asset by borrowing all or most of the

---

The 2009 US Recovery and Reinvestment Act (aka the stimulus package) extends and expands nearly all of the tax credits available for energy efficiency improvements. When the caps on energy efficiency tax credits are small, the administrative burdens to claim them were often more hassle than they were worth. The new, higher caps make the program more worthwhile. Just about any major rehabilitation should get the $1,500 max credit. The program is scheduled to sunset in 2010, but is expected to be renewed in some form.

Direct Effects of the 2009 Stimulus Bill on Tax Credits

- Existing energy efficiency tax credits are extended to December 31, 2010.
- Tax credit has gone up from 10% to 30% of qualifying costs, with a $1,500 maximum per year, up from $500.
- Qualifying energy improvement expenditures include some (but not all) windows, doors, siding, roofing, HVAC, weatherstripping and insulations.
- Products must be placed in service in either 2009 or 2010.
- The previous $200 cap on window upgrades has been removed.
- On new home construction (typically including additions) no credit may be taken for insulation, energy-efficient roofing, non-solar water heaters, air conditioning and heating systems, windows and doors.

Also

- All exterior doors, windows and skylights must have a U-factor of 0.30 or less. No historic windows doors or skylights will have this, and it would be nearly impossible to verify anyway.
- Roofs must have a basic Energy Star rating.
- Air conditioner SEER ratings must exceed 16 for split systems or 14 for packaged systems.
- Heat pump SEER ratings must exceed 15 for split systems and 14 and above for package systems.
- If claiming this tax credit for a solar water heater, half the homes' energy usage for hot water must come from the sun. Swimming pool and hot tub demand does not qualify.

Just like income tax deductions, homeowners must maintain detailed records. This means saving any Energy Star labels, all sales receipts and manufacturer's certification statements. The bottom line is that homeowners can enjoy some real savings when upgrading or remodeling, but to claim the tax credit, careful homework and record keeping must be done.

funds from a third party (other people's money, as they say). Leverage has made many Americans wealthy. When a $200,000 home bought with $20,000 down appreciated 10% in the first year, the homeowner is left with a $220,000 home. With leverage, that is not a 10% return, but a 100% return ($20,000 investment/$20,000 return).

Do you have proper insurance?

Home insurance is an important consideration with a historic house. Underwriters and brokers may debate what qualifies as a historic house, and their definitions may differ from listing on the National Register. If you insure your home as non-historic, there are some insurance clauses you need to know about. How a home is repaired after a loss matters. The industry is built on production homes, and the standards may be very inconsistent with those for historic homes. Consider the following.

- Does your insurance specifically cover a total loss to replicate original architectural elements?
- Does your insurance cover homes on the National Register?
- Do you need additional historic tax credit insurance?

Replacement cost or *replacement cost value* stipulates replacement of original features with *like kind and quality.* Unfortunately, you can count on the insurance adjuster not being a preservationist, or remotely familiar with custom woodworking. Policies tend to cover replacement with stock materials, the kind readily available at building supply chains. Labor rates are taken from *standard guidelines,* which mean production builder tables. These rates can be less than 25% of dollar value commonly required to reconstruct original built-up moldings and custom cuts.

Actual cash value generally includes *like kind and quality,* but also factors in depreciation, which is also determined by an insurance adjuster. Under actual cash value they may take a room's worth of crown molding, determine the replacement cost to be $400, then pay out $200 due to depreciation. Depreciation is a commercial tool that assumes a lowered asset value over time as the asset wears down. Real estate, however, is unlike a truck or computer, in that it is typically an appreciating asset. Crown molding doesn't deteriorate naturally, and construction costs certainly don't halve over time. So the practice of depreciation is inconsistent with historic homes. Watch out for such a clause.

Historic replacement cost is a new mechanism designed to allow for a reconstruction in line with the Secretary of the Interior's Standards for Rehabilitation: to repair and restore original features. It is a very rare offering, and your insurance agent may need to do some research to offer it.

You can also purchase historic tax credit insurance, payable in the event a loss causes the tax credit to be recaptured. This prevents the dually catastrophic situation of losing a building and the major financial benefits that its rehabilitation generated. If the tax credit is syndicated, the purchaser may require such a policy to be in place. Such an insurance policy is also a specialty product and may not be available through every broker.[6]

Sale of Tax Credits

Syndication, or the sale and transfer of credits from an owner with less tax liability to one with more tax liability, is a common practice with income-producing federal credits. For the most part, residential credits are not transferable. Rhode Island and Missouri are the only states that permit such sales. Other states permit transfer only to another person on title. While federal credits often sell at $.90 on the dollar, state credits, with their smaller buyers' markets, might generate $.55 on the dollar. Still, if the owner of a major tax credit has little income to offset with a tax credit, the credit is useless and cash more valuable. For the buyer of the credit, the credit is more useful than the cash, hence a win-win transaction. In programs of particular usefulness to low-income owners, Maryland, Ohio, Iowa and Louisiana provide a fully refundable tax credit with the full value of the credit paid out in year one. All other states cap the credit claim at the yearly tax liability of the owner, with unused portions carried forward to the next year.

In the world where houses never lost value, this all worked out great. Unfortunately, though leverage has been a great tool in an appreciating market, it can wreck owners in a declining market. When a $200,000 home bought with $20,000 down declines 10% in value the first year, the homeowner is left with a $180,000 home. With leverage, that is not a -10% loss, but a 100% loss ($20,000 investment/$20,000 loss).

Nationwide, US house prices never declined until 2008. Suddenly, appreciation is not guaranteed as it once was, and the true risks of leverage have become obvious. Deflation of asset prices, or *declining market* as mortgage underwriters refer to it, is a real pressure in formerly hot markets. Historic districts have held up better than non-historic districts. Where surrounding non-historic districts may lose value, historic districts may still see a small gain, or at worst stay flat. Historic homes, comparably, look like wiser investments with their more stable value, higher appreciation potential and lower deflationary risk.

A Sample Couple

Olivia and Trey Jones are first time homebuyers, creative class professionals. When Olivia and Trey found a project house they loved, they lost sleep over their ability to afford it. It needed work — a gut job — with new HVAC, electric, plumbing, kitchens, bathrooms and framing. The house had a large unfinished private basement that could be finished into a great recreational

Fig. 3.4: *Olivia and Trey — Projected Income and Expenses*

Annual Income		$ 100,000
Purchase Price		$ 100,000
Rehab Costs	+	$ 300,000
House Value	=	$ 400,000
Loan to Value (LTV)	x	90%
Mortgage	=	$ 360,000

room or apartment. So they did the math. Although it would need significant investment to rehabilitate, the house would qualify for tax credits and have a basement apartment to offset their mortgage.

Olivia and Trey have recognized three major financial opportunities open to them as historic homeowners. First, there is a mortgage interest deduction. Second, they could get historic rehabilitation tax credits. And third, they could generate income from an attached rental unit. Every US home buyer gets the first incentive, but few, very few, take advantage of the latter two.

Their plan considers a 3,000-square-foot fixer-upper bought for $100,000 that they will rehabilitate with $300,000.

Mortgage Interest Deduction

As a federal incentive to encourage homeownership, owners may deduct mortgage interest on their federal income tax return. Post rehabilitation, Olivia and Trey will have a $400,000 house with a 30-year mortgage for $360,000 at 6%.[7] Their monthly interest payment is $1,800. Property taxes vary widely by city, so let's just say they have an additional $300 per month property taxes, which are also tax deductible. Over 12 months, the Jones will spend a whopping $25,200 on interest and taxes, 100% of which is deductible. This tax deduction will lower their taxable income by $25,200, so they will be taxed not on $100,000 of income, but on $74,800 instead. Multiplied by their federal tax rate of 28%, the mortgage deduction creates a real dollar savings

of $7,056 per year ($25,200 x 28%),[8] or, spreading that savings out over 12 months, $588 per month ($7,056/12). Since rental payments to a landlord are not deductible to the renter, their $2,100 interest and property tax payment is the net equivalent of a $1,512 ($2,100-$588) rent payment. That gave great comfort to the Jones.

It is very important that realtors and homeowners, particularly first-time homebuyers, understand this mortgage deductibility concept. Mortgage interest deductions are the first great secret to owning any home, particularly an historic one.

Historic Rehabilitation Tax Credits

In North Carolina, for example, there is a 30% tax credit for the restoration of homes listed on the National Register of Historic Places. Essentially, when $300,000 is spent to restore a historic home in North Carolina, the state gives back $90,000 in tax credits to do so.[9]

Remember, historic tax credits are dollar-for-dollar credits. They are not, as is often and wrongly assumed, a deduction. Since the Jones filed jointly, made $100,000 in income and North Carolina has a 7% income tax, their state tax liability is $7,000 ($100,000 x 7%). That's what they pay to the state each year in taxes. Their tax credit wipes out their

Qualified Restoration Costs		$ 300,000
Tax Credit Rate	x	30%
Tax Credit	=	$ 90,000

Fig. 3.5: *North Carolina Historic Home Tax Credit*

entire state tax liability for the year. If they have already paid $7,000 in state income tax through their employer's W2 payroll deductions, they will receive a tax refund check for $7,000. Extrapolated monthly (as we are conditioned to think of our house payments) this tax credit saves Olivia and Trey $583 per month ($7,000/12). The remaining unused portion of the credits carry forward, so the next year they offset their income tax again.[10]

Historic tax credits are the single largest financial incentive available to owners of historic homes, and they are highly underused. Historic tax credits are the second great secret to making owning an historic home affordable.

Attached Rentals

Historic districts are hotbeds for students, faculty and creative class workers. Whether or not a university is present, downtown areas from Denver to Asheville are flooded with high quality renters looking for high quality renting situations. Good renters like living in secure homes in nice areas. And often high quality rentals are in short supply. Attached rentals (more technically *accessory dwellings*) come in a variety of forms — perhaps a basement apartment, a studio apartment left over from when a larger house was carved up or a flat over a detached garage. As separate housing, attached rentals all have private entrances so, to be clear, these are not live-in roommate situations.

For those open to the opportunity, the concept is very simple. If you rent a portion of your home, that income can offset your mortgage. Olivia and Trey, a young, childless couple, don't really need or want 3,000 square feet for themselves. For now, extra income from a rental gives them the option of affording a larger home, better quality finishes or a more thorough restoration. In the future they will have space to claim as their family grows while today generating income from the space they don't really need. The accessory dwelling is like an addition-on-hold space that pays for itself until needed. Further, some homeowners appreciate the security of having another person in the house, with eyes on the street, while they are traveling or at work.

The attached apartment concept is not for everyone. Some homeowners dislike the idea of someone living in their house, or at least need time to warm to the idea. Others might want all the space their large house offers. Or, they might not have a house that allows for the option.

Trey and Olivia's $400,000 house has a two-bedroom basement apartment. It is the perfect setup for graduate students — with a private entrance, a small kitchen and bath, nice finishes and even a tiny private garden. Near a university, it rents easily for $800 a month. At $800 it covers nearly half the Jones' mortgage.[11] Attached rentals are the third great secret to affording an historic home.

The Triple Play

What happens when Olivia and Trey use all three opportunities? With interest and taxes of $2,100, their mortgage tax deduction reduces net payment to $1,512. The tax credit offsets their entire tax liability to NC, giving them $583 extra, for a net payment of $929. Finally, the rented basement gives them an additional $800, for a total all inclusive payment for their rehabilitated

	Calcs		Notes
Cost of Home		$ 100,000	
Restoration Costs	+	$ 300,000	
Total costs — purchase and restoration	=	$ 400,000	
Down Payment	–	$ 40,000	10%
Mortgage	=	$ 360,000	
MORTGAGE TAX DEDUCTION			
Interest Rate and Monthly Payment	6%	$ 1,800	6.00%
Property Taxes	+	$ 300	
Interest and Property Tax	=	$ 2,100	
Tax Rate	x	28%	federal tax rate
Tax Savings	=	$ 588	
NET PAYMENT			
Payment		$ 2,100	
Tax Savings	–	$ 588	
Net Payment	=	$ 1,512	
RENTAL INCOME			
Rent Rate (Class A, 2 BR apartment)	–	$ 800	2 BR apartment
Total Net Monthly Payment (pre-credit)	=	$ 712	
HISTORIC TAX CREDITS			
Restoration Costs	+	$ 300,000	
Tax Credit Rate	x	30%	
Tax Credit	=	$ 90,000	
Owner's Adjusted Gross Income		$ 100,000	
NC Income Tax Rate	x	7%	
NC Tax Liability	=	$ 7,000	
Savings per month	/12	$ 583	
Total Net Outflows (pre-credit)		$ 712	
Tax Credit	–	$ 583	
Net Monthly Payment	=	$ 129	per month

Fig. 3.6: Net Payment Analysis including Mortgage Deduction, Rent and Tax Credit

3,000-square-foot historic home, of $129 per month. Seriously?

Yes, it seems absurd to own such a house for the cost of a week's worth of groceries. Many say it is just too good to be true and leave it at that. But very real people are taking advantage of these very real mechanisms. Clients and colleagues of mine own

1. A 1,700-square-foot $250,000 bungalow with main house owner-occupied and a detached carriage house apartment rented to a student for $725 per month. This property leaves the owner with 1,700 square feet and a net payment of $450 per month.

2. A 2,100-square-foot $270,000 restored Victorian, lower level owner occupied, upper level apartment rented to Duke PhD for $600 per month. This property leaves the owner with 1,300 square feet and a net payment of $600 per month.

3. A 2,200-square-foot $300,000 restored bungalow, main house owner-occupied, basement studio rented at $700 per month leaving the owner with 1,600 square feet and a net payment of $600 per month.

4. 4,200-square-foot $400,000 restored dual townhomes, one owner-occupied, the other rented for $1,250 per month leaving the owner with 2,100 square feet and a net payment of $700 per month.

5. A 3,100-square-foot $430,000 restored Victorian, main house owner-occupied, with attached apartment renting at $800 per month, leaving the owner with 2,300 square feet and a net payment of $350 per month.

6. A 5,500-square-foot $700,000 home, owner-occupied, with three rented units paying a total of $3,200 per month. The owner is left with 2,100 square feet and a net payment of $500 per month.

Attractive as these numbers are, few of these owners took advantage of tax credits. Obviously, there are many variables that can affect the cost of rehabilitation and the potential financial benefits of owning an historic house. However, there are under-utilized tools available to owners (and potential owners) of historic homes.

More Questions to Ask

Taking on a project like a larger house with an attached rental can cause lost sleep and make the stomach churn. It's healthy to look at the worst case scenario. If the project still works, it's safe to go ahead.

How much do similar places rent for?

Search local papers and property management firms. If the apartment has one bedroom, find out what similar one-bedroom apartments are renting for. Take a blended average of five or ten, adjusting for quality factors such as location and condition, and use that as your predicted rental rate.

What happens if the place doesn't rent?

If it doesn't rent for six months or a year, can you handle it? If such risk causes bankruptcy or keeps food from the table, it would not be prudent to proceed. If, on the other hand, you conclude that it would hurt but not make you insolvent, then such an arrangement is worthy of consideration.

Will the attached rental rehabilitation qualify for tax credits?

In cases where the attached rental is within the original historic envelope, the answer is yes. Where it is not, such as an apartment over a new garage, no tax credits will be earned. Since attached rentals tend to be small but feature an entire kitchen and bath they can be expensive spaces to build out. Of course, then they can yield a correspondingly large tax credit. Thus, when possible, inclusion in the original envelope is financially beneficial.

How secure are our jobs?

Since the upfront investment for an additional dwelling may be significant, and many use the mechanism to justify a larger house and mortgage than they would otherwise consider, it is important to consider job security. If the apartment does not rent, and you or your partner lose your job, can you afford the home? Ironically, the income from a rental can offset this blow better than having no rental at all. Still, job security is important to consider before taking on additional construction costs, assets and liabilities.

Do we have situational factors that might limit who we rent to?

Assuming you are living within ear shot, consider what sort of renter you do, and do not, want. If your kids are sleeping next door, you probably don't want a partier or musician. You may not want to rent to people with pets if you have allergies. While your and the rental spaces may be separate, the mechanical systems may not be, so allergenic particles in the air will be circulated between the spaces.

If you have a high quality space, you will attract a high quality renter. High quality renters pay their rent on time, maintain the place, are reasonable and low maintenance tenants.

Summing Up the Finances

A house should first and foremost be a home: a place to relax with family and friends. For years now, young couples have been flocking to the city to enjoy the high quality lifestyle that historic homes and their communities offer. Ultimately, people buy (or don't buy) because of these qualitative factors. Only after those criteria are met should you look upon a house as a financial investment.

As a financial investment, homes provide a (generally) appreciating asset attached to a tax-advantaged liability. Historic homes' unique and exceptional financial mechanisms can broaden the spectrum of housing opportunities available to you.

PART II: GREEN ROOMS

BATHROOMS

It is the place of blissful escape where we steal a few moments of precious privacy. It is the place to which we see to make ourselves feel good — to relax, rejuvenate, recharge. Its importance goes well beyond the mundane practical functions of personal maintenance and the rituals of hygiene; it is where we cleanse ourselves spiritually as well as physically.

— Diane Berger and Fritz Von Der Schulenburg, *The Bathroom*

They're generally the smallest rooms in the home, but bathrooms are second only to kitchens as the rooms owners most desire to upgrade. Although, when dealing with historic homes, we have to consider what *upgrade* really means. In newer homes upgrade generally means starting over, whereas, in historic bathrooms it might mean preserving and accentuating what is left of the room's original fixtures and flow. While historic kitchens are often viewed as impractical and arguably unworkable, historic bathrooms tend to be easier to preserve and adapt to modern life.

The use of the bathroom varies greatly by family. A family with kids requires a place to bathe. A young professional couple may require space for two to share a single bathroom each morning. Ultimately, the bathroom is a personal place to cleanse, relax and refresh. Luckily, with a variety of antique fixtures, tile work and trim, there are plenty of opportunities to restore a bathroom to a specific style and time period.

In quests to upgrade historic homes for modern life, there are a few possible approaches. *Preservation* involves keeping as many original items as possible, but allows for new upgrades where original aspects no longer exist. *Restoration* brings the bath back to its original state, restoring old and replacing new with original looking pieces. Or, if the existing space doesn't work, you can always modify a space plan by reconfiguring or adding bathrooms. *Reconfiguration*

Fig. 4.1-2: *A traditional restored bathroom features original double casement windows, hexagonal tile, pedestal sink, marble shower and a radiator. At right, a more modern aesthetic.*

PRESERVATION DURHAM BY SARA DAVIS LACHENMAN FOR STEVE AND RUTH CHANDLER.

PRESERVATION DURHAM BY SARA DAVIS LACHENMAN FOR ARTHUR ROGERS, ARCHITECT DAVID ARNESON OF CENTER STUDIO ARCHITECTURE

Evolving Bathroom Style

SARA DAVIS LACHENMAN

As the bathroom moved indoors in urban homes of the late 19th century, white quickly became the dominant color of choice, emphasizing cleanliness and sterility. In such a design, nearly all surfaces had easy-to-clean, high-gloss white finishes: glazed hexagonal tile on the floor, marble slabs for counters, painted cabinet trim and walls. Fixtures were white too, ☞

SARA DAVIS LACHENMAN

SARA DAVIS LACHENMAN

Fig. 4.3-5: *Bathrooms featuring original sinks or clawfoot tubs are true finds worth keeping.*

with some metal accents such as polished nickel and chrome. Tile and paint often had black accents, sometimes the only break in the color scheme.

1930s deco style brought green, pink and yellow designs with glass, porcelain and ceramic tiles, colored plumbing fixtures, mosaics and funky accessories such as recessed toilet paper holders. Depending on whom you ask, these 1930s-1950s baths are considered either fabulous or an eyesore. Such bipolar opinions illustrate that all design styles go out eventually and only need the benefit of time before their historic value can be considered. Remember that, in the 1960s and 1970s, Victorian style was synonymous with bad taste, and its overly ornate detailing was written off as frivolous. Now, of course, Victorian is one of the most sought-after styles. Mid-century modern and other 1950s homes are currently moving through this out-of-style phase and back into vogue.

Preservationist forefather John Ruskin called time out of style *the black spot of fashion.* Styles go out of favor just before coming back in. Particular historic homes styles are at most risk of being demolished when they go out of style, which is often right before their character will be most valued.

Fig. 4.6: *Replication fixtures are reliable and new, but look old.*

Fig. 4.7-8: *Hexagonal glazed tile with a custom black accent was a common touch. Replication tiles are available, some made from high recycled content or local material.*

Fig. 4.9: *Standard mounting heights for fixtures and accessories. Certain period fixtures or unusually shaped bathrooms may alter these standards.*

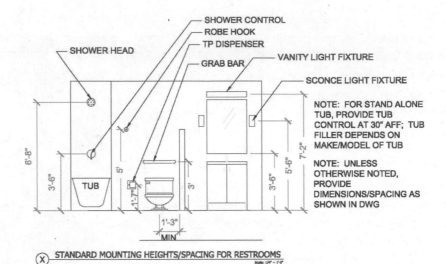

SHOWER CONTROL
ROBE HOOK
TP DISPENSER
SHOWER HEAD
VANITY LIGHT FIXTURE
GRAB BAR
SCONCE LIGHT FIXTURE

NOTE: FOR STAND ALONE TUB, PROVIDE TUB CONTROL AT 30" AFF; TUB FILLER DEPENDS ON MAKE/MODEL OF TUB

NOTE: UNLESS OTHERWISE NOTED, PROVIDE DIMENSIONS/SPACING AS SHOWN IN DWG

TUB

1'-3" MIN

(X) STANDARD MOUNTING HEIGHTS/SPACING FOR RESTROOMS
Scale: 1/4" = 1'-0"

involves rearranging fixtures within its existing footprint. *Addition* involves a new footprint, either by expanding an existing bathroom or installing a new bathroom where previously none existed.

In the 21st century, environmental concerns are as important as style and character. Fixtures may be pretty, but they must be efficient. With respect to green restorations, this chapter will demonstrate how to

- Use water more efficiently
- Minimize energy use (and wait time) for hot water
- Reduce moisture and improve air quality
- Minimize environmental footprint through fixtures, salvage strategies and thoughtful design

Questions to Ask

- Are there original fixtures or finishes in my bathroom?

- What style is my bathroom design?
- Do I prefer an historic looking period bathroom, or something more modern?
- Do I prefer vanity or pedestal sink?
- Do I prefer custom or off the shelf shower enclosures?
- How much storage do I need?
- How quickly will hot water arrive in the bathroom?
- What systems and fixtures can I install to minimize energy and water waste?
- How is moisture managed in my bathroom?

Due to their compact size and concentration of finishes and fixtures, bathrooms are a great focal point for a green restoration. I'll discuss green building issues and solutions, and how they relate to preservation concerns. The reader will also find information about bathroom styles, reconfiguration strategies and what to look for in salvage materials. Lastly, note that some concepts applicable to bathrooms are also discussed in the Kitchens, Electrical and Plumbing chapters.

Minimizing water use

Water conservation requires us to consider how much we use and how we can lower our demand.

- How much water do I use per day, month and year?
- Is this below or above the national average?
- What can I do to lower my usage?

According to the EPA, the average family in the US spends $484 a year for 60,000 gallons of water. That is, for most, pretty cheap, especially when compared to gas and electric bills. Some dwellers in cities in the Southwest spend four times that, as do the citizens of many countries in Europe. Many argue that the low cost of water in the US has encouraged wasteful, inefficient fixtures and lavish, artificially-irrigated grass lawns. The true cost of water is buried elsewhere: water and sewer infrastructure is expensive and is often subsidized by general levies such as property tax. The cost of pumping water to (or sewage from) houses requires massive amounts of energy. As our general population grows and suburban sprawl requires more and more gallons of water per person, water becomes scarcer and prices rise. There is no shortage of experts claiming that water rights may be a major source of world conflict in the 21st century.

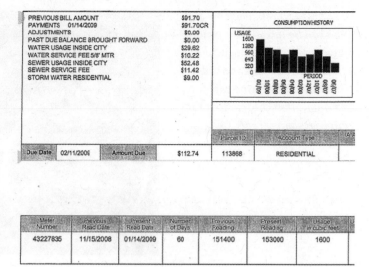

Fig. 4.10: Above and opposite page, *water bills that visually track usage give close to real time data about demand spikes or leaks, which can lead to conservation. Municipalities that graphically show usage on their bills have better educated clients, resulting in more water-saving efforts.*

Few expect water costs to go down, and water is now being recognized by governments as a limited resource. So what can be done?

Toilets

Of the water used inside the home, roughly $1/3$ is used to flush toilets. Before 1950, toilets averaged over seven gallons per flush. The 1992 US National Energy Policy Act mandated that toilets flush a maximum of 1.6 gallons per use, the usage rate of most toilets today. Many legacy toilets are still in existence today, including some old high-tank water closets (common before World War I) which can produce a waterfall of up

Fig. 4.11-14: *A relatively modern toilet can be mixed with historic features. All other finishes are period specific — an original, rehabilitated medicine cabinet and replication chrome fixtures with porcelain accents.*

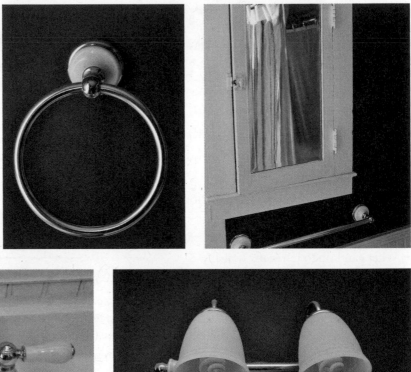

to 10 gallons per flush. Even new replication high-tank water closets are a showpiece for visitors but unfortunately do not come in low flow, water-minimizing versions. The high tank was replaced by the china, ceramic and porcelain toilets commonly used today. Original toilets are somewhat of a rare find, still, unless the old toilets have a fabulous historic aesthetic, it may be worth upgrading to a low flow toilet just for the water saving benefit.

There are some great replication toilets for a period restoration with hundreds of stylistic options. Yet, while period toilets are available, some homeowners choose to install a commonplace toilet in a bathroom and spend their preservation dollars for tile and clawfoot tubs.

Low Flow Toilets

Somewhat recently, the plumbing industry introduced two water saving toilets.

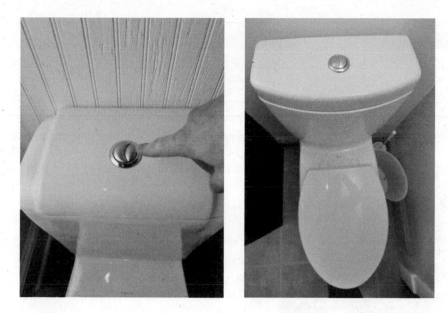

Fig. 4.15-16: *A dual flush toilet has two buttons, allowing the user to choose how much water is necessary to clear the contents of the bowl. Sometimes a challenge to design cohesion, most efficient toilets tend to be very modern looking.*

1. Low flow pressure-assisted toilets can use as little as .9 gallons per flush.
2. Dual-flush toilets offer the user the choice of .9 gallons per flush or 1.6 gallons executed via dual buttons located on top of the tank. In actuality, very little water is needed to flush pee. Why use more water than necessary?

The switch to a dual-flush toilet can save as much as 25% of your water bill, costs only slightly more than traditional toilets and pays for itself in three to five years. The technology is standard in much of Europe. More and more municipalities offer rebates for the installation of water-saving toilets, paying for some or all of their installation.

Strikingly, these water-saving toilets are still not carried by the big box home supply stores in the US. But you can order dual-flush toilets online, and plumbers can get them through trade stores. And as proof of water-efficient fixtures moving into the mainstream, in 2008, Sam's Club started selling a dual-flush model for $100.

Low Flow Fixtures

Shower, bath and faucet fixtures are becoming more efficient, too. Low flow fixtures restrict water flow so, relative to a conventional fixture, less water moves through the fixture per each second of use. Fixture manufacturers have paid minimal attention to water conservation over the years, resulting in showerheads that use more water than is really needed. The luxury home market has pushed multiple showerhead systems that are extraordinarily wasteful, with the vast majority of the water never touching human skin.

Fig. 4.17:
*Low Flow vs.
Conventional
Plumbing
Fixtures*

US DEPARTMENT OF ENERGY

Fixture	Low-Flow	Conventional	Savings
Toilets	1.6 gallons of water per flush	3.5 gallons per flush	1.9 gallons per flush
Showerheads	2½ gallons of water per minute	Between 4 and 5 gallons per minute	Between 1½ to 2½ gallons per minute
Faucet Aerators	2½ gallons of water per minute	4 gallons per minute	1½ gallons per minute

Fig. 4.18:
*Tub faucets are
great preserva-
tion pieces.
Unlike
showers, water
efficiency isn't
an issue.*

Low flow showerheads save significant quantities of water, using roughly half the water of a standard fixture. It is simple and inexpensive to install a low flow showerhead. Unfortunately, most low flow showerheads have thusfar lacked fashion, and choosing between having an inefficient beautiful showerhead or a dull one that uses less water has not helped people make the move to conserve water.

Finally, water conservation depends on the user just as much as on the fixture. For example, a 30-minute shower with a low flow showerhead uses more water than a ten-minute shower with a conventional showerhead.

An antique or replication tub faucet makes for a brilliant preservation visual, while also not wasting water resources. Bath faucets don't need to be low flow because they fill up a defined space. A low flow bath fixture would just take more time to fill the bath.

Minimizing Hot Water Waste

Hot water usage requires us to consider source, transfer and usage of hot water.

- How long does one have to wait for a hot shower in the morning?
- How much water is wasted waiting for hot water to flow?
- Does it irritate you to stand in a cold bathroom in January waiting for the shower water to heat up?

On average hot water consumes 15-25% of a home's utility bill (slightly less if you use gas). Conventionally, cold water is delivered to a large 40-80 gallon storage tank, where it is heated by electricity and stored until needed. Keeping that large amount of water at 140°F demands significant energy, whether you are using it (in the morning for showers) or not (on vacation). In that sense, conventional water heaters are quite wasteful.

Tank storage water heaters are the norm. They cost about $300 and are the default solution for builders and plumbers concerned more about easy installation today than paying the utility bill tomorrow. Since poorly designed hot water systems waste energy *and* water, there is a lot of room for improvement.

Solar Hot Water

Solar hot water systems are often tied to a radiant floor system, which is a great way to receive natural and inexpensive heat. Piping is looped through flooring, and a transfer medium, usually concrete, is then poured around the piping. Concrete is fantastic at absorbing heat and releasing it slowly. Many old tile floors sit on top of four- to six-inch slabs of concrete. Unfortunately, retrofitting radiant piping into existing slabs isn't easy or friendly to existing finishes, so it's an approach best reserved for a major job

Fig 4.19-20: Top, *a traditional storage water heater uses electricity (or gas in this case) to heat water. Bottom, a solar water heater uses the sun.*

Storage Water Heater

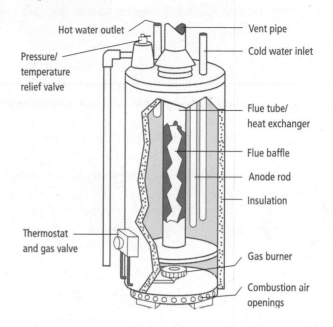

Active, Closed Loop Solar Water Heater

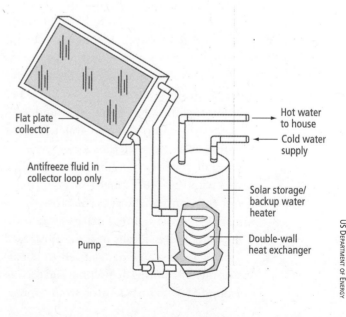

US Department of Energy

US Department of Energy

where a re-pour of concrete is planned. Radiant floor heating can be difficult to retrofit even in new construction, so consult an experienced installer.

There are significant state and federal tax credits for solar hot water systems, making them very affordable. Solar hot water heaters are one of the few items for which you can potentially claim a tax credit for both energy efficiency and historic rehabilitation. Tax incentives make these systems no-brainers for new construction projects, and they can be a wise choice for historic homes too. Every state features its own revenue code, so be sure to verify qualifying expenses with a local tax expert.

Retrofit Recirculating Hot Water

A traditional recirculating hot water system, which generally can only be installed in a gut job, runs hot water within six feet of each fixture in a return loop to the water heater. A retrofit recirculating kit system is a simple and inexpensive way to get instant hot water in the morning. A thermometer gauges the hot water line temperature, and upon reaching a low point of around 95°F, crosses over into the cold water line for return to the hot water heater via a pump. The hot water heater fills the supply line void with 120-140°F water, ready the instant you turn on the shower. The crossover is installed at the fixture farthest away from the water heater, ideally near the most-used morning shower. Being relatively unobtrusive, rarely requiring demolition and costing around $500 to install, this retrofit recircu-

lating system is a great choice for those looking to upgrade but not do major work. The technique requires no wall demolition. Temperature gauges are also available with timers, so the pump will only work certain times of the day (since it is wasteful to run a pump at 2 AM).

Improving Air Quality

The bathroom yields some of the lowest air quality in the home, which requires conscious odor and moisture management. Ask yourself

- Does steam linger in your bathroom after a hot bath?
- Is your shower curtain home to some weird growth?
- How often are bath fans run?

Green or not, there's no getting around the fact that the bathroom is a wet place. Showers, toilets, baths and faucets all have water sources and waste lines, each providing an opportunity for leaks. Even when the plumbing is functioning properly, everyday hot showers suspend enormous amounts of moisture in the air. Unmitigated, this moisture causes problems.

Mold and other bacteria require organic material, moisture and heat to thrive; all are readily in attendance in the bathroom. There's an entire chemical industry built on fighting mold and bacteria growth, particularly in the bathroom. It is ironic that we treat one environmental concern (mold) with chemicals that cause another (pollution and contamination) particularly when the problem is easily avoided with little more than proper ventilation. Luckily, there are simple solutions.

Ventilation Installation and Automation

Mechanical ventilation involves a wall- or ceiling-mounted bath fan that sucks moisture out of the bathroom and dumps it outside the home. Modern building codes require minimum ventilation for the bathroom to be a window of at least three square feet of which 50% is operable, or a mechanical ventilation system that moves at least 50 cubic feet per minute, ducted to the outside.

The extra expense and hassle is why cheap buildings feature a minimum-sized window to avoid having to install any mechanical bathroom venting. But this assumes that the occupant uses the window. And do any of us actually open a window after each shower? And who uses natural ventilation when the HVAC is running on cold winter nights or hot summer days? This is why all baths should have mechanical ventilation. The logic is shared by the 2009 International Mechanical Code, which deletes the window exception, effectively requiring mechanical ventilation in all bathrooms.

Perhaps even the presence of a bath fan is not enough. For those of us that do have a bath fan, how often do we actually use it? My wife thinks it just makes noise, so she never turns it on. A simple approach is to install an automated switch. Upon leaving the bath and turning the light off, the fan

Fig 4.21: *A basic ceiling mounted bath fan is rated for 110 cfm, recommended for bathrooms up to 100 square feet. If ceilings are exceptionally high, a larger fan should be installed.*

automatically runs for a set amount of time, usually ten to 20 minutes. This sucks low-quality air out of the house, of the moist or aromatic variety, and requires no conscious thought by the home's occupants. At roughly $30, the automatic switch is a helpful addition to any bathroom and can be a huge boost for a home's general indoor air quality.

Few historic homes have mechanical venting, therefore it is recommended that a bath fan be installed. It is equally important to ensure that the fan be properly sized. Fans are sized by how much air they move in cubic feet per minute (cfm). Bath fans are typically sized from 50 cfm to 400 cfm. Most are sized by the square feet in the bathroom, a two dimensional calculation. This is problematic for historic homes with high ceilings, which require a third dimension in the calculation. Most newer homes have eight- to nine-foot ceilings, whereas an old home's ceilings might be ten to 14 feet high. Since fans move air based on cubic feet, not square feet, contractors should install larger than recommended fans in tall baths. Venting requires subcontractor coordination — a mechanical subcontractor (aka *sub*) to install the fan and vent and an electrician to wire the unit. Exterior carpenters may need to coordinate the exterior vent with the mechanical sub.

Environmental Footprint Considerations

Life cycle analysis leads us to consider the greater impact of our material selections.

- How can I consider the life cycle of plumbing systems and fixtures?
- How long did the last plumbing system last?
- How long will this new plumbing system last?

- Will new fixtures look good with some wear and tear?

There's been a great debate about plastics and plumbing. The leading supply pipe today is PEX, and the leading waste line is PVC — both plastics. Plastics in general are shunned by green industries for environmental concerns over manufacturing and disposal processes and are shunned by preservationists for the ruinous effects of vinyl siding on historic homes. The United States Green Building Council recently facilitated a public debate on whether to deduct LEED

Fig. 4.22-25: *Recycled glass manufacturers offer substantial style with minimal footprint. Glass mosaics are strikingly modern, but penny rounds give an older feel.*

Common Ground Green Building Supply Center

- Can I repair an old fixture to work again?

applicants a point for using plastic PVC waste lines. USGBC's rating system is based on earning or not earning points, with no mechanism for deduction, so the proposal was an unprecedented and unusual first. Though USGBC ultimately decided against the deduction, the debate was indicative of the flaws of such scoring systems and the general distaste for plastics.

The problem is that the alternatives aren't any better, so the general consensus is that plastics are a lesser evil. The alternative to PEX is copper, an expensive material which has a very dirty manufacturing process, is highly recyclable but is costly to install. Waste lines are almost universally PVC now, replacing the cast iron systems used through much of the 20th century. Cast iron also has a dirty manufacturing process and corrodes over time. Any of these plumbing materials can be recycled, although, with the exception of high-value copper, they rarely are.

Finding the perfect finish fixtures for a restored bathroom can be a real expedition. There are many internet sources for replication materials, and local architectural salvage stores supply old sinks, baths and sometimes electrical fixtures. Rejuvenation, Restoration Hardware, Vintage Plumbing and Van Dyke's Restorers are all excellent suppliers of replication fixtures.

Replication fixtures are new, but look old; salvage fixtures are old and look old. Few new resources are required for salvaging a fixture, and its embodied energy is already spent. So the reuse of a salvage fixture can dramati-cally minimize the environmental footprint of a project. Consistent with the theme that runs through this book, a salvage approach is one of the greener things you can do, and I highly encourage it.

Preservation Issues

Old bathrooms have great content to work with. Clawfoot tubs are a favorite fixture to restore or retrofit. Antique sinks, with their unique profiles and non-standard sizes, are also returning to popularity. Bathrooms are showcases for tradespersons' craft too, featuring custom tile work with unique material, accents and patterns that indicate something about the time they were built, the style of the original owner or builder, and the cultural mores of the day.

Bathrooms are, by definition, subjected to the pressures of water. Over the course of 100 years they wear out faster than rooms without plumbing. Rotten floors, peeling paint, failing window sills, leaky plumbing, rusty mirrors and bacteria growth are all problems that need to be addressed and that may require demolishing original elements to fix the problem.

Fig 4.26: *Original hexagonal tile covered by vinyl squares, a prime opportunity for restoration.*

SARA DAVIS LACHENMAN

SARA DAVIS LACHENMAN

Fig 4.27-28: *Top left, a gorgeous master bathroom in a historic home need not feature historic styles. Because it is not in the considered historic living space, there is more flexibility with design. Top right, in the same house, a guest bath has more of a restoration feel, with period pedestal, accent tile and (unpictured) clawfoot.*

Fig 4.29: Bottom left, *space for a powder room bath is forged by claiming unused space under a primary stairway.*

Furthermore, modern bathrooms are safer places than they were 100 years ago, thanks to improvements in code and safety standards. Many old fixtures are OK to reuse in a new bathroom, though some require modification or replacement for safety reasons. Plumbing fixtures have to ensure that water won't backflow into the supply lines, and electrical fixtures have to be rated for damp locations.

The lifespan of bathrooms is less than that of drier rooms in the home, so it is a treat to find a bathroom in its original state. If you do have original fixtures and tile, go out of your way to preserve them. While they might not be the same style you would install if building from new, keep in mind that once an original part of the home is gone, it is gone forever. It's irreplaceable, by definition. Aside from being wasteful in a cultural and environmental sense, it might affect resale value for potential buyers who look for historic qualities. It also generally costs much more to restore than to preserve. Plus, you can brag to guests *Can you believe that's the original sink?*

While preservationists appreciate every effort to restore and accentuate original aspects of the home, SHPOs do recognize the need for modern amenities and offer significant flexibility to upgrade and reconfigure bathrooms. It's undisputed that today's homeowners demand modern bathroom features such as showers. After all, who has time for a bath every morning? Technically, you can have a totally new, even modern bathroom in an historic home and still qualify for tax credits. Or you may install a simple bathroom in an effort to save preservation dollars for other parts of the house. When taking a blank-slate approach, still look for opportunities to recycle, reuse or donate any fixture from the old bath.

Reconfiguration and Additions

Original bathrooms tend to be larger than today's standard five- by seven-foot bath, offering ample elbow room for rearranging. Though they tended to be larger, it was rare that a home built before 1920 had more than one bathroom. Baths were seen as a luxury, and even the wealthy saw multiple bathrooms as frivolous and unnecessary. Today, even most starter homes have two and a half baths. This modern standard puts quite a strain on preservation designers. There is often no obvious place to add one bathroom, let alone two. Claiming portions of a room in a house in order to add a new bathroom often makes an original room

look uneven and tacky. Given that centered windows are so large and defining to a room's character, this design strategy rarely works.

When restoring, expanding or reconfiguring, it is best to keep bathroom projects from affecting the core historic living space of the house. Preservationists allow more flexibility to change a *private* bedroom into another use than, say, to divide a *public* dining room in order to add a bathroom. With respect to tax credits, SHPOs tend to be strictly against the reconfiguration of rooms in historic living spaces, rarely allowing it. Conversely, they generally offer flexibility in bedrooms and other private spaces. Bathrooms are considered private spaces, allowing for necessary modifications.

To preserve the public spaces, bathrooms are often placed in nooks and crannies, such as under stairwells, where they are somewhat hidden and don't dramatically alter the feel of home. Where you might consider a new bath, consider the following questions first.

- Is it necessary?
- Is the space currently unused and out of the way?
- Can I style the bathroom to the existing house?
- Will the addition cause damage to other historic aspects of the home?

Often bathroom additions are part of larger reconfigurations, such as a kitchen, which might offer a new and larger space plan. Sometimes an original single bath is large enough to be split into two: one serving as a public powder room, the other serving a private bedroom. When that is not possible, you might look at building a dormer (but not viewable from the street), perhaps squeezing fixtures in with minimum roof clearance or access. In small spaces, retrofitted bathrooms regularly end up with cozy, unique and interesting designs.

KITCHENS

Living green is about opening the spirit, or the heart, to ways in which we can direct our energies toward creating places that are healthy, vibrant and joyful.

— Jennifer Roberts, *Good Green Homes*

With today's trend towards more open floor plans, people spend more time in their kitchens than in any other room of their house. Over the last century the kitchen has evolved from a very private place into a very public one. Whereas in 1910 the kitchen was little more than a practical space, today it must also be beautiful. Kitchens grab the emotions of homeowners, home buyers and guests. People often buy a home because they fell specifically for the kitchen.

No room is used more frequently or intensely than the kitchen. All four sustainable building principles are at play. Indoor air quality is affected by cooking as we breathe in kitchen air, be it scented by freshly baked cookies or burnt grilled cheese. Kitchens demand huge amounts of energy to freeze our ice cream, microwave popcorn or fry an egg. They're the primary recycling room for the home, aggregating paper, metals and plastics prior to our weekly pickup. Life cycle considerations are paramount, as kitchens have the shortest lifespan of any room of the house and are often remodeled every 20 years in the name of style, functional obsolescence or system upgrades.

Sometimes, though rarely, features of an original kitchen may still be in place. If this is the case, a design can benefit from the reuse of fixtures like old farmhouse sinks, butler's pantry or stove hood. Whenever possible, it's best to recondition original fixtures and reuse them. Such rehabilitation saves and showcases historic materials.

Questions to Ask
- What style is my kitchen?

Fig. 5.1: *A newly remodeled kitchen features a pleasant blend of old and new. Traditional cabinets, countertops and windows match the house and time period, while modern appliances and lighting are added for aesthetic accents and function.*

- Are there any original features?
- How was the original kitchen laid out?
- What do I love (and not love) about the current kitchen?
- What are my favorite cooking tasks?
- Will the kitchen remodel be coordinated or staged with a larger rehabilitation project?
- Is the size of the kitchen sufficient or will a relocation, reconfiguration or addition be necessary?
- How will the new kitchen address function, beauty and energy efficiency?
- What specific storage needs do I have?
- Where do I collect recycling?

Systems

In terms of complex systems the kitchen is Grand Central Station. It features more fixtures, appliances and automation than the rest of the house combined. It's a complex space to design and construct, which is why it's the most expensive room to remodel, and typically designed and built by specialists.

Plumbers and mechanical and electrical (PME) subs each spend a disproportionate amount of their time roughing in and finishing kitchens. Notably, kitchens are subject to frequent code and safety improvement requirements, which means that even recently remodeled kitchens may not conform to code. Ground fault receptacles are now required on kitchen countertops, for example, but are nearly non-existent in old kitchens. Any room that is remodeled must be brought to code, work that falls more on PME subs than any other.

The plumbing of a kitchen is extensive. A *plumber* installs a waste line for the sink — usually shared with the dishwasher — and a dedicated waterline for the refrigerator. A growing trend is a water supply line over the stove, allowing large pasta dishes to be easily filled on the stove top. Additional plumbed fixtures may include water filtration and garbage disposals. The kitchen sink is the most frequently used hot water valve in the house, so, to limit hot water delay it's best to place the hot water heater as close as possible to the kitchen.

The *mechanical subcontractor* installs range venting, ductwork for vents and appliance gas lines. Gas lines may be used for ranges, cooktops and ovens.

The *electrician* installs receptacles and lighting and hardwires each appliance. Each appliance has specific amperage requirements so it's best to print installation instructions for the electrician prior to rough-in. A modern kitchen can have five or more dedicated circuits because every appliance exceeding a ½ horsepower motor (including the refrigerator, dishwasher, electric range and garbage disposal) requires its own. A separate circuit should serve receptacles, which must be ground-fault (GFCI) protected because of the presence of water. Lighting circuits should be run separately from the ground-fault receptacles circuit; otherwise, a trip in the GFCI will shut off all the lights. The electrician also wires smoke detectors, which should be placed near, but not directly in, the kitchen. A smoke detector in the kitchen would trigger too frequently from day-to-

A Brief History of Kitchens

Early kitchens were as much about survival as pleasure. Originally, the home was a one-room structure where dwellers cooked, slept and ate. Even in larger homes in the US during the Colonial period, people worked in the kitchen from morning until night, preparing, cooking, feeding, even making soap and candles.

Victorian inventions greatly simplified kitchen work. By the mid 1800s, the first cast iron stoves made cooking significantly easier, retiring the fireplace as a cooking element and negating the need to haul heavy iron pots and pans to stacks of burning logs. For those who could afford it, servants performed most kitchen chores. As the industrial revolution grew, servants moved into factory work and housewives took on more kitchen duties.

Busy homemakers demanded simpler ways to prepare food and to clean. With electricity came the first major wave of appliances and electric tools for every daily task. Recent advances of appliance technology pale in comparison to those occurring at the turn of the last century. By the roarin' 1920s, women had a wide array of *helpmates*: iceboxes, carpet cleaners and toasters. Water was, for the first time, heated mechanically rather than boiled on a fire. Food was purchased at the grocery store rather than grown.

Preservationist Guy Ladd Frost has noted that first appliances were invented and then rooms were built around them. Kitchens have become more public throughout the 20th century. By the 1930s, kitchens were established as the nerve center of the house, evidenced by carefully decorated (more than functional) built-in cabinets. After World War II, the Levitt brothers (of Levittown's famous production homes) moved the kitchen from the back of the house to the public front. The move of the kitchen from private space to public, coupled with the sheer scale on which the Levitts were building, changed the role of the kitchen forever.

The sexual revolution is also credited for making the kitchen quickly a more public, open space. When more women joined the workforce through the 1980s, they were not home as much. Thus, deletion of wall barriers between the cooking and living space was thought to bring the family closer together during those precious evening hours. Such open design concepts are prevalent today.

Structural Concerns

Analyze kitchen floor framing prior to a major remodel. Modern kitchens are extremely heavy. Old kitchens may have had a few cabinets, countertops and small appliances and relatively little weight. New designs may double or triple the amount of cabinetry, include solid surface countertops and massive appliances to boot. The additional weight will stress an underframed floor. It's an easy necessity to overlook. The solution is to add more framing, either through sistered joists or a mid-span girder.

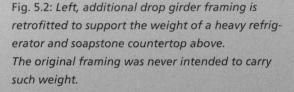

Fig. 5.2: *Left, additional drop girder framing is retrofitted to support the weight of a heavy refrigerator and soapstone countertop above.*
The original framing was never intended to carry such weight.

Fig. 5.3: *Right, an island in the middle of a floor span can cause a floor to sag. Additional support is warranted.*

day cooking. Lastly, a properly installed and sized vented range hood should control smoke.

Design

Good kitchen design is a highly skilled trade. A good design will consider space planning, specify cabinetry and countertops material, targeted task lighting, durable floors, efficient and practical appliances. Such design should take craftsmanship cues from the existing home and include a functional layout and style customized to the homeowner.

Designers from the International Interior Design Association (IIDA) or National Kitchen and Bath Association (NKBA) have a proven educational background that documents such skills. As with all professionals, ask about their historic home experience and request photos of their work.

Space Planning

Kitchen design starts with space planning. Where does everything go? First and foremost, consider how people flow through the space, then consider how people flow

Kitchen improvement projects

Low-hanging Fruit

- Clean cabinets, replace hardware
- Add organizers to cabinets and drawers: silverware, spice racks and Lazy Susans
- Replace incandescent lights with dimmable CFL or LED lights
- Install water filtration (or replace aged filters)
- Clean hood filter and refrigerator compressor coils
- De-clutter: get rid of everything you don't use or know to be valuable

More Involved

- Paint
- Replace appliances
- Reface cabinets
- Weatherstrip old doors and windows
- Install backsplashes

Major Undertaking

- Replace cabinets and counters
- Replace/refinish floors
- Reconfigure space, relocate kitchen

within the space. We might enter the kitchen through hallways, exterior doors, porches or mudrooms. Very often the kitchen might be passed through without being used, so you might want to minimize obstructions on the thoroughfare. When considering kitchen flow within the space, the kitchen triangle has long been the bench mark of design, meaning that the range, sink and refrigerator should all be easily accessible to one another.

A newer design school divides the kitchen into zones, often referred to as a diamond layout. Separate areas are dedicated for storage (pantry and refrigerator), food preparation (often a butcher-block surface), cooking (cooktop, pots, pans, stone surfaces) and cleaning (sink, dishwasher, stainless steel surfaces).

Once a preliminary space plan is complete, highlight sightlines or vistas through windows and doors. Consider what can and cannot be seen from the kitchen work space.

- Can children be seen in the backyard or playroom?
- Can children conduct homework in view?
- Are other core entertainment areas in view?
- Are there nice exterior vistas that can be captured with design modifications?
- What is the vista from the sink window?
- What functions do you not want visible (such as dirty dishes piling up from dining)?

Finally a few design basics will ensure a functional and entertaining space for years to come.

1. The *work triangle* ties together the stove, sink and refrigerator. It's long been the guiding concept in kitchen design. Some use microwaves more than stoves, so some now refer to a *work diamond* that can incorporate an oven or food prep

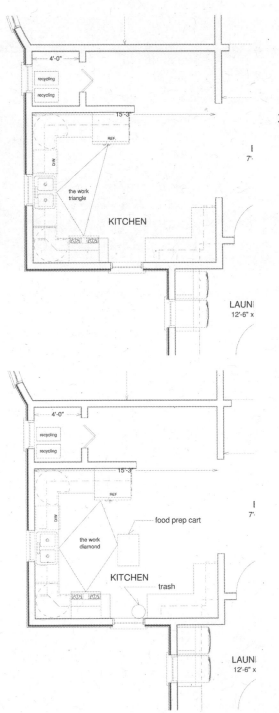

Fig. 5.4-5:
The kitchen work triangle has long been a guiding space planning concept. Recently, designers have sugested the food preparation area be included, forming a work diamond.

area as a fourth point. (Your author spends more time at the food prep area than at all three other elements combined, so finds its inclusion quite worthy of design consideration.)

2. Appliances are used constantly in tandem while cooking, so they should be close together. They also require adjacent counter space. Ideally, there should be three to eight feet between the stove and refrigerator, three to six feet between the refrigerator and sink, and two to five feet between the stove and sink. In a very large or small kitchen you will need to alter accordingly. Though rarely discussed in print (or by kitchen designers), kitchens can be too large. A massive kitchen suffers from large distances between appliances and prep areas, making it less functional. Also, an island constructed within the work triangle or diamond can block the cook's movement from one point to the next.

3. A dinner table should allocate an area 24 inches wide by 12 inches deep for each person. When seating, between 36 and 42 inches is the ideal distance from the table or counter edge to the nearest obstacle, allowing others to walk behind. If there is no need to allow people to pass, 24 to 30 inches is plenty.

4. Design for plenty of countertop space next to the stove and microwave and space on each side of the sink for dirty and drying dishes. A sink directly adjacent to a wall or appliances is very impractical.

5. In traditional design, kitchen sinks were generally placed under a window. Contemporary designs sometimes place the sink facing inward so the cook can face and talk with others who might be in the kitchen.

6. Kitchen cabinets usually extend up to 84 inches off the floor. Space above the cabinets is either filled with a soffit or left open. High cabinets will be reachable only with a stool, but provide excellent long-term parking.

7. Doorways should be 32 through 36 inches wide to allow for appliances, large serving trays, groceries and general egress.

Lighting

Kitchen lighting is a complex art, given that it must simultaneously provide task lighting for cooking and ambient light for entertaining. General lighting design includes three primary types of light, each serving a different purpose: 1) ambient lighting, 2) general task lighting and 3) targeted accent lighting. A good whole house lighting design mixes these options, sometimes with all three in a single room. Sustainable practice encourages fixtures that can provide multiple types of light, eliminating the need for additional fixtures or wiring.

Ambient lighting is a soft, often dimmable, light designed to set moods for entertaining. It includes over- or in-cabinet lighting, cove lighting above a soffit shelf and indirect pendants or wall sconces. Indirect pendants direct ambient light upward, whereas downward-directed pendants tend to be task lights. Cabinetry lighting and cove lighting

Fig. 5.6-7: *Over-the-counter pendants, and an over-the-table chandelier serve as task lighting and ambient lighting simultaneously. A dimmer raises the light output for reading, cooking and food preparation and lowers it for entertaining.*

Fig. 5.8-9: *Ambient LED under-cabinet lighting sets moods and softens the effect of harsher task lights.*

focused beam of light. Accent lighting is a relatively modern design feature, rare to find in old homes. Its inclusion in an old house plan is often determined by owner preference, specific to a person, piece of art or activity.

Track lighting is often errantly installed as a task light in kitchens, which is problematic since it really provides only accent light. Track lighting is very targeted, meaning that it will cast directional light on a few areas and leave adjacent areas under-lit, often called the *museum effect*. When track lighting is used, it is best reserved for accent lighting. Also, nearly all track lighting features incandescent halogens, which are hot-burning energy hogs. Since kitchen lights are some of the most frequently used lights in the home, efficient fixtures are necessary.

Task lighting is functional work light targeted at specific activity spaces, such as book reading or food preparation. It is the most common type of lighting in residential design. It might be as simple as a chandelier in the middle of the room or a row of can lights strategically placed over work areas. Though most task lighting is simply placed in the center of a room ceiling, good design is a bit more complicated. Functionally, the best place for task light is between your head and the task at hand. Light above your head will cast a shadow, making it less effective. This is an important consideration for placing reading lights, particularly over a bed where the reader's head can cast a shadow. High light output is essential for task lighting (75-100W incandescent or

are typically pucks or fluorescents, while sconces can feature exposed or concealed lightbulbs. Ambiance is only part of a deeper equation; a complete design requires other types of light. A room with only ambient lighting makes everything look bland, flat and without depth, sometimes called the *cloudy day effect*.

Accent lighting highlights plants, artwork or tables, typically using track lighting or adjustable recessed fixtures with a narrow equivalent), so energy-efficient bulbs pay dividends. Consider dimmer controls, too, since dimmable recessed lights and pendants can serve as both task and accent lighting.

Finally, plan for a consistent color temperature within each room. An awkward lighting mix can result from the combination of cool CFLs and warm halogens. There is more on lighting options and color temperature in the Electrical chapter.

Cabinetry

No part of a kitchen is more stated than its cabinetry. Cabinetry can be basic or extravagant, stained or painted, unique or ordinary, economical or expensive. The same kitchen might cost $10,000 with cabinets from IKEA or $50,000 from a custom cabinetmaker. The options are countless.

Manufacturers commonly offer formaldehyde-free wood, stain and paint grade finishes and a variety of styles, made of medium-density fiberboard (MDF) or plywood base with veneer. Newly ordered stain grade cabinets are often less expensive than paint grade, because paint grade cabinets require the further step of painting at the factory (counterintuitively, stain grain wood trim, like crown and baseboard, is actually more expensive because it is solid wood and has few if any imperfections). Drawers and doors are usually made of solid wood, while cabinet boxes rarely are. Solid wood cabinets are extremely expensive and rarely made anymore.

Urea Formaldehyde is toxic chemical compound commonly found in today's building materials. It's found in adhesives, finishes, MDF and molded trim. It is coveted for its tensile strength, water resistance and volume stability but is a known cause of cancer and is classified as a probable human carcinogen by the US Environmental Protection Agency. Though present in a naturally occurring state in most wood (in nearly inconsequential amounts), its widespread use makes it one of the greatest foes of indoor air quality. Its off-gassing can cause flu-like symptoms, including runny nose, itching, headaches, memory loss and nausea. It is also allergenic, so is commonly included in standard allergy testing.

Fig. 5.10: *About 200 cabinet manufacturers have the Kitchen and Cabinet Manufacturers Association's (KCMA) label. Green cabinet manufacturers that go above and beyond such designations include the Breathe Easy, Neil Kelly, Holiday and Executive brands.*

COMMON GROUND GREEN BUILDING SUPPLY CENTER

Consider in a cabinetry design

- Where will silverware go? Is it easily accessible from the dishwasher?
- Where will the trash bin and compost go?
- Where will recycling go?
- Where will small appliances be stored?
- Will any wall cabinets be glass-faced?
- What sort of corner cabinets are best (Lazy Susan, diagonal, flush)?
- Where will primary pantry storage be?
- Will the refrigerator, oven, microwave and cabinet doors easily open? When opened, will they create hazards or obstruct traffic?
- How can my cabinetry style match my house style?
- Do I like open shelves or doors on upper cabinets?
- Do I prefer built-in cabinetry or furniture?
- Do I have furniture or family heirlooms to incorporate into my design?

Formaldehyde-free cabinets might demand a 10-20% premium, a small price to pay considering you will be eating off plates and dishes stored in these cabinets for decades to come.

Cabinet styles are varied, and should be cued from the house style. A Shaker style cabinet, for example, would look more appropriate in a Craftsman bungalow than in a Victorian house.

Pantries are often designed as small separate rooms adjacent to the kitchen. If no such room is available, a group of large full-height cabinets is a strong alternative.

Common Countertop Types

Countertop food preparation surfaces continue to evolve with a multitude of new, particularly green, materials entering the marketplace. Colonial kitchens had no countertops, but by the turn of the 19th century wooden counters and drainboards were being manufactured and used as kitchen work surfaces. Being wood, they easily warped and split and demanded constant conditioning or replacement. That's why longevity and durability are behind today's designs. Today's kitchens feature different materials serving specific purposes. Wood is preferred for food preparation, solid surfaces are preferred near the range for hot plates and stainless steel is preferred near the sink for cleaning. The mixing of permanent countertop surfaces is a recent trend, with some kitchens even featuring two, or even all three, surface types. Since countertops can be large and heavy, sourcing is a sustainability concern. Materials that are extracted regionally, or at least nationally, are more desired that those that are imported.

Woods

Butcher block has the end grain facing up for dimensional stability. It offers a great cutting surface that ages well with each whack, making it a highly desired food preparation surface. Plus, it won't break glass as easily as stone might. Pine, oak and maple woods are all popular. Some exotic woods such as purpleheart can be used for panache. Butcher block has a tendency to blacken when repeatedly exposed to water and is not hot plate proof. Avoid exotic hardwoods unless FSC-certified. Seal with a mineral oil, but never use polyurethane on a food surface as it will poison you.

Stones

Natural and synthetic stones are heat resistant, unique and long lasting. Soapstone, slate and marble have a 100-year-old history in kitchens, while shiny granite is more recent. While synthetic or aggregate materials will have a consistent appearance, natural stones vary greatly. Always hand-select natural stones from the building supply yard. Color and veining vary significantly, so the only way to be sure you'll like your stone is to select it yourself.

Starting around 1850, *soapstone* was used for sinks and butler's pantry counters and was a popular countertop material for science labs. It can scratch under extreme circumstances and requires a treatment of mineral oil every few months to keep its dark color. Freshly cut stone requires a few months to oxidize before

Fig. 5.11: *Soapstone is a dark, often black surface with unique veining that is traditionally honed to a finish.*

Fig. 5.12: *Center,* concrete *is a formed material that is either poured in place or custom fabricated off-site and delivered. Though high in labor costs, its material cost is so small that it's almost negligible.*

Fig. 5.13: *Bottom, raw concrete can be mixed with nearly any aggregate from pennies to glass, so finish designs are only limited by material availability and your imagination.*

taking on its final charcoal color. Nevertheless, soapstone is a great traditional choice. It's sourced from the US Northeast (so it's relatively local in the US) and South America (not so much a local source).

Slate is a solid work surface commonly used in backsplashes. It was used in dry sinks before indoor plumbing. It can scratch and does require sealing. Slate is more common (and cheaper) in the slate-producing Northeast US.

Granite is available in a wide variety of patterns, often struggling to work well with a classic, historic-looking kitchen. Its mining and fabricating requires diamond cutting, which is one reason it was not readily available until the 1970s. Granite is the dominant upscale solid surface countertop material today. Though it's plentiful, critics point out that granite manufacturing and transport is wasteful. Increasingly, granite is coming out of China.

Tile is a solid surface generally requiring grout lines, and grout lines pose cleaning problems. Still, a butt joint with no grout line is the cheapest way to get a heat-proof,

solid surface countertop. Modern epoxy grouts are stain resistant, while Portland cement-based grouts are not and will stain easily over time.

Metal

Stainless steel was introduced in the 1920s, lasts forever, won't stain, won't rust and is easy to clean. It does require custom fabrication, which can be expensive. Stainless steel can scratch and looks industrial and modern, arguably making it stylistically inappropriate for many period kitchens. Still, I've seen some designers have success incorporating stainless steel into old kitchens. If you like such styles, check with commercial restaurant suppliers, who may have prefabricated tables and countertops.

Laminates

A final material worthy of discussion is laminate, made from craft paper glued with resins, which has been installed in kitchens from the 1920s through today. Laminates (also commonly called Formica for its primary manufacturer) are cheap and widely popular. When laminate colors boomed in the 1950s, it quickly became the stock material of post-war production building. Of the six million homes built in the US from 1945 through 1952, fully 30% had Formica counters. Laminates are neither scratch proof nor heat resistant, so they are not as durable as pricier options.

The newest versions certainly do not look old, but a few tricks can create an historic Formica look, particularly for mid-century

What makes a product green?

Green kitchen counters and flooring are sustainably harvested, manufactured locally, off-gas little, are easy to clean and will last decades if not centuries. Products that are not green have harsh sourcing and manufacturing processes and are often shipped long distances. High levels of formaldehyde, VOC content and adhesives make them neither durable nor cleanable.

projects: trim the outer edge with aluminum and use aluminum strips to bond the counter and backsplash.

Today's Green Countertop Options

Quartz is a visually comparable and more environmentally friendly alternative to granite. Why? Granite is mined in whole slabs, a process that produces large amounts of waste. Also, little granite is mined locally. Most slabs come from South America, and the cheapest slabs (which are poised to dominate the market) come from China. Conversely, nearly all quartz countertop material is mined in the US.

Similar distinctive products are the result of regional material supply, waste demands and creative concrete artistry.

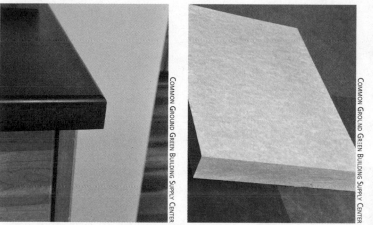

Fig. 5.14-15: *Top left and center,* paperstone, *made from recycled paper with a water-based resin. It is heat resistant, easily cleaned and zero-VOC. Paperstone has great strength for cantilevered applications, and can be cut as thin as $3/8$ of an inch. Some manufacturers source wood waste from FSC-certified wood, advertising 100% post-consumer application.*

Fig. 5.16: *Top right,* glass and concrete counters *use recycled glass products as accents for a countertop with a concrete base. Given a three month lead time, one client used the countertops as an excuse for a wine and liquor party, drinking from the bottles that would one day be their permanent counters (do so at your own risk, I suppose).*

Fig. 5.17: *Bottom right,* bamboo countertops *with a decorative middle ply leave no need for facing. Rapidly renewable, bamboo is unique looking and long lasting.*

Fig. 5.18: *Above, wood waste and natural countertops, clockwise from top left: Wheatboard, oriented strand board (OSB), more OSB, Dakota Burl (sunflower seed shells), sawdust and more Dakota Burl. Each is an inexpensive, natural product. It is pressure-treated with acrylic resin that makes it durable and water resistant. Many versions are not heat resistant, so uses may be limited near the stove top.*

CHATHAM™ 76

NOTTINGHAM™ 7120

ASHFORD™ 7620

PRESTON™ 2220

Fig. 5.19: *Above, quartz is mined as a granulated aggregate, then assembled with a nontoxic epoxy (which does have a petroleum base), a process that creates nearly zero waste.*

Fig. 5.20: *Center left, butcher-block countertops from antique salvaged wood feature a beautiful reddish-hue. The material is all natural, glued with nontoxic wood glue, ages well and can be refinished. It is protected by a simple covering of mineral oil, applied periodically. Wood is an ideal food prep surface.*

Fig. 5.21: *Bottom left, Riverstone uses rock dredged from the base of a dam in Virginia. As silt builds up, it puts pressure on the dam, which has to be periodically relieved of the force. Concrete fabricators use the unique brown rock in various shades of concrete, serving as an incredible accent to brown cabinets.*

Flooring

A well-chosen floor goes a long way, particularly in the kitchen. The kitchen floor will be subjected to spills, breakage and stains. It will also have a larger volume of traffic than anywhere else in the home. When choosing kitchen flooring, consider its cleanability, durability, look and feel, and off-gassing, as well as design cohesion with other kitchen features and the rest of the home. Just about any material other than carpet is fair game, including bamboo, wood, tile, concrete, stone and linoleum.

Among all the choices, few beat the cost, durability, look and feel of old-fashioned wood. Wood material can range greatly in cost, from around $2 per square foot to $20 per square foot. On the lower end are pine and oak products. On the higher end are old-growth, exotic species and salvaged materials with stunning color.

Furthermore, wood is a flexible and reusable product. One local company salvages old logs from a river, where they have been submerged for over a century, and mills them into spectacularly unique flooring (wood requires oxygen to rot, so completely

Fig. 5.22-24: *Linoleum offers the wide range of colors and designs otherwise limited to synthetic vinyls.*

Fig. 5.25: *A Marmoleum floor, a linoleum product that is solid all the way through (no plies), backed by a strong, long lasting hemp-fiber. It's manufactured at a reclaimed 300-year old hemp factory in Scotland. There's a huge variety of colors and it is non-static, so nothing sticks to it. Being true linoleum, it is made with pine tar, linseed oil and wood flour. It is 100% natural and biodegradable, so you can throw it in your compost.*

submerged wood does not decay). Other companies deconstruct old buildings and resell the salvaged flooring, a process that saddens hard-core preservationists.

With more environmental savings, wood can easily be salvaged within a single home.

Cork	Rapidly renewable, moisture and fire resistant, easy on dropped glass, easy installation, good for acoustics and minimizing sound transfer.	Harvested in Europe, often manufactured with formaldehyde. Some are vinyl laminates with cork on a single layer. Can off-gas a minor odor.
Linoleum	Made from renewable resources, durable, historically accurate and available in many colors. Can be purchased in rolls, tile or tongue and groove (TnG) panels. Easy to maintain and clean.	Some varieties off-gas VOCs and linseed oil odor. Manufactured primarily in Europe. Higher first costs. Note that many mistakenly refer to plastic sheet vinyl (a plastic product) as linoleum (a natural product).
Tile	Made from clay, an abundant resource. Can be repaired, wide range of colors, styles, textures, regional sourcing. Can provide thermal mass, low toxicity.	Grout can stain and be difficult to clean. Manufacture is energy-inefficient. Some mortars and sealants contain high VOC content.
Solid Wood	FSC products available. Salvaged material readily available, wide range of styles, colors and woods manufactured, long lasting (200 years +). Refinishable Old-growth wood is very hard and stable.	FSC-certified products are expensive. Solid wood flooring production exacerbates deforestation. Manufacturer's claims difficult to verify. Reclaimed old-growth wood is more expensive than new.
Engineered Wood	Engineered products use wood waste, creating less material demand than solid wood. Most are pressure-treated to be durable and long lasting.	Can be refinished far fewer times than solid wood. Sub-layers are made from young, fast growing trees, making this wood less dimensionally stable. Glues may off-gas.

In a major remodel, wood may be taken up from one room and reinstalled in another.

Linoleum was a popular product in the early part of the 19th century and is recently resurgent. It is made primarily from linseed oil, a natural renewable product. It is an expensive product, but a beautiful one and a great historically accurate option to consider.

Appliances

We take for granted how much appliances do for us. Just about any kitchen features a range and refrigerator, but dishwashers are also now standard, and there are an overabundance of other options, including microwaves, trash compactors, garbage disposals, washers and dryers, ice-makers, freezers and so forth. In specifying, it's important to consider each appliance's ease of use, energy efficiency, size and style.

Ease of use is crucial. With many appliances, simplicity has virtues. Some refrigerators now have onboard TVs, timers, water filtration, digital thermostats, beverage chillers, dedicated freezer drawers and connect to the internet. Each layer of complexity makes breakdown more likely and repair more expensive. The irony of such smart technology is that it makes a simple device complex to run. All you really need the thing to do is keep your vegetables cold and your ice cream colder.

Also, don't confuse upgrading with supersizing. Larger appliances take more room and use more energy. It's a poor allocation of remodeling dollars to buy more than you need or more than is appropriate for the home. A massive appliance in a modest kitchen looks like a race horse on a NASCAR track — beautiful, but out of place.

Appliances use up to 20% of a home's energy, so the purchase of energy-efficient models has a large effect on the power bill. Today's refrigerators are better insulated and have more efficient compressors; they're far more efficient than units just ten years old. Since the refrigerator runs more frequently than other appliances, it should be a priority for upgrade. The US Environmental Protection Agency and US Department of Energy have set up a website that helps calculate energy savings and outlines potential utility rebate programs for appliance upgrades.[1] Finally, not all appliance suppliers will recycle what they remove (as required by law in most states), so check before you buy.

Energy Star is the US government's benchmark standard for helping businesses and homeowners protect the environment

US Department of Energy, US Federal Trade Commission

Fig 5.27: The most efficient appliances receive the Energy Star certification, indicated by this label.

US Department of Energy, US Federal Trade Commission

Fig 5.28: Most appliances in the US will feature the EnergyGuide data, which indicate how efficient the unit is relative to its peers.

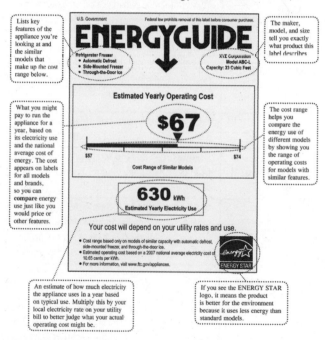

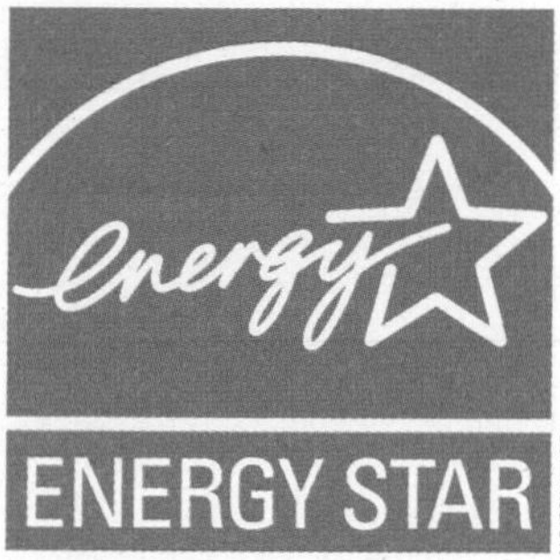

Fig. 5.29: *Choosing Your Appliances*	**Considerations**	**Width**
Gas Cooktops	Gas heat is instantaneous and can burn hotter than electric. High-BTU gourmet ranges are all gas, more expensive than electric and require an additional gas line.	Typically 30", luxury versions 48"– 60".
Electric Cooktops	Does not require additional gas line, less expensive than gas. Require 220V electricity, inefficient, not as high heat output, take time to heat up.	Typically 30", luxury versions 48"– 60".
Oven	Duel fuel models feature gas cooktops and electric oven. Convection models can cook more evenly and quickly. Some feature a separate broiler and self-cleaning functions. Review cleanibility, ease of use, complexity of controls. Electric ovens require 220V lines.	Typically 30", luxury versions up to 48".
Range Hood	Properly-sized version (generally sized to cooktop) deposit smoke and odors outside the envelope, increasing indoor air quality. Decorative versions are available. Concealed downdraft versions allow for placement of cooktops in interior space (when not on an exterior wall, as typical). Ventless versions suck air up and shoot it out at the cook's eye level, and should be avoided.	Typically 30", luxury versions 48"– 60".
Refrigerator	Energy Star versions are very energy efficient. Exterior ice and water supplies are convenient, but put a hole in the insulated shell, causing the unit to consume more energy. Usually set at 36°F for refrigerator, and 0°F for freezer. Water/Ice service requires additional water line.	30" small, 36" large. Small versions available for secondary kitchens/bars, larger luxury versions available.
Dishwasher	Technology-heavy versions are expensive to repair. Medium to high end units have double the capacity, meaning the unit runs less frequently.	24"
Garbage Disposal	Used to break up food scraps prior to sending to the sewer. Often omitted from design as it encourages the disposal of organic matter through the sewer, when it is better rubbished to the compost bin.	12"–18"
Microwave	Uses radiation to heat certain items in a fraction of the time of the range. Quality of heat makes many foods soft or watery. It's an energy hog, so if you use the microwave a lot, purchase an Energy Star version. Built-in, above range versions have onboard venting for range below.	30", typically to fit over range.
Trash Compactor	Compacts trash so it will occupy less space in the landfill. It's an extra expense and possibly redundant if local trash service also compacts.	18–24"
Deep Freezer	Good for long term frozen storage, freezes at temperatures cooler than regular freezer (-13°F). Deep freezers use a lot of energy, so they're best reserved for larger families; smaller families are better off buying smaller amounts of food less often and not having an additional freezer.	Varies, vertical and horizontal styles available.
Clothes Washer	Front loaders are far more efficient, using less energy and water. Consider the size of the unit to make sure it will fit, and the capacity, which should be sized to your family. Stackable dryer combination units save space.	27–30"
Dryer	High end units use magnets to accelerate the spin cycle while using less electricity. Gas dryers, though rarer, are more efficient. Electric dryers require 220V line.	27–30"

through energy efficiency. One of the primary roles of the Energy Star service is to rate the energy efficiency of products in more than 60 categories ranging from refrigerators to ceiling fans. Energy Star refrigerators, for example, use 20% less energy than the required federal standards and 40% less energy than conventional models sold in 2001.

Craftsmanship

During a kitchen remodel any preexisting architectural details should be kept and, if possible, accented. Continue moldings, such as baseboard and crown, from other living spaces through the kitchen. Keep old masonry work in place where possible. Sometimes the kitchen remodel is so thorough that the new version looks nothing like the old. Often a kitchen may be in the back of a house or new addition where historic craftsmanship doesn't exist. In such a case, the design decision would either consider existing house features or differ from them altogether.

Generally speaking, a complete stylistic change may be awkward. A fantastic contemporary kitchen worthy of *Dwell* magazine is bound to feel awkward in an otherwise wholly Tudor-style home. It is best to keep some style with the house, even though the cabinets, for example, may not be completely period consistent.

Preservation Issues

Since it does not fall into the core living space of the home, a kitchen's architectural

Fig. 5.30: *A retired masonry chimney has been exposed, serving as a ghostmark of the home's previous systems and a nice architectural detail.*

Fig. 5.31: *A butler's pantry was once used for kitchen storage and food preparation. It features large original cabinetry, and a small eating nook. Such a room may risk being demolished for the sake of a larger kitchen.*

integrity is of less concern to preservationists. Preservationists do realize that a 1910 kitchen is probably not consistent with the needs of modern life and that upgrades will be desired. Historically speaking, kitchens were not the public space they are required to be today. Still, when relocating kitchens, demolishing old features or conducting work that does affect the core living space, be sure to obtain prior SHPO approval.

Fig. 5.32: *Cabinets are temporarily protected from construction with foamboard (which can then be reused as insulation).*

Generally speaking, there is generous tax credit flexibility with kitchen remodels as long as the proposed remodel does not adversely affect adjacent public living spaces, such as the dining room. Kitchens are the most expensive room in the house to remodel, and all expenses except appliances should qualify for tax credits.

Because the kitchen is the most frequently remodeled room in the home, it is rare to find any original features in a 100-year-old kitchen. When old or original sinks or butler's pantry cabinetry are found, make a strong effort to keep, rehabilitate and reuse them. Whenever getting rid of old cabinetry and appliances, be sure to deconstruct and donate. Habitat for Humanity regularly picks up such items and reuses them in their own projects or sells them to fund their operations. Donations to such nonprofit organizations yield a tax deduction for the homeowner.

LIVING SPACES

Other than rehabilitation to meet the expectations of modern living or the urge to restore to recapture lost architectural splendor, owners of historic houses do not redecorate or remodel as often as do occupants of more modern homes. The homeowner's satisfaction with an older house usually reflects a recognition that the house has qualities that are hard to replicate in a new house or new location.

— Hugh Miller, *Caring For Your Historic House*

The integrity of an historic home's public living space is paramount. Public living space is a somewhat technical, often interpretive term, but it generally includes the entryway/foyer, living rooms, dining rooms, stairwells, main hallways and any parlors. The private living space includes bedrooms and private bathrooms. Grey areas include the kitchen, which was private 100 years ago but is public today. Public living space is one of the three major focal points of preservation review. For preservation's sake, these core living spaces must be kept intact.

In her widely acclaimed *Not So Big House* series, Sarah Susanka advocates small houses with higher quality and well-designed layouts and finishes. She goes on to argue that you should not build new space without first considering how to better use existing space. Often design solutions as simple as deleting a wall can make a kitchen and living space function better, negating the need for a large addition project.

While historic homes have much synchronicity with the *Not So Big House* philosophy, they also come with special limitations that do not exist in non-historic housing stock. This is most evident when considering what to do with the wall between a dining room and kitchen. Historically, this formed an intentionally private divide between either the servants or housewife cooking and the public entertaining areas. The kitchen was once a place to be neither seen, smelled nor heard.

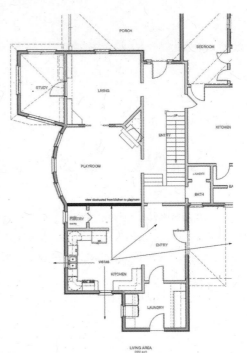

Fig. 6.1:
*Formal
living and
dining rooms
are often
integral to
the historic
character of
a home.*

Fig. 6.2:
In Not So Big
*fashion, a
previously
underused
space was
claimed for
a high-
functioning
office nook.*

PRESERVATION DURHAM BY SARAH DAVIS LACHENMAN FOR ARTHUR
ROGERS, ARCHITECT DAVID ARNESON OF CENTER STUDIO ARCHITECTURE

Fig. 6.3: A *wall separates a kitchen from a
living space, in this case a formal dining
room remodeled into a children's playroom.*

This can be frustrating for young couples
with kids who play in a room that is invisible from the kitchen where mom and dad
prepare food.

Many wish to knock down walls to create
a more modern cohesion between the kitchen,
playrooms and living space. This is categorically denied by most SHPOs. Still there is
some flexibility to widen a doorway, if the
casing and doorway detailing are kept. Others
opt to reconfigure a rear portion of the home
that may already be private, either by means
of an addition or to incorporate a non-public

Oh, how things have changed. Through
shifting cultural mores, women moving into
the workforce and the desire for families to
be closer together in informal settings, the
kitchen is now the favored gathering place
in the home. But in old homes, the kitchen
remains largely separate from other rooms.

historic portion of the home, such as a bedroom. Such an approach may not run into the same public living space protections.

Questions to Ask

- Where is the core historic living space?
- What makes my public living space special?
- Where are the transition points from public to private space?
- Stylistically, how would I describe the interior trim architecture?
- Are the chimneys functioning?
- What are the conditions of the floors?
- Is the plaster cracking?

Fireplaces[1]

For centuries, buildings have been warmed by burning wood or coal directly in the

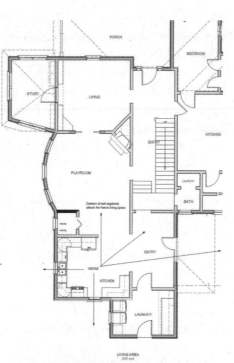

Fig. 6.4:
Ideally the children could play in view of parents working in the kitchen, but the removal of the wall negatively affects the historic integrity of the living space. Such a proposal would likely be denied by a SHPO.

Fig. 6.5-6:
Wood-burning stoves

room the resident intends to heat. This localized control is actually a rather green principle, allowing the user to heat a single room instead of an entire empty house. Because of their original core function in heating a home without a central system, it is not uncommon for even modest historic homes to have five or more fireplaces. Like any other interior fixture, fireplaces can be purely functional or rather majestic. Old fireplace mantles often feature meticulous trim carpentry, making modern stock units appear manufactured and sterile. Historic mantles are customized by nature, meaning it is difficult, if not impossible, to find an exact match. Fireplaces tend to be one of a kind, unique to the home and a defining input into its greater character.

Rehabilitation

When undertaking a fireplace rehabilitation, first review the system's overall existing condition and ask yourself

- Is the firebox in good shape?
- What sort of materials are present, and are they original?
- What sort of fuel was last used?
- Do I want to continue using that fuel or convert to something new?

The *hearth* is the horizontal member that protrudes beyond the chimney footprint into the living space. It is made of non-flammable material, typically concrete, tile or stone. It is often decorated with original tiles.

The *firebox* is the chimney opening and planes directly adjacent to the combustion source. The side and back walls of the firebox must be coated with a fireproof material — either firebrick, fire paint or refractory cement. Additionally, the firebox must be dimensioned properly and angled slightly to reflect heat into the room. Firebrick, tightly joined with 1/8-inch grout lines, is used for most modern fireboxes and reconstructions.

The *mantle* is a decorative trim piece made to cover rough transitions between the plaster, floor, hearth and firebox. It may consist of wood, tile, metal or brick.

The *damper* is the mechanical device that opens and closes to regulate drafts.

The *ashpit (ashdump)* receives ashes swept from the fire where they can be removed at a later time through a cleanout door. Water tightness and frequent cleaning are critical; if old ashes get wet they can cause an offensive odor.

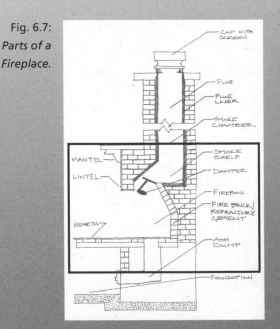

Fig. 6.7:
*Parts of a
Fireplace.*

- Does adjacent framing, the hearth size or firebox present a health or fire hazard?

Many old fireplaces are retired coal boxes. Since we don't burn coal in the home any longer (it's a major personal and environmental health hazard), the only viable options are to convert to an alternative fuel or keep the fireplace in a state of nonfunctional obsolescence.

Gas, either natural gas or propane, is a popular fuel choice for its clean burning and low maintenance qualities. There is no wood to haul or split, no ashes to clean up and the chimney doesn't need to be cleaned. Wood is revered for its natural, organic feel, its smell, sound and genuineness. Wood requires more maintenance, of course, including regular cleaning of the firebox and ash dump. Wood also poses a greater fire hazard.

Safety is the paramount concern when reconditioning a fireplace. Fire is a huge risk in any house but particularly risky in balloon-framed houses that lack fire blocking in the walls. Because of the absence of fire blocking in historic homes, a two-story Victorian can burn to the ground in as little as ten to 15 minutes. Special care to limit or remove risks is well warranted. Building codes require minimum clearances between fire and wood framing and floors, prescribing specific hearth clearances and framing gaps around chimneys.

Coal fireplaces are almost always too shallow to be converted to wood fuel use. Wood is large and stacked randomly, so it can fall outside a shallow firebox. While burning wood in a coal box, a stray ember is likely to land outside the hearth and onto a wood floor. Some rather incompetent framing may run floor joists directly into the ashpit, where they can easily catch fire. This is rather rare (and completely prohibited by modern codes), but check the floor framing around your chimney before burning any wood, just to be sure.

A wide variety of gas logs are available to fit just about any size firebox. Be sure to check manufacturer's specifications prior to buying, since many standard gas logs will not fit old fireboxes. Required clearances must be followed.

Carbon monoxide is another serious concern. It was never a significant risk in historic homes because large leaks in the envelope prevented the buildup of poisonous gases to lethal levels. Once the house is properly tightened, carbon monoxide poisoning becomes a real risk. It usually originates from one of three sources.

1. Attached garages, where car exhaust leaks into the home
2. Failing chimneys that do not allow fireplaces or furnaces to exhaust
3. Ventless gas logs

Architects didn't start attaching garages to houses until the mid-20th century, so an attached garage shouldn't be an issue on a historic home unless found on a newer addition. Chimneys often need a simple cleaning or damper repair. Gas logs come in vented or ventless varieties. Ventless logs are cheaper to install since they negate the need for a functional chimney. They are often installed by sealing the damper permanently shut with brick or concrete board. If run for short periods of time, there is minimal carbon monoxide risk. However, burning ventless logs is the equivalent of running a high Btu range (which should also be vented) without its vent. When either appliance is run for long periods of time without venting, carbon monoxide can become a hazard. For this reason, vented logs are greatly preferred.

Lastly, children love fire, and that is a good and bad thing. Children can be as much a danger to a fire as the fire is to them. The author's own son once threw a plastic toy on gas logs that resulted in a discernible, and not so enjoyable, odor. Luckily, the toy wasn't paper, which could have caused real harm to him and the house. Take special care with kids in the home. It is best not to allow children to play unmonitored in a room with a fire.

Fireplace Restoration

In this project, a landlord had carved a large Craftsman into three apartments and rented it as a de facto fraternity. As is common with landlords, the fireplaces were deemed high risk in a home where both residents and structure were particularly flammable, by way of alcohol and balloon framing, respectively. So the fireplaces were bricked over and made non-operational. New owners repurposed and restored the fireplaces.

Fig. 6.8: *A landlord sealed the fireplace so fraternity members would not burn the house down.*

Fig. 6.9: *The owners opened the cover and installed vented gas coal baskets, giving the appearance of coal burning. Vented chimneys vent harmful gases, making them preferred and superior to ventless alternatives.*

Interior Paint[2]

There are many different questions to ask regarding interior paint.

- What kind of paint currently exists?
- What condition is it in?
- Where has it failed and why?
- Is lead present?
- Is it just time to repaint, or are there underlying problems that the paint failure is indicating?
- What sort of look, feel and texture do I want?
- What color schemes work best with my home and personal property?

The condition of a home's existing paint can tell you many things. It may be telling you that it is time to repaint, or it can tell you when it was last painted. Wall stains can indicate water damage and the need to investigate something further. If the top layer of paint is lead-based (verified with a five-dollar home test readily sold at big box stores), you'll know the home has not been painted since the mid 1970s.

Remember, lead was mostly an additive in glossier paints and white paints. This makes lead paint far more likely to be found in trim and doors and less likely to be found on walls. Gloss oil paints give a heavy look which is more historically consistent with old houses and perhaps desired in a more authentic restoration in spite of its much higher off-gassing. Oil paints are also more likely to have lead, which was less commonly added to latex paint. Latex paint was only around for about 20 years before lead was banned, another reason lead is far more likely to be found in oil paints.

Glossier texture walls are easier to clean, which is why they are found in kitchens and baths. Flatter walls capture less light and show fewer imperfections. Living space walls and ceilings are typically painted flat or eggshell. Trim, doors and windows are painted semigloss or gloss. Sometimes oil paint may be used as trim paint for the core historic living spaces such as the entry foyer, while the rest of the house is painted with more pliable and less hazardous latex. Unless the thick look and feel of oil is desired, there are not many other reasons to stray from latex.

Low-VOC paints are more important on the interior of the home, where they are beneficial to both applicators and occupants. Exterior paint is by definition exposed to exterior air, where its off-gassing dissipates with limited threat to occupants. The same goes for lead, which is a concern everywhere, but more of a concern inside than out. Lead must be tested for, and as this book went to press the US Environmental Protection Agency was in the process of implementing unprecedented restrictions on all tradespeople working on pre-1978 homes, particularly those homes with children. Lead is of most concern in homes with children under six. Often overlooked, it's also important to address lead around construction workers with children under six. There are cases of carpenters collecting lead dust on a work site and transferring it to their personal home by way of their work clothing. Dust

Fig. 6.10-12: *Mythic, Safecoat and Yolo Colorhouse are all zero-VOC paints. Mythic advertises zero toxins and zero carcinogens, too. Most confuse no-VOC for nontoxic, and there are many low-VOC products on the market that are still toxic. Yolo Colorhouse emphasizes sustainable practices throughout their process, including zero-emissions manufacturing and shipping only by energy-efficient means such as rail.*

COMMON GROUND GREEN BUILDING CENTER

COMMON GROUND GREEN BUILDING CENTER

COMMON GROUND GREEN BUILDING CENTER

commitment. First, you must decide whether the finished work will be paint-grade or stain-grade. Paint-grade stripping requires only a smooth surface to paint on while stain-grade requires every speck of paint to be removed, a far more laborious process. The stripping process is accelerated with chemical strippers and proper tools. Professionals dip wood into a highly toxic solvent (methyl chloride is often used) in a stripping tank. For homeowners, a quality five-in-one painter's tool should do most of the work, with an orbital sander for the finishing. Since a good many doors and trim had lead at one point (and probably still do), strip with care. A three-dollar disposable painter's mask should be considered one of the necessary tools for the job. A charcoal filter or HEPA filter mask is even better. I have met many young couples who stripped paint and joked about all the lead they probably inhaled. Know what you are working with and take precautions for your health and the future occupants of the home.

Wood Flooring

Tongue and groove (TnG) wood flooring is the dominant flooring in historic living spaces. Wood was, and still is, popular for its beauty and longevity, and it is easy to clean. While today's carpets and linoleum last five to 20 years, wood looks great a century on and has a reasonable lifespan of 200-plus years.

Just about any tree can and has been made into flooring. Today, pine, oak and

can linger long after a project is complete, so a thorough cleanup is essential.

Paint stripping is a particularly popular activity for preservationists to pursue. No blood, sweat and tears are truly sacrificed on an owner's rehabilitation until they have hand stripped a door or casing. It is a true labor of love and a task that requires serious maple are most common, while walnut, mahogany and other regional specialties such as redwood and ipe are also available.

Lumber is either *flatsawn* or *quartersawn,* a quality that is most noticeable in flooring grains. Most wood flooring is flatsawn, which leaves wavy grains in the wood. Flatsawing is a much simpler and cheaper production process. Quartersawing requires specialty equipment and a rotation of lumber through the milling process, making quartersawn timber rarer and more expensive. Quartersawing produces consistent and straight grain lines, as many as 30 per inch, a quality highly desired in flooring.

Old-growth trees have thicker heartwoods, making for tighter grains and stronger wood. Old pine floors are relatively hard compared to newer species. Century-old trees are rarely timbered today, so the more dimensionally stable old-growth wood is no longer coming out of the mills. New red oak flooring regularly sells for around two dollars per square foot, but I have seen old-growth quartersawn heart pine, which has a highly desired dark reddish hue, sell in the salvage market for $10-20 per square foot.

Wood flooring comes in different widths, difficult to match exactly. Where I work, 3½-inch heart pine is very common in old homes. Newer pine is a much lighter yellow in color, and comes in 3½-inch nominal widths, about 3¹/8-inch actual. The nominal/actual differential is important in rehabilitation: if trying to seam in a new board with the old, it will be ³/8 of an inch

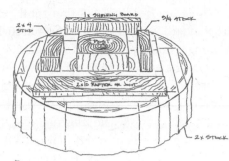

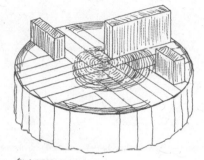

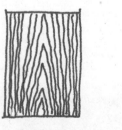
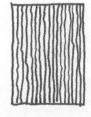

Flat sliced   Quarter sliced

Fig. 6.13-14: *Flatsawn and quartersawn lumber.*

too narrow. Try to match the existing as closely as possible, particularly in historic living spaces. Sometimes wood needs to be specially milled. In other areas, reflooring with newer products may be permissible, but you can be quite certain that proposals to carpet the living room floor will be rejected categorically by your SHPO.

Three-quarter-inch 4x8-foot subfloors are standard floor structure today, but such framing is not always present in old homes. Most of the homes I've worked on feature 1x strip subfloors, structurally comparable to plywood sheets. Some houses have no subfloor at all; finished flooring runs directly over and perpendicular to the joists. As the house settles over time, you may actually be able to see through the floor to the crawl space. Houses with no subfloor are far more likely to be underframed and overspanned, with saggy and creaking floors. If the floors look to be in good shape and have stood the test of time no repair work may be necessary; however, a thorough review of the structure should be considered before adding weight (such as solid surface countertops or a heavy Sub-Zero refrigerator) to underframed floors.

Sometimes, either due to laziness or a known environmental hazard, a newer floor will be installed directly over an existing finished floor without removing the existing floor. Old kitchen floor tile may have asbestos material or be secured to the floor with an asbestos mastic. In such a case, it may be best to install new flooring directly over suspect material, effectively encapsulating the hazard. This practice can produce significant offsets in floor heights, requiring some creative offset thresholds.

Floor rehabilitation generally involves patching, repairing and refinishing. Patching is needed when the floor is damaged or a few strips have exceeded their useful life. Wood may be damaged from moisture, furniture, fire or insects. To strip in pieces of new wood, old wood must be removed, with particular care given to protecting adjacent boards. The replacement wood must match in width, or a large gap will result. The tongue of the adjacent board is sawn off, and both the new and adjacent boards face nailed.

Fig. 6.15: Original maple meets new oak.

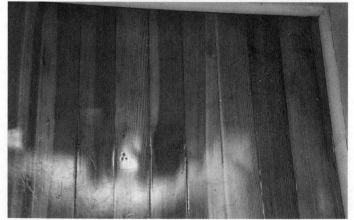

Fig. 6.16: Reddish gold quartersawn heart pine, with 20-30 growth rings per inch.

Face nailing carries its own problems. Tongue and groove flooring has no exposed nails because it is the unexposed tongue that is nailed, which sits below the finished floor level. Face nailing involves nailing the finished floor. To avoid viewing an ugly nail head, a small head trim nail must be used. Face nails are likely to tear up sandpaper when refinishing, so their heads should be countersunk below finished floor level, the holes filled with wood putty and stained to match the surrounding wood.

Refinishing is a multi-step process that typically involves three separate sandings, each with progressively finer grits (often 80 to 150 to 220 grit). A drum sander is used for the open floor and an edger for the wall areas. Each sanding takes off +/- $\frac{1}{16}$ of an inch, meaning a ¾-inch thick piece of wood could be fully refinished five to ten times before it became too thin. Finished every 20 years (and it's rare to see sandings so frequent) a wood floor should last 100-200 years. Softwoods like pine may have never been refinished. For years refinishing entailed waxing with a linseed oil or painting, but no actual sanding.

Sanding is a learned skill. For the amateur operator, it's very easy to put divots throughout the floor, which will then require professional sanding. Rather than rent the equipment and use your floors as a training ground, it's best to subcontract this skilled work out to someone who sands floors day in and day out.

After sanding the floor smooth a top-coat sealer is applied. Traditionally this was done with varnish, shellac and oils. In the 1960s, polyurethane synthetics hit the market, and they remain the dominant choice today. If you prefer a natural look, water-based polyurethanes are better than oil-based products. Water-based polyurethanes provide a

Fig. 6.17: *A gorgeous wood floor lies under vinyl tile, the latter installed by someone who wrongly concluded the vinyl was easier to maintain than wood. As the photo shows, it was not.*

Fig. 6.18: *A wood patch ghostmark intentionally shows the placement of previous radiator piping*

clearer finish with less odorous VOCs. They're quick to install, clean and dry. The recommended four coats of water-based

Fig. 6.19: *The door casing on a modern house requires six pieces of trim made of a single material, typically synthetic brick-mould.*

Fig. 6.20: *The casing on this historic home requires 16 pieces, made from five different moldings: 5/4 plinth, 1x6 casing, 1x2 lintel base, 1x8 lintel and lintel crown. Old trim is grand in size and detail, while modern trim lacks an emphasis on quality, revealed by its nickname,* speedbase.

polyurethane can be applied in a day. If you prefer amber tones, an oil base is better. Oil-based finishes produce a thicker finish with more color. They are disruptively slow to dry, requiring five hours between coats and 12 to 24 hours after the final coat. Some consider that oil produces a warmer glow than water-based material. Oils are half the cost of water-based polyurethanes. Since oil is thicker than water and penetrates the wood, two or three coats suffice. Oil is believed to be longer lasting.

Trim Carpentry, Stairs and Doors

Trim carpentry can define a home. Door and window casing can be distinctly Victorian or Craftsman. Functionally, trim carpentry exists to cover rough transitions between different surfaces or planes. Unfinished edges exist between plaster and doors, flooring and windows. Trim covers these transitions and makes them look finished, which is why applying trim is called *finish carpentry*. Often the entire interior carpentry package may be performed by a single carpentry crew, including doors, window rehabilitation, stairs, wainscot and moldings.

Doors are a popular item to source at architectural salvage yards. Each era and style has a dominant door type, such as five-panel horizontal or two-panel rectangular. When modifying a home, you may need a couple of old doors to match existing ones. Salvage yards take such material when people have more than they need, or a house is being demolished. They then recondition and resell the doors. These old doors have a look and

Fig. 6.21: *Any interior trim should be select #1, clear and better grade wood free of knots with minimal imperfections. Knots will bleed through paint after a few years.*

Naming Trim

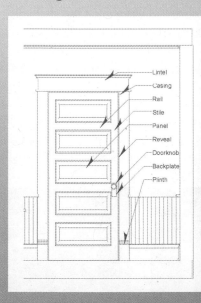

Lintel
Casing
Rail
Stile
Panel
Reveal
Doorknob
Backplate
Plinth

Fig. 6.22: *Top left, parts of a Door.*

Fig. 6.23-24: *Top and bottom right, Typical Trim Details.*

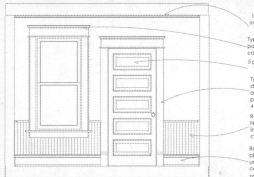

1-3/4" Picture Mold, stock material.

Typical 1920s Craftsman multi-part window surrounds with 1x5 casing and 1x8 lintel.

5 panel solid core door

Typical Craftsman multi-part door surrounds with 1x5 casing and 1x8 lintel. Note decorative plinth blocks, replicated from 5/4 stock.

Retain existing wainscot in place. New wainscot made from 4" SYP, in place of sheetrock, using chair cap. Stock materials.

Retain existing baseboards in place. All new to match existing using 1/8, 1/4 round and base cap, stock materials.

TRIM DETAIL   SCALE 1/2" = 1'0"

feel unmatched by factory-made replicas, so salvage yards do a lot of business in doors.

Old doors installed on a new addition can really help tie old to new. One of my project manager's favorite activities is doing such a good job replicating old details in a new addition that building inspectors struggle to figure out what part of a home is new and what part is old. Doors are a major part of the trick.

All historic doors are solid core, meaning there is solid material through the entire door section. Most are built on a rail and stile system with floating panels filling the gap. Modern doors are mostly hollow core. They are far lighter, have a cheaper feel and offer less sound privacy. Even when looking at new doors, solid core doors are more appropriate for an old home.

Solid wood doors, if paint grade, are easily repaired and modified. It's common to purchase a few five-panel salvage doors, patch any penetrations for deadbolts, hinges and doorknobs, then start fresh so the doors can match. Conversion latches are available

that allow old door knobs to fit a modern latching mechanism. It's similarly easy to expand or trim a door by subtracting or adding wood to any of its four sides. Such modifications are not possible with stain-grade doors, which require consistent wood throughout. Any patch or transition will be obvious and thus unsuitable for stain.

Trim, being made of wood, is generally easy to repair. Wood filler can patch minor gaps, while molding epoxy can do larger jobs. Sometimes a portion of wood requires replacement, in which case you'll have to match with stock materials or have a molding custom-milled. Replacement trim has different profiles and fewer imperfections than old, so rarely will it be an exact match. For look, feel and principles of reuse, reconditioning is always preferable to total replacement.

A lot of skilled trim work goes into stairwells. Stairs consist of risers and treads, newels, balusters and handrails. They are often custom-constructed, and repair work can be expensive. Some architectural supply houses carry stock newels and balusters,

Fig. 6.25-26: *If removed, trim should be carefully inventoried and stored for reuse.*

as will salvage yards. Other materials have to be custom-lathed.

Stairs in old homes are very likely to fail modern code clearances of 80-inch head height, minimum widths of 36 inches above the handrail and 32 inches below. Risers must be no more than 7¾ inches tall, and treads must be at least ten inches. No riser or tread may be more than ³⁄₈ of an inch larger or smaller than any other. Handrails must be between 34 and 38 inches above the treads. Landing and balcony guards must be 36 inches if the fall is greater than 30 inches. Balusters may not allow passage of a four-inch sphere. For the most part, if you are not modifying the stairway, its inconsistencies with the code will be grandfathered in. If you are modifying the stairway, or adding significant living space that will rely on the stairway for egress, an inspector might

Fig. 6.27: *Original built-ins should be preserved in place. The glass may be too valuable and fragile to move.*

Fig. 6.28-29: *Parts of a Stairway.*

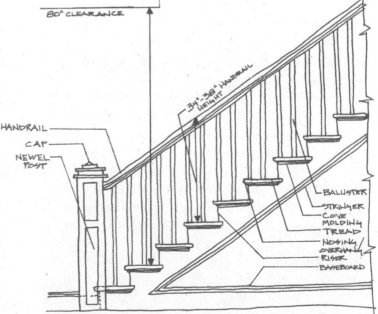

make you upgrade to modern standards. Of course, if the stairway is full of irreplaceable detailing, this would be a torturous directive from a code official. Such a dilemma may require getting a preservation organization involved or looking at alternatives.

Rehabbing old hardware?

When rehabilitating old metallic hardware, be sure to clean gently, as you can destroy a finish or patina that has been a century in the making. Chemical strippers can do particular damage to metals. Use superfine steel wood and water-based materials whenever possible.

Fig. 6.30: *An original glass doorknob can shine again with some affectionate paint stripping.*

Bedrooms and Closets

Historic homes are notoriously short of closet space. This is a chronic problem in master bedrooms. Many houses don't even have a distinct master bedroom much less the *master suite* universal in today's designs. Historically, many owners used wardrobes instead of closets. Such solutions don't work for owners with large clothing collections. Owners might require space planning to solve this problem. Closets are claimed from the oddest places: under stairwells, in underframed, low ceiling gables, even auxiliary bedrooms. Though it's difficult to do tastefully, I've seen an entire secondary bedroom annexed into a master suite, then broken into a master bath and his/her closets. With modern demands for closets and empty nesters buying large homes, an entire 15x15-foot bedroom may be claimed for a glamorous walk-in closet.

Plaster

Plaster was the most common wall material for historic homes through World War II. It is, unfortunately, an art form that all but disappeared with the advent of sheetrock. Still, preservationists love plaster. They argue that the natural look and feel of plaster cannot be replicated by wallboard. Plaster helps deaden sound, gives mass to the house, feels natural and organic and involves less manufacturing. It can also serve as a thermal store, helping to heat and cool the home.

Plaster was typically applied in three coats over a series of horizontal wood strips called lath. The scratch coat was trowled to create a corrugated look, helping it bond with top coats. Scratch coats often added horsehair for strength, the same way rebar is used with concrete today. Brown coats were heavy in sand, but jagged, making them excellent for creating a rough finish. Finishing coats were lime-heavy and floated smooth.

Plaster tends to be between ¾ and ⅞ inches thick, and the thickest stock sheetrock is only ⅝ of an inch, so replacement of plaster with sheetrock requires either the furring out of studs, modification to trim, built up layers of sheetrock or large tacky caulk lines. The latter is obviously highly discouraged.

To Gut or Not to Gut?

When the house requires major structural repair or systems replacement, a gut job may be the best option. We have all heard about gut jobs that require every inch of plaster and systems to be removed. But why would a homeowner go to such extremes? Plaster is extremely difficult and expensive to work around. Keeping plaster in place may hide faulty wiring or environmental hazards and can make tightening the envelope difficult. Many subcontractors are reluctant to make penetrations through plaster, and they certainly jack up their prices to route their trade through existing plaster walls.

Once the decision is made to gut, it is best to do it all at once. It's an awful task. Air quality is terrible, plaster dust saturates the lungs and makes the skin itch. And it is very possible that old plaster can be coated with carcinogenic coal soot or lead from old paint. US Occupational Health and Safety Administration (OSHA)-approved respirators and disposable coveralls should always be worn, and cleanup should be performed with a wet mop and a US EPA-approved HEPA-filter vacuum.

There are many reasons not to gut a house. The amount of material a gut job produces will amaze you. As much as half a home's weight can be in plaster. On a single 3,000-square-foot Victorian gut, we estimated that 30 tons of plaster and lath were demolished and disposed of, requiring seven full dumpsters.

Some agricultural companies will take plaster or sheetrock scraps and recycle their lime as an agricultural additive. These companies are sometimes hard to find, they won't take any hazardous material and you probably have to haul to them. But if you

Dumpsters		8.5
Avg Tons per	x	6
Total Tons	=	51
% plaster and lath	x	60%
Plaster & Lath Tonnage	=	30.6

Fig. 6.31:
Plaster and Lath Tonnage in One 3,000-square-foot Home

have a lot of material you want to keep out of the dump, it's a great option.

The historic qualities of plaster should always be considered first. If it's in good shape and you can make the house reasonably functional without gutting, then don't gut. If, on the other hand, you have major work to do on a severely depressed structure, gutting may be the only prudent choice.

Rehabilitation Options

Plastering is an advanced trade, and the magic you can do with the material is beyond the scope of this book. Properly protected from moisture and supported by a sound structure, plaster can last forever. When it does fail, look for one of the following reasons.

- The 1½-inch lath was not installed in staggered bunches of a half dozen or so, creating stress cracking.

Fig. 6.32:
A house in the process of a gut job — a messy, hazardous and major waste-producing procedure.

- Underframed ceilings can fail to support the weight of plaster, or the bounce from people walking above may cause plaster to deanchor from the lath.
- Water leaks from plumbing or roofs can damage plaster.
- Sometimes it's nothing more than building settlement, seasonal expansion and contraction.
- In particularly dry years or wet years the earth may move more and create plaster cracking on 100-year-old plaster that has never had such a problem.

As long as the plaster is secured to the wall or can be resecured easily, it generally makes the best sense to repair rather than replace. Regardless of the source, there are two problems overwhelmingly common with plaster.

1. Plaster can crack. Sheetrock joint compound will take care of small cracks, as long as it is installed over fiberglass tape. Larger cracks require further excavation to create an area large enough to replaster with the traditional three coats.
2. Plaster can separate from the wall or ceiling. Sometimes lath nails rust away, other times vibrations loosen the bond. In most situations, drywall anchors can be used to reattach the assembly using a wide head that is then plastered over. Loose ceilings are a major concern. Each square foot of plaster and lath can weigh ten pounds, so the ceiling of a typical 200-300-square foot room can weigh in excess of a full ton (2,000 pounds). If that ceiling falls on you, you'll be lucky to survive.

Sustainability and Preservation

Like exteriors, interior living space defines the home and contributes to its aesthetic longevity. It exhibits the charm we value, giving it permanence.

In keeping original elements we win on two fronts. We demand less material from mines, mills and factories which lessens our environmental footprint and keeps old material out of the landfill. And, rehabilitation and trim carpentry is labor intensive, which supports the local economy through the hiring of tradespeople, many of them small businesses.

Keep what you have, for the sake of both movements. Plaster demolition is particularly wasteful on both counts, sending up to half the weight of a house to the dump, while losing the historic benefits of the finish and putting remaining trim at risk by causing such a major disturbance.

The Secretary of the Interior's Standards are of paramount importance in the historic living space. Alterations to the core living space are largely prohibited, particularly if they spoil the original look and feel of the home. Whenever possible, repair rather than replace. Original trim should be retained and rehabilitated. It should be replicated where material condition or costs make it necessary.

ATTICS

Attics are the large, typically unfinished areas defined by the top floor's ceiling joists, roof rafters and gables. Finishing such a space can add living space without adding any space to a footprint or envelope. Since historic houses sit in urban areas, many are restricted from expanding outward. There's often no space to do so. Furthermore, historic covenants, tax credit restrictions, lot lines, setbacks or just consideration of neighbors' space can prevent a homeowner from adding on. Sometimes the only option is claiming an attic.

On historic homes, attics are almost exclusively stick-framed, meaning each framing member was assembled individually, rafter by rafter, on-site. Today's production roofs are framed with factory-built trusses, built off-site, trucked in and boomed in place. While building at the factory causes less waste and uses less material, most modern trusses have structural web supports that forbid any future finishing of the space. In this sense, truss framing is less adaptive, less flexible for future uses.

Old stick-framed houses have huge unobstructed spaces. There is almost always more space in the attic than appears from the street. Nearly every attic I've been in with a client yielded a *Wow, there's more space up here than I thought* epiphany. Additionally, sloped rooflines, chimney and

ground, which may require load paths through finished living space necessitating some plaster demolition. New footings can also be difficult to install due to limited crawl space access.

To the homeowner who needs space and has few other options, the attic is a great choice. Isolated from the primary living space, it makes great away space for a teenager; think of an attic room as a Greg-and-Jan-Brady room. The space can make guest rooms, a media room, art space or an office.

Questions to Ask

- How big is my attic?
- What are the framing sizes of the floor joists and rafters? Can they support finishing?
- Is the insulation currently at the attic floor level, or in the roof rafters?
- Is the attic sealed or vented?
- Are there mechanicals, wiring, chimneys, plumbing stacks or other obstructions in the space?
- How can I access the attic?
- What is the headroom at the ridge and proposed walls?
- What is the roof pitch?
- What would I use the space for?
- Would it be worthwhile to finish?

Design

Designing and building an attic can be difficult. Documenting existing conditions requires constant measurement and verification. Attics can have odd roof slopes,

Fig. 7.1: *Old home attics make fantastic nook-and-cranny spaces for custom hobbies. Here, an attic is a paint studio.*

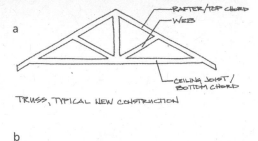

Fig. 7.2: *(a) a modern truss-built attic leaves no option for future attic finishing. (b) an old stick-built attic leaves a large open space that can be claimed for living space.*

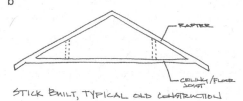

gable nooks all generate unique spaces, each excellent opportunities for custom design.

Claiming an attic can be exceedingly complex. Attics are, after all, spaces that were never really intended for occupancy. Floors are underframed, sometimes seriously, and rafters may not be large enough to support the weight of even sheetrock. All structural weight must be carried to the inconstantly sized framing members and unknown structural characteristics. Traditional floors deal in vertical walls perpendicular to horizontal ceilings, but attics add roof slope as a critical third dimension. This tends to be an unforgiving dimension if measured inaccurately. If the roof slope is thought to be nine in 12, but actually turns out to be seven in 12 it will encroach so much on headroom that the space becomes unusable.

Verification of existing conditions should be done through multiple reconciliation methods. First, conduct a rough measurement of the floor spans, ridge height and roof slope. Sketch all penetrations through the space, including chimneys, mechanical equipment, condensation runs and plumbing vents. Each of these can be moved, but budget may dictate the need to work around them. Note the floor joist depth and conclude if larger floor joists or closer joist space will be required. If framing must be added, make note of how it may affect head height. Going from a 2x4 joist to a 2x10 eats away six inches from ridge and ceiling height. It can make a tight space tighter and may guide the decision to proceed or not.

A professional designer is a huge help in such complex spaces. Nooks and crannies must be precisely designed, and a designer can help ensure everything first fits on paper. These days, most designers work with computer aided designer (CAD) programs, which can easily generate building sections that measure roof slopes, ridge heights and head clearances. Such visuals are valuable when planning such a complex space.

After a plan is completed, verify dimensions again. And again. Then, after floor framing is complete, mark proposed walls, cabinetry and desks with painter's tape. Make adjustments prior to framing vertical members.

Stylistically, what to do with an attic is a tougher decision. One camp argues that new interior space should replicate the details of the original home, making seamless transitions throughout the structure. The other argues that the space is new and should be treated and designed as such, since any replication of historic trim will just give a false sense of time. The Secretary of the Interior's Standards state that

9. New additions, exterior alterations, or related new construction shall not destroy historic materials that characterize the property. The new work shall be differentiated from the old and shall be compatible with the massing, size, scale, and architectural features to protect the historic integrity of the property and its environment.[1]

There's some debate about whether or not attics qualify as *related new construction,* which would make them subject to this guideline. I generally consider new construction an expansion of the envelope, which an attic is inherently not. Still, if the guideline applies, then it makes the case for differentiating new work from the old.

Some old house owners love to use the attic as the one space they can feel a bit freer to design as they want. With all the cultural burdens inherent in being the steward of an old house, sometimes it's nice to have an away space that you can design any way you want without negatively imposing on historic parts.

The bottom line is that attics can be tastefully done in both old and modern style. Either approach can work. A modern approach might include flush line sheetrock with no trim, track lighting, chic flat face cabinetry, an explicitly sustainable floor such as bamboo or sorghum board and skylights.

Skylights are particularly popular feature and the simplest way to get light into a converted attic space. Some skylights qualify for egress (emergency escape), meaning you can legally use the room for a bedroom. Unfortunately, skylights are stylistically inaccurate on both the interior and exterior of most historic homes. They can actually cause tax credit problems if they are placed on a front-facing roof slope or if visible from the street.

Furthermore, skylights can be inconstant with principles of sustainable building. Yes, they let in natural light and some are operable, which promotes air flow. But on the down side they can add incredible heat gain in the home and must be placed in a manner that will limit the amount of direct radiant heat that transfers through. Skylights on northern roof slopes let in light and avoid direct heat gain. South-facing slopes cause the most heat gain. In cold climates such heat gain may be desirable, but not so in hot places. Many green architects actually shy away from skylights because they cause so many problems with management of heat gain. Moreover, skylights basically poke a hole in what is arguably the important surface for a tight envelope: the roof. While a well-insulated roof will have an insulation assembly exceeding R-30, a skylight might have an R value of R-2. Since the roof is under pressure from the stack effect, convection and radiant heat beating down on the shingles, a big hole in the envelope can negate some of the envelope tightening gains described in other chapters. Bottom line: tread carefully with skylights.

Stairways are another challenge to many attics. The author's own attic would be great space for kids and guests, but there is no logical way to get there. A common solution is to stack one stairway over an existing stairway. This may or may not cause a tax credit problem, depending on how significant the original stairway is and how much a new stairway would hamper its character. In other instances, a stairway may seem to fit but cannot be made to satisfy modern codes. The 80 inches of head height required on any new staircase can be a challenge under many rooflines. You'll feel like 70 inches will be enough since you might not have family members who are six-foot-eight, but building code officials are likely to balk. For some smaller attic spaces, a ladder may be the best option. This is particularly feasible when the space is primarily for kids. Ladders are a huge space saver, an interesting architectural detail and just plain fun. The building code offers no language on ladders, nothing for or against. It's left to code officials to interpret. In my experience, they will allow ladders to storage space, but not to living spaces. Because so much is left to interpretation, it's good to check with you local regulator prior to construction.

Lastly, strategic placement of the attic's mechanical, plumbing and electrical systems requires intelligent anticipation. In a typical two-story house, the upstairs HVAC system comes with a large spiderweb of ductwork. In an unfinished attic, HVAC installers place systems where there is least challenge, usually right in the center of a proposed living space. To finish the space, a system's ductwork must be rerun to fit behind the knee walls. Depending on how much space the attic conversion adds, a larger system may be required, though insulation can negate such a need. A mechanical sub can conduct load calculations. Plumbing vent placement is more restricted, since the vents serve fixed toilets and baths below. Electrical wiring may need to be completely redone. The original electricians likely ran

Fig. 7.3: *Toilets require a six-foot-eight-inch clearance at the front of the bowl, a measurement that requires precise planning*

Fig. 7.4: *Stairways may require too much space. Ladders can be used for access to an attic space, though they cannot be used for egress. Inspectors may require egress if the attic appears habitable.*

Fig. 7.5-6: *An attic is converted to work space. Structural beams are painted to give a more finished look. Knee walls are great for built-in storage.*

wires over the floor joists rather than through them, figuring no one in their right mind would ever finish this space: After all, the place was wired before air conditioning. Even if the floor joists were properly sized for attic finishing, you cannot install sub-floor on top of electrical wire so new wire needs to be rerun through the joists.

Sketch the existing and proposed attic, make note of existing and proposed system alterations, then call on some good trades-people to talk through options.

Structural

Structural issues are the primary headache in old home attic finishing. Floors and rafters are underframed. Rafters can be too small and lack knee wall support. Floor studs may be balloon-framed and lack a top plate. Framing can be invisible behind plaster or flooring or may lack structural stamping. Since the attic will be finished for the first time, code officials have license to require it meet modern codes. Of course, in such hard-to-quantify conditions, little if any of the work can be prescribed by reading guidelines in the code. In such a case, pro-fessional structural engineering is needed. An engineer will take what is known, make reasonable assumptions about what is not (or require selective exploratory demoli-tion) and formulate a specific construction plan.

New floors must meet modern code. The original builder framed the unfinished attic's floor to be ceiling joists, not a floor. Ceiling joists are not sized to carry people, so they are smaller. You may find 2x8, 2x6 and even 2x4 ceiling joists spanning lengths that requires 2x10s as floor joists. Here, new joists must be sistered alongside the old effectively negating the smaller joists' ability to carry floor loads. Original ceiling joists may be kept in place to carry the plaster or sheetrock of the ceiling below. In a gut job attic conversion, there is little reason to keep old joists, so they are commonly deleted in favor of a cleaner working surface.

Figuring out load paths is a learned structural skill. It's like a GRE logic ques-tion, requiring lots of sketches and trial and error on the way to concluding the best answer. Some carpenters love the process of figuring load paths and tracing them to earth. While laying out the attic floor may be simple, figuring out where rafters, gird-ers and headers bear, and how much weight they carry can be extremely difficult, inva-sive, maddening and expensive. This is why attic completions are far easier in a gut job where exploration and installation of such load paths are not nearly as destructive.

Insulation

Building codes require insulation around any new conditioned space. Many old attics are partially finished without a thermal barrier, making them tremendously uncomfortable, if not unusable, in hot and cold seasons. Some homeowners simply shut down the space when it's too hot or cold, only using it in spring and fall, but this defeats the pur-pose. Today, we like to build for all four seasons.

Dormer and Gable Windows

Unique, character-defining windows are often found in the attic gables or dormers. Inspect your attic windows. You might be surprised what a pleasant vista is available from your attic. If attic windows are original, keep them. Storm windows can always be added for efficiency. Any new dormers should offer a complementary design.

Fig. 7.7-13.

If you are considering finishing an attic at a later date, you have one more reason to consider a sealed attic. The sealed attic, explained further in the Envelope chapter, installs insulation under the roof deck instead of the more traditional attic floor. Insulation can be attached to the roof deck in a non-vented assembly, or one can install a thin baffle run to create a vent channel for a traditional vented roof. Both techniques insulate the attic space. For non-vented roofs, states vary on permeability ratings for insulation, so be sure to check with your local inspector prior to installing. An insulated roof deck is a great insulation strategy even if the attic is not being finished, as it helps the house and attic mechanical systems operate at more consistent and manageable temperatures.

Preservation Issues

Generally speaking, SHPOs and preservationists are very enthusiastic about claiming already existing space within the envelope for additional living space. Any project that helps meet the spatial needs of the homeowner while keeping the exterior unaltered, all the better.

The view of what qualifies for tax credits may vary by state program. In North Carolina, any space within the preexisting house qualifies. The SHPO recently clarified that they interpret qualifying space in three dimensions (an envelope) rather than two dimensions (a footprint). Thus, a small dormer bump-out might not qualify (though it wouldn't negate a large project if sensibly placed on the structure). In the dormer proposal illustrated, the ceiling, electrical light fixture and small portions of the paint, trim and insulation would need to be backed-out of a tax credit claim. It all gets a bit absurdly technical, which is why it's often best to communicate with your SHPO reviewing architect and work with a CPA.

Attic Case Study #1

This attic had been framed with 1x8 lumber, 16 inches on center, spanning 15 feet - sufficient for an unfinished attic space, but not for living space. The floor had to be reframed. Major structural engineering was required to carry floor loads and roof loads to earth. Engineered laminated veneer lumber (LVL) was installed at the roof valleys. With all loads coming down on eight points, each required a new footing to meet modern code. The structural work was significant, and the results were striking. The attic ridge was so high, at about 18 feet, that it allowed for not one but two additional floors in the attic, adding 1,500 square feet to the home. The attic features a highly customized

Fig. 7.14: A dormer bump-out proposal expands the envelope. This state's SHPO declared that all costs inside the pre-existing 3D envelope qualify, while costs outside do not.

Does NOT qualify for tax credits

Qualifies for preservation tax credits

Fig. 7.15-20

design to the client's unique needs: two efficiency apartments — one for a live-in nanny and the other for frequent long-term guests — two simple kitchens, two bathrooms and three nook-and-cranny private office spaces tucked within the gables.

Attic Case Study #2

This Queen Anne Victorian featured lots of claimable space in the attic, but no great way to get to it. Part of the motivation for the addition design was to solve this problem. The addition gable was designed to tie into the original home, forming a continuous media room and guest suite. As with most attics, all original framing had been undersized. The floor joists were 2x5, 16 inches on center, spanning up to 16 feet — barely enough to support a human. Rafters

were random, ranging from 2x4s to 2x6s. Since the rafters on the addition were framed with 2x8s, a transition was required between the old and new ceilings. Floors were reframed, and new loads were carried to the ground on new footings as directed by a structural engineer. Even though this house was built in 1910, it had non-traditional balloon-framed studs actually bearing on chimney ledges, a practice that was largely retired in the 1850s. Rather than retrofit these studs, new headers were installed to bypass the awkward framing, carrying the entire attic floor load on just a few concentrated points. In so doing, the framing in the attic is now not directly dependant on the old framing beneath it. Thus, the attic is built to modern standards, while the old rooms below (which were functioning fine) are structurally separated and did not require upgrading to the current standards.

Since the attic was sealed the space was conditioned whether it was finished or not. The finishing of the space, then, resulted in the addition of 600 square feet of living space without adding any additional heating or cooling expenses.

Fig. 7.21-23: *Ceiling joists in the attic replaced with beefier floor joists. Rafters are sprayed with open cell foam in a sealed attic assembly. Skylights are placed on the north slope to let in light while restricting heat gain.*

EXTERIOR

What is it about old houses? What strange spells do they cast, so that otherwise perfectly rational human beings are compelled against all sanity and sense to commit large amounts of energy, money, and time to their rebuilding?

— George Nash, *Renovating Old Houses: Bringing New Life to Vintage Homes*

Nothing differentiates interesting historic homes more than exterior architectural detailing. Homeowners articulated themselves through their homes, their personal character expressed through material, rich style and color — much as Americans do today with their automobiles.

Exterior systems are complex; they involve varying functional and aesthetic materials serving multiple functions. Materials of architectural flair are also functional, keeping the home dry, safe and livable.

Preservation work on the exterior of an historic home requires careful consideration and review. *Streetscape* is the portion of the house viewable from the street. For preservation of the community as a cultural asset the streetscape must be retained, and protecting it is a core preservation tenet. Therefore, it is most important to retain materials, rehabilitate and minimize alterations to the exterior part of a house.

Questions to Ask

- What elements of the streetscape are unique?

- How does my home fit with the neighbors', and are there things (such as paint colors) I could choose to complement the neighborhood?

- What style house do I have, and what are the defining characteristics of this style?

- Are there non-original elements on the exterior? Are there original details I can restore or accentuate?

- What materials comprise the exterior?

- What kind of roofing material does the house have, what condition is it in and how long should it last?
- What kind of exterior paint does the house have?
- Where are exterior materials failing or damaged, and why?
- Are the chimneys safe and operational?
- How do shade trees and landscaping affect the aesthetic and performance of my home?
- Are replication materials available through stock suppliers or will they require custom carpentry?

Evolution of Exterior Styles

American architectural styles and substyles, from Colonial houses of the Revolutionary era through Contemporary, are far beyond the scope of this book. For the most part, house styles are labeled and otherwise defined by their exterior detailing, which is why the alteration or deletion of such saddens preservationists. *A Field Guide to American Houses* by Virginia and Lee McAlester is a phenomenal resource for identifying such detail. A home's details identify it within a period and style of American architecture, and each style has a litany of substyles.

1. Colonial (1600-1820) style includes Dutch Colonial, French Colonial, Spanish Colonial, Georgian and Early Classical Revival. This style varies greatly by region.
2. Romantic (1820-1880) style includes Greek Revival, Gothic Revival, Italianate and Octagonal.
3. Victorian (1860-1910) style includes Second Empire, Stick, Queen Anne, Shingle, Richardsonian and Folk.
4. Eclectic (1880-1940) style includes Colonial Revival, Neoclassical, Tudor, Beaux Arts, French Eclectic, Italianate Renaissance, Mission, Monterey, Pueblo Revival, Prairie, Craftsman, Modernistic and International.
5. Contemporary (1940-) style include Modern, Neoclassic, Contemporary Folk, Post-Modern, Ranch and McMansion.

Typically, each historic district is dominated by a few styles. In central North Carolina, for example, many historic districts are dominated by Queen Anne Victorians, Craftsman Four Squares, Bungalows and Colonial Revivals. Many homes have elements of more than one style, an indicator of variety in professional designers and tradespeople working on the home. Homeowners must understand their home's details before undertaking major exterior work.

An example substyle is the Queen Anne Victorian, a dominant style of building from 1880-1900, decreasing in popularity through 1910. Its defining characteristics include

1. A steep roof of irregular shape, usually with a dominant front-facing gable and secondary cross gables.
2. Cutaway bay windows designed to avoid long smooth exterior walls. This led to interesting irregular floor plans, frequent bay windows, towers, insets and projections, all facilitated by asymmetrical

façades made possible by the growing use of balloon framing.

3. Large windows were typical, sometimes with a large pane surrounded by many smaller panes in the upper sash. Exterior doors usually had decorative detailing and a single large pane of glass set into the upper portion.

4. Some Queen Annes have detailed spindle-work ornamentation at gable, columns, frieze or porch ceiling. Often referred to as *Gingerbread*, about a third of the homes are defined as Free Classic with no spindlework and classical columns, 5% are half-timbered with large timber columns and 5% are decorated with patterned masonry.[1]

A preservation designer or consultant can help identify these characteristics. It's smart to identify such features early on so they can be incorporated into your restoration plan. Exterior components can be broken down into three categories: siding and trim, porches and roofing. Each can be simple or gloriously ornate; restoring original features in a sustainable way offers great rehabilitation opportunities.

Siding and Trim

Exterior surfaces on historic homes are mostly brick masonry or wood. Wood typically comes in overlapping horizontal rows, otherwise known as *clapboard* (aka beveled or lap siding). Wood shakes are also common. Pine is a very dominant wood material, though redwood and cedar are

also regionally popular, particularly in the West.

Wood is renewable (if harvested correctly), biodegradable and nontoxic. With proper care, it lasts centuries. Care can be as simple as paint, usually every four to ten years, depending on exposure. Where wood is damaged, individual pieces can be repaired with epoxy or locally replaced. Nearly all repair is simple carpentry. Wood is one of the most repairable materials in the building trades.

Sadly, old home exteriors in the modern era have a habit of devolving into plastic boxes. The artificial siding common on today's homes has caused headaches for many preservationists. Restoring exteriors by removing artificial siding can be one of the more rewarding tasks of a rehabilitation. The good news? Covered wood siding tends to be in good structural shape, just needing a paint job. The paint job is usually the reason owners put on artificial siding in the first place. The bad news? Artificial siding

Fig. 8.1: *Gingerbread detailing, a defining characteristic of the Victorian style.*

Artificial siding is a product manufactured out of vinyl or aluminum, usually made to imitate clapboard siding. Like replacement windows, the faux siding industry is rife with nonsense-promising, too-good-to-be-true products. It's a production industry that makes money by doing lots of jobs cheaply. They'll say there's an insulation value, which there is not. They'll say their siding saves energy, but the US Federal Trade Commission filed suit against one manufacturer for making false energy conservation claims. They'll say it's maintenance free, but aluminum easily dents, and a simple rock from your lawnmower will go straight through vinyl. Neither vinyl nor aluminum is repairable. Damage to either material requires complete replacement of the damaged member.

Additionally, aluminum and vinyl have a polluting manufacturing process. Vinyl is toxic when burned, ☞

Fig. 8.2-3: *A botched vinyl siding installation covers up all but one of the home's windows.*

installation is extremely destructive. You can be sure that Mr. Vinyl is not a member of your local preservation commission. All the detailing common to historic homes is put at risk and may be damaged. In some cases woodworking may have been completely removed.

Apart from the technical reasons not to use artificial siding, it just looks bad. The US National Park Service sums up the preservationist position.

Changes to character-defining features of a building ... have an impact on more than just that building; they also alter the historic visual relationship between the buildings in the district.[2]

Once artificial siding is placed on a number of buildings, the historical character of the entire district as a whole may be seriously damaged. The retention of original materials and their craftsmanship must be of primary importance. When artificial siding conceals the historic fabric it will always subtract from the integrity of historically and architecturally significant buildings.

and aluminum siding can confine a fire to the structure and literally turn your house into a furnace. The National Fire Prevention Agency has stated that aluminum siding makes it difficult for firefighters to locate a fire within a wall cavity.

The one redeeming quality of artificial siding is paint maintenance. Vinyl requires no paint, and though aluminum siding does, it holds no moisture, is not subject to seasonal expansions and contractions and thus should last longer between paintings. In my experience, artificial siding does not directly cause structural failure. However, because it can mask wood rot or insect damage, it can allow a visible problem to be swept under the rug, where it could eventually destroy structural members.

Fig. 8.4: *After restoration.*

Fig. 8.5: *An old house in the process of siding restoration.*

Fig. 8.6: *A siding restoration reveals the damage vinyl siding installers do to original woodwork. The skirt board is destroyed, skirt sill detail deleted, window sills chopped and lintel detail deleted. Vinyl casing requires destruction of original woodwork. Artificial siding decreases door, window frame and cornerboard projections, eliminating shadow lines and creating a flat exterior. Good restorations aim to restore the craftsmanship.*

Fig. 8.7: *Asphalt shingle siding, the original artificial siding.*

Proposals violating preservation principles may completely disqualify a project from historic tax credits. Artificial siding is one of the most commonly rejected requests by historic commissions.

Trim

Exterior trim defines the home more than the siding. Depending on the style of house, you may see gingerbread detailing, elaborate corbelling and brackets, decorative lintels and flamboyant windows and doors.

Skirtboards, cornerboards, door and window casing, friezes, soffits and fascia were typically cut from stock 1x, 2x or $^5/_4$ boards, then trimmed with a molding detail. Matching original molding detail can be a real wild goose chase. Big box stores have a limited selection, so you may have to dig deeper for specific profiles. Take a sample to match, and ask your supplier for a trim profile book which offers many styles not out on the shelf.

Sometimes a trim detail will be a specific depth not available in stock sizes. When this is the case, you have a few options

1. You can plane a larger piece of wood down to size.

2. You can keep the basic pattern with a slightly different depth.

3. You can artificially fir out trim to give the impression of greater depth. A $^5/_4$-inch cornerboard furred out ¼ inch gives a matching shadowline to a 1½-inch original cornerboard. Or, you may use a crown on the lintel that is the same size as the original, but with a slightly different profile.

It's always preferable to match exactly, although budgets sometimes limit the ability to do so. SHPOs are usually cooperative in this area so long as the intent to rehabilitate and replicate is clear.

Be sure to check *cornices,* the area where rake meets eave, a very problematic spot for decay. Squirrels, bats and insects love to enter the attic at this point. It's a particularly

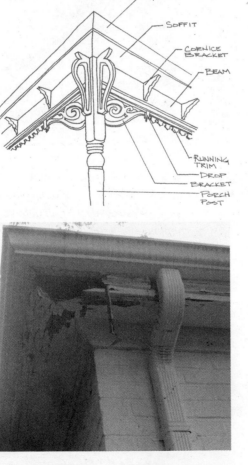

Fig. 8.8:
Historic eave details can feature incredible craftsmanship. Comparably, eaves on today's homes feature a simple soffit and fascia, production built and lacking character.

Fig. 8.9:
Cornices, where insects and animals meet wood rot and ornate, custom woodwork, require particular attention.

difficult repair that usually requires high skill and specialized or no-longer-available molding, all performed 15 to 25 feet in the air.

While artificial siding is prohibited by strict preservationists, *composite trim* is the subject of an ongoing debate. Manufacturers like Azek and Miratec make trim boards made of synthetics that are virtually indistinguishable from wood once painted. They are long lasting, require less painting, more dimensionally stable and are not attractive to insects. And, for some of the larger trim boards, composites can actually be cheaper than wood. If you replace a rotted 1x10 painted pine skirtboard with a 1x10 painted composite board, visually no one will know the difference.

On the other hand, fake trim fits in with the whole artificial and synthetic plastic houses vibe which many preservationists vehemently oppose. Plastic is generally written off as not natural, green or renewable. It is manufactured, which makes it more perfect and free from defects, not necessarily desirable when trying to replicate the look and feel of wood. I would recommend composite materials if the trim board must be in contact with earth, as is common on some porches and skirtboards. Otherwise, there is no true match for the randomness of wood.

Roofing

Roofing sheds water to the ground by a system of overlapping surfaces. When the surfaces fails, through wear or obstruction, leaks happen. Today, roofing serves the

Fig. 8.10-12: *A rotted return is repaired, flashed and painted.*

important functional task of keeping us dry and little more. Sadly, it's now rare to consider the roof as a place to show character, and distinctive styles such as slate or copper roofing are all but retired. The unique roofing of historic homes is all too often replaced with something bland and ordinary. On top of this, we generally consider the darkest shingles the most attractive, ignoring the fact that they are the most inefficient and a major contributor to heat gain. For both preservation and sustainability, there is much to improve about the way we do roofs.

Many materials have been used for roofing, including metal, slate and clay. Wood shingles dominated construction through the US Civil War. The asphalt shingle popular today began service around 1900. Metal comes in flat seam, solder-seam and standing seam varieties. *Flat seam*, featuring an exposed fastener, is cheap and common in rural areas on barns and outhouses. *Soldered-seam* is often found as an original material in

Artificial Siding — A Typical Historic District's Finding

To determine if aluminum or vinyl sidings are appropriate materials for use on existing structures in a Historic District, the Historic Preservation Commission has reviewed applicable information provided by the North Carolina Department of Archives and History, The Preservation Foundation of North Carolina, Inc., and the National Trust for Historic Preservation, and has inspected structures within the District on which artificial sidings had been installed. Following this review and inspection, the Historic Preservation Commission releases the following findings:

1. The application of artificial siding over wooden siding may cause moisture retention and eventual deterioration.

2. The insulation value of artificial siding and "insulation" applied behind the siding is minimal.

3. Artificial siding may cause fire to burn longer and be more difficult to extinguish.

4. The techniques for installing artificial siding are likely to cause permanent damage to the original siding over which it is installed.

5. Artificial siding prevents detection of deterioration of original materials that have been hidden from view.

6. The textural and visual quality of artificial siding is neither consistent nor compatible with the recognized textural and visual characteristics of the various siding materials historically used in the District.

7. The physical characteristics of artificial siding do not allow the flexibility to duplicate moldings, curved corner boards, raised panels, and other architectural elements, thus contributing to the loss of integral architectural details which are characteristic of buildings in the District.

8. When artificial siding is installed on some surfaces with original architectural details left exposed (i.e. window/door casings, cornices, corner boards, etc.), the incompatibility of characteristic materials and artificial materials diminishes the historic character and integrity of the structure.

9. Inappropriate, uncharacteristic and incompatible materials and inappropriate alterations or loss of architectural details adversely affect the character and environment of the Historic District.[3]

use a century after installation. *Standing seam roofs* feature a unique locking system that keeps the anchoring mechanism protected from the elements, preventing leaks and extending longevity. With little more than paint, standing seam roofs can last forever, and the average metal roof lasts four to six times longer than asphalt shingles. Clay roofing tiles are popular in parts of the country with roots in Spanish culture. Slate roofs are more traditional and extremely long lasting.

Where original roofing is found, review options to rehabilitate and continue its service. Few materials exposed to a hundred

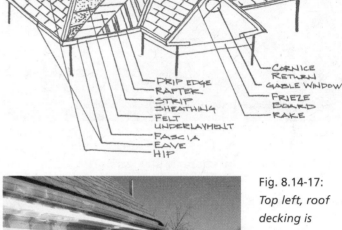

Fig. 8.13: *The Many Parts of a Roof*

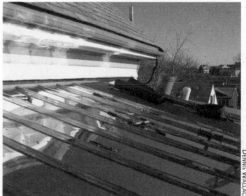

Fig. 8.14-17: *Top left, roof decking is found to be in good shape. Top right, new felt and a copper standing seam roof is installed. Within a season copper will patina to a golden green. Bottom left and right, an entryway roof is redone.*

Fig. 8.18:
A 130-year-old home, where the locals swear the slate roof is original. High pitches shed water and snow better, making materials last longer.

years of elements survive, but some do. Slate can last up to 200 years.

Wood shingles are now used for specialty applications, offering a unique look and key architectural detail. Interestingly, old wood shingles can last 40-60 years because their material was cut from old-growth trees. However, new wood shingles are dimensionally unstable, typically installed on lower roofs without skip sheathing and are expected to last only ten to 15 years.

Longevity is a key consideration in selecting your material. Most roofing warranties range from ten years to lifetime. Cash-strapped folks usually request 20-year shingles, but 30- or 35-year materials are available for only a few hundred dollars more. In quoting a roof, the roofer will account for waste, flashings, overlapping shingles at the hips, accessibility and the costs of demolishing and disposing of the existing roof. Some areas have recycling centers for old shingles, which can be regenerated into asphalt

roads. Most roof replacement jobs also include the demolition of old shingle and paper, installation of new paper and a drip edge. Some jobs require partial deck repair. If an old roof deck is in particularly poor condition, replacing the complete deck is warranted. Roofing is quoted by *square,* each square equaling 10x10 foot coverage area, or 100 square feet.

Shingle color is also an important consideration. Black or charcoal are popular color choices for their classy look. But black absorbs heat, so these colors are inefficient choices for hot climates. A lighter shade of shingle should be considered. White would be stylistically inappropriate, not to mention tacky by most standards, but some lighter shades of gray, tan and green are widely available.

Penetrations through the roof are made for chimneys, vent stacks, skylights or solar panels. Roofs are most likely to leak at these transitions and penetrations. Each opening must be properly flashed and sealed. All roofing transitions must be well flashed, and eaves and rakes should feature a clean line drip edge or gutter.

Installing new roofing over the existing one (without removing old shingles) can save in labor and disposal costs, but can generally shorten product life. For many asphalt shingles, a roof-over will void the new roof warranty. Some metal roofs allow for installation directly over old shingles. This is a serviceable approach when a new roof is needed but the costs of demolishing the old roof are prohibitive.

Old roof sheathing, aka the roof deck or *strip sheathing* is typically made from 1x6, 1x8 or 1x10 wood butted against each other. Less common is *skip sheathing,* where gaps exist between the wood. Newer homes use 4x8 sheets of plywood or OSB, typically ½-inch thick. Plywood creates a more uniform surface with fewer penetrations. Old roof decks can warp or sag, particularly under the pressure of a heavy finish material such as slate or years of deferred maintenance. I often find roofs that failed decades ago still in service (loosely speaking) through a variety of resourceful patches from tarps to duct tape. Such repairs usually indicate the urgent need for roof work.

A drip edge is an L-shaped flashing installed under the first course of shingles on the eave and at the rake. When installing gutters, shingles should extend ½ – ¾ of an inch beyond the fascia to ensure proper runoff. If shingles are cut too short, water will leak onto the fascia and cause rot, potentially leaking behind the siding and into structural elements. Drip edges are very inexpensive to install, but many roofers still consider them an add-on, so be sure to ask.

Gutters are molded material designed to catch roof water runoff and direct it away from the house. They vary in shape, size, installation details and necessity. Old versions were made of wood and copper. The modern market is almost entirely vinyl and aluminum, available in seamless and seamed

Fig. 8.19-20: *Strip roof sheathing supports 15-pound roofing felt and three-tab shingles.*

Fig. 8.21-22: *Copper is molded to fit an original wood gutter form.*

DENNIS WALLACH

DENNIS WALLACH

varieties. Seamless gutters provide continuous material between corners. Seamed gutters come in fixed lengths which produce potential leaks at each seam, an inferior design.

With proper overhangs and grading, gutters are not necessary. Many old houses never had gutters, and installation of guttering may inappropriately cover architectural detail. The large overhangs common in Craftsman and Prairie homes, for example, drop water between three and four feet away from a foundation adequately without gutters. Still, some jurisdictions require gutters on new construction, and enforcement officials may require gutters on major rehabilitations, local ordinance trumping historic preservation.

Retrofitting gutters can be tricky. I often see a three-inch crown molding on the fascia obstructing the preferred placement for a gutter. Remediation options include removal of the crown detail or installing the gutter below the crown. Removal of the crown can leave a huge shingle overhang of two to three inches, half the width of the gutter. This looks awkward and may prevent the gutter from performing in a heavy rain. Installing the gutter beneath the crown can look a bit funny, often dropping the bottom of the gutter lower than the bottom of the fascia. Neither choice is a great option.

Most residential gutters are five inches in width, with four-inch and six-inch models also available. Four-inch gutters are too small for most applications, and you don't need a six-inch gutter unless you live in a castle. The typical, and most structurally stable, shape is a box with an angled front. Decorative shapes, such as U-shape copper, are more aesthetically pleasing but bend easily when the first ladder is leaned against them.

Flashing is a thin piece of sheet metal used to prevent water from leaking into a structure at an angle or seam. Flashing is used at roof valleys, penetrations, windows, doors and sills. Materials typically include aluminum, galvanized steel, copper or zinc alloy. Lead flashing is still available, despite its well-documented environmental issues. Manufacturers promote lead's malleability and durability, noting that lead lasts many centuries, whereas other metals might fail in two decades. Because of its inherent hazards, however, lead is rarely used in the US. Even so, it still may be appropriate to use lead to flash a point that is extraordinarily cost-prohibitive to access.

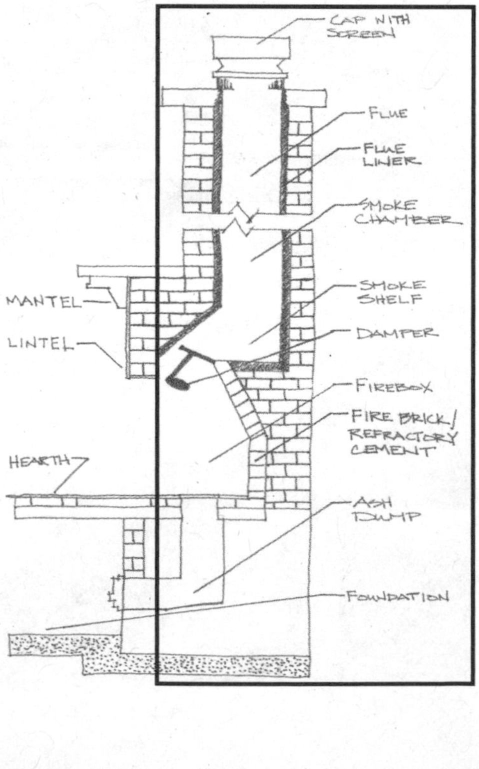

Fig. 8.23:
Parts of a chimney.

CAP WITH SCREEN
FLUE
FLUE LINER
SMOKE CHAMBER
SMOKE SHELF
DAMPER
FIREBOX
FIRE BRICK/REFRACTORY CEMENT
ASH DUMP
FOUNDATION
MANTEL
LINTEL
HEARTH

Chimneys

Chimneys are built to vent hot gases and smoke sourced from combustible fireplaces, furnaces, boilers or stoves. Their vertical structure allows hot air to flow directly up, called the stack effect, or, appropriately, the chimney effect.

Chimneys require special attention when converting an old system to modern use. A substandard chimney can collapse, cause fires or leak poisonous gases into the house. Since many chimneys in historic homes have been nonfunctioning for decades, they require a thorough inspection by a professional before being returned to service.

Inspections may reveal a multitude of problems. Obstructions are most common, including fallen bricks, bird nests and dead animals. *Creosote* is the buildup of carbon materials from the combustion of coal or wood tar. This buildup can cause a chimney to fail, clogging a chimney the way plaque clogs arteries. *Efflorescence* is proof that moisture has pushed soluble salts in masonry to the surface. Either creosote or efflorescence signal that a chimney lacks proper lining.

Inspections take place by visually analyzing the damper at the fireplace, the brick foundation in the basement or crawl space, looking through the chimney cap on the roof and/or by removing brick in certain areas. When doing the latter, it's best to make penetrations in easily repairable walls that are not core to living space, such as closet interiors.

Pre-1920 chimneys may feature refractory (heat resistant) mortars poured or parged

over rough brick joints. Over time the mortar can fail, or the rough joints collect so much creosote that the chimney clogs and can set the surrounding framing members on fire. Clay liners were installed from 1920 on and feature smooth surfaces that expedite smoke, capture less debris and allow for longer time between cleanings. Also, their infrequent joints mean less risk of fire or smoke leakage.

During a basement inspection, you may see how chimneys have changed function over time. While coal fireboxes may have been retired by the mid-20th century, the same flue may now be used to vent gas furnaces and water heaters. When this is the case, you cannot reopen the flue for the fireplace without rerouting the flue for the heating appliances. Old chimneys often routed venting for multiple fireplaces through a single flue, a practice that is not allowed today. Retroactively, this may lead to placing one fireplace back into service, while closing the others sharing the flue.

Fig. 8.24:
A *chimney being reconstructed.*

Relining is the most common application for restoring or repairing a chimney. Coal gases were tremendously corrosive, making them incompatible with metal liners. Clay or mortar mix is best for wood-burning fireplaces.

There are three options, depending on purpose and budget.

1. *Cementous lining* (fireclay parging) uses a molded balloon-like form inflated to fill the cavity with spacers, keeping it just

lightly off the walls. Refractory mortar is then slowly poured over the balloon to reline the chimney.

2. Installation of *clay tiles* requires demolition of the chimney at key intervals to gain access to install tiles, creating such a mess that the method is rarely used in retrofits.

3. Rigid or flexible *stainless steel pipe* comes in a single continuous piece and can be snaked or fished through a chimney to create a new flue. Steel flues are less expensive than clay or mortar retrofits, but their use should be limited to oil and gas combustion fireplaces.

Chimney caps are installed at the top of a chimney to prevent water from draining into the chimney or animals from nesting inside. They can be ornate or simple. Modern caps are almost exclusively metal, but some old chimneys use decorative masonry caps. Since chimney caps and chimneys above the roofline are often seen from the streetscape, any ornamentation should be preserved.

Tuck pointing is the process of renewing a masonry mortar joint. Brick mortar does not last as long as brick itself. Old mortar was generally made with sand and lime, notably lacking cement. It is less structurally stable than the modern replacement and is thus prone to problems. Bricks can collapse on themselves when mortar fails, leading to structural failure. Two hundred years ago brick and mortar were soft; 100 years ago bricks were still soft but mortar was hardened with cement. Today, both the brick and mortar are hard. Soft mortar and brick

Fig. 8.25-26: *Chimney caps vary from non-existent to simple to ornate. Chimney detailing, such as brick corbelling, is commonly overlooked in a large project. Masonry caps are particularly nice and worthy of rehabilitation. Metal caps are the modern norm, fabricated with common materials. Some feature bird screening. In the bottom photo, the left chimney has exposed clay tiles, indicating it was relined at some point.*

give some flexibility, allowing a building to contract and expand with the seasons. When today's hard mortar is used to repoint old soft brick, the result is a short-lasting joint and brick failure. It's important to identify the material and work with a mason skilled in old materials.

A chimney that requires a total reconstruction is best rebuilt with old salvage bricks to match existing masonry. New modular brick is slightly smaller than most old brick, and surface texture is hard to duplicate. When matching is necessary, local masonry supply stores usually have dozens of color and texture options. Any masonry detailing such as corbelling should be duplicated. If the chimneys are prominent from the streetscape, deletion or alteration may disqualify a project for tax credits.

As to building code, the height of an active chimney must be two feet taller than any roof point within a ten foot horizontal run. If it's not, and the chimney is being reconditioned for reuse, it must be built up to modern code clearances. Old chimneys that have been in continuous use should be grandfathered. Of course, if the chimney will not be in use, there's no code requirement to extend its height.

Porches

Porches can serve as a public and private space, a place to quietly read a book, to entertain or communicate with neighbors and passersby. Front porches, in particular, were coveted and representative of early 20th-century design. Unfortunately they

and the cultural benefits that come with them have been almost entirely removed from today's architectural lexicon.

Structurally, porches are often under assault more than the rest of the house due to exposure to weather, low-slope roofs, under-built framing and foundations or excessive use. Since the porch is outside, problems are usually written off as low priority. While a leak in the kitchen is immediately

Fig. 8.27: *A veranda is a roofed structure open to the exterior and structurally supported by columns.*

Fig. 8.28: *After restoration, a sleeping porch, originally built for lounging and cooling off on a hot day via natural breezes. The modern substitute is a sun room, often built of inferior construction with little detailing, intended to bake us with UV rays.*

dealt with, a leak in the porch roof may be ignored for years.

Tongue and groove (TnG) porch flooring is most common on old houses, though concrete slabs also exist. In my area, painted 1x4 TnG pine is the dominant wood material. Three-quarter-inch depth flooring should be used when joists are 16 inches on center and $5/4$-inch flooring when 24 inches on center. Ceilings are often finished with a TnG beadboard detail.

Columns are decorative structural members that hold up the porch roof. Column bases are prone to failure. A *plinth and torus* comprise the column base, which takes the brunt of falling rain and water runoff from floorboards. If the base hasn't been painted, caulked and sealed regularly, it will rot and wick water into the center of the column. This requires reconstruction of the column, either by wood replacement or epoxy. Exact matches for columns are difficult to find at salvage yards and can be exceedingly expensive to replicate.

Porches are commonly underframed relative to the houses to which they are attached. It is common to see structural spans between columns greatly exceeding modern span tables. While this overspanning may not be an issue if the porch shows little sign of deterioration, if a major repair is being performed an inspector may require new headers of structural lumber or steel to be installed.

Landlords have been famous for carving large historic houses into multiple apartments, and in attempts to maximize rentable space often claimed front porches for living space. The practice created low quality rooms with leaky, structurally unsound and uninsulated floors, not to mention obliteration of the historic streetscape. Such a finding offers a unique and gratifying opportunity to restore the front porch.

Fig. 8.29-30: Left, the porch structure on this transitional Craftsman had failed because the supporting 6x6 posts were wicking water and causing decay. Right, the 6x6 members were reconstructed and set on a small metal base that allows water to drain away underneath.

Relatively speaking, many porch rehabilitations can be done fairly easily. Since porches are typically covered by nothing more than a roof, the structural load is light. Since framing is exposed to the elements, only pressure-treated framing should be used. If porch framing is original, it is not pressure-treated. Use kiln-dried-after-treatment (KDAT) approved pressure-treated lumber. Non-KDAT wood has too high a moisture content, which causes it to fail sooner. Of note, up until 2003, pressure-treated wood was dipped in arsenic, a material hazardous to human contact and surrounding soils. It has now been replaced by copper dipping, which is less harmful to the environment.

Porch floors must be sloped to allow for water to drain. Often the original slope is extreme, as much as a two-inch rise for a 12-inch run. Some slopes are uncomfortable and can be reframed for lesser slope. When doing so, ensure a minimum slope of ¼ of an inch over 12 feet, which will ensure water runoff. Because there is no subfloor under exterior flooring, all flooring must run

Fig. 8.31: *Since porch flooring must allow for drainage the length of the board, and framing must run perpendicular to the flooring, porch framing requires installation of a mid-span girder.*

Appraisers

Appraisers calculate value by finished heated square feet, meaning that front porch square footage is generally ignored in calculating home value. This is the main reason new home builders rarely build large porches. Old houses can have 1,000 square feet or more of porch space, a characteristic that makes modern appraisal practice incompatible with historic homes. As Albert Einstein noted, not everything than can be counted counts, and not everything that counts can be counted.

Fig. 8.32-33: Top, *wraparound porches fall prey to landlords maximizing rentable space. The house originally had a 1,000-square-foot wraparound porch on three sides of the house. The expansion of apartments decreased it to 150 square feet. Below, a reconstruction restored the old porch, fundamental to the home's character and integrity.*

Fig. 8.34: *A paint mock-up shows the client or designer different colors. Paint looks different in interior and exterior light, on wood as opposed to paper and in morning and afternoon light. All these are good reasons to do a test swatch on the building wall prior to choosing final colors.*

Volatile organic compounds (VOCs) are harmful gases emitted into the air from certain solids and liquids. Concentrations of VOCs are up to ten times more likely indoors than out, particularly from interior paints, cabinets, stains, sealers and cleaning products. US Environmental Protection Agency studies concluded VOCs cause "Eye, nose, and throat irritation; headaches, loss of coordination, nausea; damage to liver, kidney, and central nervous system. Some organics can cause cancer in animals; some are suspected or known to cause cancer in humans. Key signs or symptoms associated with exposure to VOCs include conjunctival irritation, nose and throat discomfort, headache, allergic skin reaction, dyspnea, declines in serum cholinesterase levels, nausea, emesis, epistaxis, fatigue, and dizziness."[4] The long-term effects of VOCs are just now becoming known. Low or no-VOC paint is widely available for a small price premium. The strong new paint smell is noticeably absent with these paints and is an indication of a healthier product.

perpendicular to joists. For drainage purposes, flooring must run the short length of the porch, whereas inside the house you'd typically frame the shortest distances to minimize the framing lumber required. Thus, framing for porches is usually designed counterintuitive (and perpendicular at 90 degrees) to interior framing logic.

Lastly, wood end grain should never be exposed to the elements. End grain soaks up moisture, which will shorten the service life of the wood. Flooring end grain should be covered with an end cap, and exterior trim boards should be mitered to keep water from entering wood through the end grain.

Paint

Few restoration tasks are, or at least seem, as simple as painting. Perhaps no task makes such a positive difference between before and after. A fresh coat quickly turns a rough-looking home into an attractive one. Some careful forethought about multi-color schemes can do wonders for the neighborhood's streetscape. Choosing high quality material ensures that installers and occupants breathe healthy air and will enjoy a finished product that lasts eight to ten years or more.

Using quality paint is one of the more obvious choices to make. According to a Paint Quality Institute study, spending $700 on top quality paint materials instead of $400 on an economy brand dramatically reduces your cost per year of service life from $1,350 to $570 on an average house. Labor, at $5,000, is estimated to be 80-90%

of a painting bill. So for an extra $300 up front, you save $780 per year. Big historic houses will cost much more than that to prep and paint, so the savings will vary depending on house size.

A general inspection of the exterior should include a visual analysis of paint condition. Look for mold, moss, algae and peeling paint. Where water damage exists a problem exists. Usually the problem is obvious: a leaky roof, clogged or leaky laundry vent, failed gutter installation, missing flashing or landscaping too close to the house.

Unfortunately, paint is often used to conceal underlying problems. A deceitful seller may intentionally mask a problem with a coat of paint. If you're looking at purchasing, try looking for inconsistencies in the exterior, particularly areas that look like they've experienced significant patching. When you probe the suspect areas with a screwdriver, any area requiring work will feel far less solid than good wood.

Paint (especially oil) is relatively impermeable so any water vapor that pushes through the wood will loosen the paint's grip and cause the paint to bubble. Such bubbling indicates a need for moisture remediation strategies. It's most common to see moisture and humidity assault the exterior walls of bathrooms, laundries and kitchens.

Paint preparation is the most crucial and overlooked part of a good paint job. All flaking, loose and uneven paint must be removed prior to any primer or new paint being applied. On old homes, prep work can

Oil vs Latex

The US Department of Agriculture Forest Product Laboratory concluded that the most durable application for new siding is two coats of acrylic latex over a 100% acrylic latex primer. The paint will not crack with seasonal expansion, and should last eight to ten years. Some manufacturers and painters still believe an oil primer is best and that it adheres to chalky, glossy and inconsistent surfaces better. Still, due to VOC issues, oil is being pushed farther and farther out of production.

Oil paints are longer lasting, thicker and offer a more historic feel. Oil is much higher in parts per million of VOCs, penetrates wood better, glues to objects, hides knots better and dries slowly, minimizing brush marks. On the downside, oil requires paint thinners (which dilute colors and emit VOCs of their own) and is basic food for mold and mildew.

For better or worse, oil paints form a vapor barrier, which can have unintended moisture management consequences in a wall assembly. Cleanup causes disposal problems. Oil paint's market share has shrunk so much that certain materials may be hard to find. Modern use is typically limited to primers on exterior surfaces or high-use glossy surfaces such as kitchen cabinets.

Latex paints are cleaner and available in low or no-VOC formulas which are better for the environment. Latex is cheaper and does not require thinners. It is flexible and can be cleaned with soap and water. Even the regular formulas are much lower in VOCs relative to oil. Latex paint breathes, allowing moisture through, which makes it less likely to blister over time.

Fig. 8.35-36:
Top, the paint job has exceeded its useful life and must be stripped to a smooth paintable surface. Bottom, pump jacks and walkboard makes the job of stripping paint easier. Notice how the old paint has been almost entirely removed, a necessary process for any long lasting paint job.

DENNIS WALLACH

DENNIS WALLACH

Paint Texture

Paint texture describes the glossiness of the paint, caused by a difference in pigmentation. The more pigment, the flatter the texture. As a rule, glossy paint is reflective and easier to clean. Flatter paints better hide defects such as nail pops and bumps. In previous eras, glossy paint was seen as more luxurious and would have been less common in proletarian housing. You'll commonly see flat and eggshell textures on interior wall surfaces. Satin, a popular mid-texture, is found on siding and interior wall surfaces that require cleaning such as the kitchen, playroom and bathroom. Semi-Gloss is seen on interior trim, windows and doors, while gloss paint is common to exterior trim, windows and doors.

be the biggest part of the job. While newer homes are typically just power washed before painting, old homes require additional steps. Often only a portion of suspect paint is removed, leaving the painter to apply new paint over failing flakes of old paint. There's no better way to have an eight-to-ten-year paint job last only three years or less.

First, you must know what you are working with. Lead paint is of most concern in homes with young children. Lead paint was common in high-end applications and is most commonly found in glossy paint and white paint. Unless proved otherwise, all old white or glossy paint should be treated as if it has lead. However, old paint is not, repeat not, inherently lead-based. It's possible an old house in a working class neighborhood never had lead paint simply because the former residents couldn't afford it. Lead paint was banned by the US federal government in 1978. According to the National Paint and Coatings Association, high-quality older paint could be as much as 55% lead. A single gallon of lead paint would weigh over 40 pounds. Today a gallon of paint averages just ten pounds.

Second, failing paint must be removed. First, the ground should be prepped to catch falling debris. There are many different ways to remove the paint. Scraping by hand is laborious, but a preferred method of painters for generations. Sanding can cause a mess of dust and is discouraged when working with lead. If sanding, wet sanding helps by limiting harmful dust. Heat guns are a great way to burn down your house while also giving your neighbors lead poisoning. If you insist on using such a tool, make sure a fire extinguisher and water source are readily available. Chemical strippers strip paint off without making much of a mess; they are applied overnight and yanked off the next day. There are a couple of proprietary paint shaver products that use a rotary grinder tool with a concealed broom and vacuum to capture all debris as it is shaved. They are expensive but the most thorough way to get back to pure wood prior to repainting.

Finally, once back to bare wood or solid surface, painting follows the same procedure as for a new house. Prime, caulk and apply two final coats of paint. A preservation consultant can help by performing a paint color analysis of the paint preparation debris to document past colors of the home. Using an original color scheme is an inexpensive way to restore a home's old characteristics.

Exterior Lighting

Exterior lighting can highlight architectural accents in the evening, while lighted pathways offer security and set moods. SHPOs offer some flexibility in exterior lighting. While the preservation ethic requires us to make efforts to rehabilitate historic details and not give a false sense of time, life in 2010 generally requires more lighting than it did 1910. As long as the general style matches, you should be able to install additional exterior lighting without any problem.

Low voltage (12V) lighting is a popular addition that allows for lights to be placed in the yard without the burden and expense

Fig. 8.37-38: *Top, a simple test swabs a suspect area to detect lead. Within seconds,* red means lead *(pink too). Bottom, a paint shaver removes eight decades of paint in two passes, suctioning the debris into a HEPA-filter vacuum.*

of the electrical conduit required for high voltage (120V). These low voltage circuits are installed with a step-down transformer that can include an automatic timer. From a sustainability perspective, lighting should be limited to what is necessary, in terms of number of fixtures and hours operated, and should make use of energy-efficient CFL or LED bulbs. Bulbs must be rated for exterior use, and security floodlights should be on motion sensors.

Sustainability and Preservation

The ultimate goal of sustainability is conservation, and that common end is best on display in a building's exterior. Houses that

Fig. 8.39-41: *This homeowner pre-ferred the three column massing sketched above. Historic research indi-cated that sided columns (bottom) were original defining characteristics of the home. SHPO denied the three-column design and requested the original columns be restored (right).*

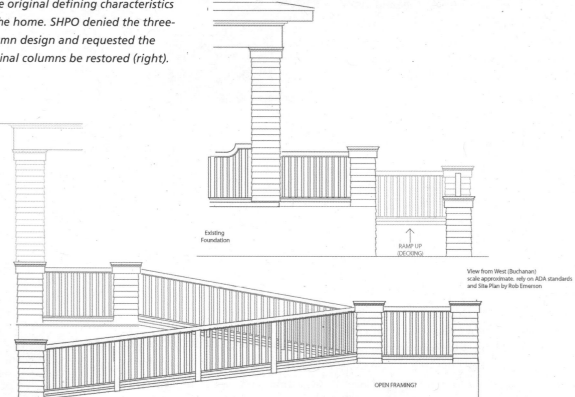

Existing
Foundation

↑
RAMP UP
(DECKING)

View from West (Buchanan)
scale approximate. rely on ADA standards
and Site Plan by Rob Emerson

OPEN FRAMING?

View from South
scale approximate. rely on ADA standards
and Site Plan by Rob Emerson

last for centuries serve both movements. Houses that are healthy last longer, as do their occupants.

Still, SHPOs will really hammer exterior plans if they are deemed inconsistent with the Secretary of the Interior's Standards. For other preservation boards, such as those that regulate local historic districts, the exterior of the home may be all they care about. It's common that artificial siding proposals are rejected outright, while some stickler boards may debate and require the owner to install certain profiles, moldings or material types. My company had a column replication proposal rejected because it was deemed not true to the original design. Even though it fit the style of the house and surrounding neighborhood, it was clearly not the column design original to the home. Of course, plans that rehabilitate what is already there or propose to restore a building's facade to its original detail get approved with little problem.

The approval process for additions varies greatly by jurisdiction. Additions should not affect the streetscape, and are generally relegated to the rear of the building. Sizing and massing should be complementary to the house and surrounding buildings. New should be differentiated from old, and an addition should be engineered so that a future owner could remove it without adversely affecting the historic portion of the home. Try not to lose too many original windows and doors in the process. Sometimes old windows can be deconstructed on the old house and reconstructed on an addition.

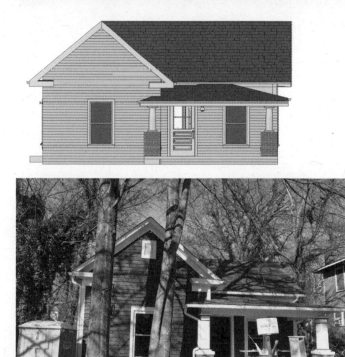

Fig. 8.42-44: *All things great are created twice. Quality restorations require the creation of a well thought-out plan as a pre-cursor to any successful construction project. Before photos, plan sets and after photos can document a chain of logic.*

The cultural benefits of sustainability and preservation are at play on an historic home's exterior. Craftsmanship detailing American architecture, art, workmanship, history and culture are all present. Where these qualities exist, work should be pro-tected and enhanced. Where they are notably absent we feel no connection, no emotional attachment and less objection to bulldozing. In this way preservation reinforces sustain-ability, in and of itself.

PART III: GREEN SYSTEMS

STRUCTURAL

9

It is the pervading law of all things organic, and inorganic, of all things physical and metaphysical, of all things human and all things superhuman, of all true manifestations of the head, of the heart, of the soul, that the life is recognizable in its expression, that form ever follows function. This is the law.

— Louis Sullivan, "The Tall Office Building Artistically Considered"

Questions to Ask

- What kind of foundation does the building have?

- What condition is the foundation in?

- Where are water problems most likely?

- What type of framing was used for my home?

- What size and spacing of floor joists does the house have, and is it overframed or underframed?

- Are the floors particularly bouncy, and is additional support warranted?

- Do the exterior walls, windows, doors or roof noticeably sag?

- Is there evidence of previous structural repair, and if so, why was it performed?

Old homes were designed with structural logic much different than today's. New homes are designed with strict adherence to the lumber sizing and spans listed in the building code. Old homes were built with common sense, logic and feel. Most homes built between 1880-1930 were built on inferior footing. These old footings offer foundation walls little support, which then may support often overspanned joists and girders. Historic home foundations were subject to improper load calculation, inferior footings and substandard mortar. Old framing systems can be vastly over- or under-built. Each is a potential point of failure. It is crucial to understand such risks during a rehabilitation.

Structural failure is a phrase that scares the average Joe. Unfortunately, most structures subject to a century of seasonal expansions, water, humans, animals, deferred maintenance, improper storage and poor footings are destined to have some structural issues that need to be addressed. Combine construction flaws, time and the dreadful soil of central North Carolina, and it's rare that I see an old home that doesn't have some sort of structural problem. Structural issues can all be addressed, however, and most are simple but laborious fixes.

The structure of a building is formed by foundation and framing.

The *foundation* is a structure that transfers loads to earth. It keeps earth and wood apart. The concept is simple: a house is heavy, so a foundation spreads that load over an area suitable for the earth to handle. The average two-story Queen Anne Victorian weighs between 30-60 tons, enough for three 20-ton jacks to support the whole thing (theoretically, but don't try it at home).

The *framing* forms the structure, defines separate rooms and carries the floor, wall and roof loads to the foundation.

Fig. 9.1:
Typical Structural Construction in the Southern US.

I'll discuss the most common foundation and framing techniques, common problems and how each is typically fixed. I'll also discuss basic preservation and sustainability issues related to the structure.

Footings and Foundations

Foundations are constructed of footings and foundation walls. *A footing* is the below-ground mass, generally made of concrete or brick, that supports the foundation wall. It is sized to transfer the weight of the entire structure to ground. A footing must sit on stable soil and not backfill, which compresses easily. If the soil is not stable, the footing is more likely to fail. Today footings are eight inches wider than the wall or pier they support (e.g., a 12-inch-wide wall requires a 20-inch-wide footing) and deep enough to sit below the *frost line,* the depth at which groundwater is expected to freeze in a respective climate.

Footing construction varies greatly on old homes. Larger stately homes may well be on large and well built footings, though it would be rare to find the metal *reinforcing bar (rebar)* required today. Many houses sit on a *soldier course,* which is nothing more than an extra course of bricks at the bottom of the brick pier or foundation wall. Soldier courses are commonly found above the frost line and are prone to mortar breakdown, especially under pressure of water.

The *foundation wall* carries loads from the exterior sill beam framing to the footing. *Piers* support interior girders and are made of a variety of materials — stone,

	1900	2010
Footing	Two soldier courses of brick, no rebar, no concrete footing	Continuous 20x24 footing with reinforcing bar
Foundation	Pier and curtain wall, sills span as much as 10' between load points	Continuous foundation
Framing	Non-treated, balloon frame	All wood in contact with earth must be treated, platform frame

masonry and poured-in-place concrete are all common. Mortar joints offer little resistance to unbalanced lateral forces (such as a backfilled basement wall), so tall, thin, unreinforced masonry curtain walls are prone to failure.

The foundation wall also defines the area underneath the main living space. In the northern US basements are common, while in the South crawl spaces are more typical. A below-grade basement or crawl space is intrinsically unstable and problematic; the pressures of earth and groundwater are predisposed to assault its footing and wall. Based on their porosity, soils hold and shed varying amounts of water. The basement floor can actually be below the water table, most likely in spring when snow is melting both on the roof and ground.

Water causes nearly all problems in foundations. Water against a foundation wall exerts *hydrostatic pressure* — water trying to get from areas of high pressure (poor draining soil) to areas with less (your basement). *Frost heave* happens when water

freezes in poorly draining soil, then expands and pushes the footing, foundation and house upward. Any footing above the frost

Fig. 9.2-3: *Top, a pier and curtain wall. The piers bear the weight, and the curtain is not load-bearing, though in practice this house has settled and does bear on the curtain wall. Bottom, two freestanding piers bear interior girders; the pier in the background has failed and must be reconstructed.*

Fig. 9.4-6: *Left, a new 24x24-inch footing is formed. Center, freestanding CMU block piers await framing for an addition to an historic home. Right, a continuous footing will support a load-bearing exterior wall.*

line will rise and fall with the freeze thaw cycle. Typical frost lines vary from four feet in Maine to less than a foot in the Southeast, and footings must be at least as deep as the frost line to avoid frost heave.

Fig. 9.7-8: *Top, this pier failed and was then subjected to some, well, rather hopeful engineering. Repair involved replacement with a new pier on a proper footing. Bottom, the curtain wall caved in due to hydrostatic pressure from the outside.*

The best solutions for water problems are to grade, divert roof runoff, dampproof or waterproof the foundation.

Grading refers to the slope of earth around the foundation. Code requires a 5% slope to six feet around the foundation, and many old homes fail this bench mark. Any place where a slope does not meet such grade is subject to water problems. Solutions include *swales*, which create a low point six to 12 feet from the foundation to capture water, and *French drains*, a subsurface swale covered with perforated pipe and drainage gravel, allowing surface grading to remain unaltered.

Roof runoff (rainwater) is diverted away from the foundation by either gutters or proper grading. In cold climates gutters cause ice dams which can result in roof leaks and eave damage, which is why some forgo gutters in favor of ground-based drainage often involving plastic water barrier protection covered with decorative gravel or a continuous pitched concrete grade.

Foundation failure

Foundation walls of masonry or poured concrete fail for different reasons.

1. Hairline cracks are the result of curing too rapidly, poor concrete mix or settlement. As long as the crack is not increasing, it can be repaired with hydraulic cement.
2. Vertical cracks are more likely because of hydrostatic pressure.
3. Horizontal cracks likely occur because of settlement.
4. V- shaped cracks are evidence of frost heave.
5. Pyramidal cracks are evidence of footing failure, often from water saturation.

For major cracks, it's possible to shore the wall without reconstructing it in its entirety, using steel jack posts or timbers and screw jacks (typical hydraulic jacks do not work horizontally, while hydraulic ram jacks do). Backhoe operators are needed for some jobs, but be sure to hire a competent one. Mechanized equipment plus old foundations have led to some unhappy endings.[1]

Dampproofing keeps most water out of the foundation, but allows water through in a torrential rain. A perforated pipe is set just below the exterior of the footing, sloped to direct water away via gravity or sump pump. A dampproofing approach may or may not include a latex waterproofing paint on the foundation wall, now required by many local ordinances on new construction.

Waterproofing keeps all water from entering the foundation and is necessary if using the basement as finished space. It is much more involved than dampproofing. Waterproofing can be done inside or outside the foundation wall; it's better to stop water before it enters the structure though that does requires a more expensive exterior waterproofing. First, a thick, impermeable dimple sheet is installed to keep water out of the foundation. Next, just below the footing, a perforated pipe is set which captures groundwater and drains it to either daylight or a sump pump. A *sump pump* is used to remove water accumulated in a sump pit, commonly placed at the low point in a basement, crawl space or exterior.

Bentonite clay is a natural waterproofing material that functions by suspending water in a gelatinous form. Less natural but more common is extruded polystyrene foam

Fig. 9.9:
Exterior waterproofing detail.

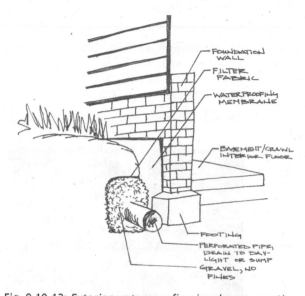

Fig. 9.10-12: *Exterior waterproofing involves excavation, hydraulic cement, insulation board and a drainage mat to direct water to the footing drain. The drain is buried in clean gravel, with no fine particulate matter, and covered with a filter fabric. Water exits the drain to daylight or sump pump.*

board insulation (XPS), which is a cheap and common detail on new foundations, particularly in northern climates. It is non-permeable (except at its seams), helping resist water infiltration.

It's important to differentiate between problems caused by surface water runoff and a high water table. The first can be fixed rather simply, the latter may be impossible. High water tables enter the structure through the wall and the basement floor. Concrete is

Fig. 9.13: *A sump pump sits in a sump pit. Basements or crawl spaces are graded to direct water to this pit, where it is pumped to the exterior and away from the house.*

Always call your local *One Call* service before digging. In some areas the service is known as *811*. Utility workers will come out and mark buried lines. Typically, the color markings they use are

Red – Electrical service
Yellow – Gas and oil
Orange – Communication
Blue – Potable water
Green – Sewers and drains
Purple/Violet – Reclaimed water and irrigation
Pink – Survey markings
White – Proposed excavation

porous, and no match for such pressure. Today, vapor barriers of four- or six–millimeter (mil) thick polyethylene are installed under slabs and are an excellent tool against such an assault. Old homes won't have such a barrier. A possible fix is to install a vapor barrier and pour a new slab. Still, while it's feasible to waterproof a new footing and all its transition points it's nearly impossible to waterproof an old footing. Footing drains outside should relieve some of the pressure, but not all. If there is evidence of a high water table, it's recommended that you leave the basement unfinished. Finished basements require a 100% success rate against water, and the costs to insure such a rate would be too excessive.

Lastly, a wet basement can occasionally be caused by a blocked drain tile, failed sewer or stormwater line. Unfortunately, private lines are not easily explored by anything short of excavation. Plumbers do have pipe camera tools that can avert a major dig, though many are cautious about sending an expensive piece of equipment up a pipe with an unknown blockage.

Basements

Questions to Ask When Finishing a Basement

- What will finished head height be?
- Will utilities be easy or difficult to access?
- Will plumbing lines and ductwork encroach on headroom?
- Does the basement have water problems and why?

- Will my basement allow for egress in case of emergency?
- Is a floating floor, concrete floor or carpet best?

Our basements served very different purposes before the invention of refrigeration and furnaces. A basement floor, up to eight feet below grade, has a far cooler surface temperature which helps to preserve foods and cool the house. Thermal lag, from the temperature conditioning of the surrounding earth, keeps the basement from freezing. Historically, the cellar, as a basement was more commonly called, was an ideal storage place for potatoes, onions, cabbage, smoked meats, canned items, wine and cider. Modern versions of food storage, called bermed pantries or root cellars, are reappearing in some functionally retro designs.

Finishing basements was never considered. Today, it is. In many climates where basements are the norm, a simple interior waterproofing may be all that is necessary. In the clay-dominated South, more serious measures are necessary, typically including exterior waterproofing.

Short of pouring a new slab and installing a footing drain, there is no 100% certain way to waterproof a basement floor. Waterproof paint is often installed in lieu of polyethylene under the slab, a less than perfect solution. And, with the water risks basements pose, it's best to tread cautiously in choosing material finishes. Materials that absorb and retain moisture should be avoided. Wood should not be installed directly on a slab and requires either a vapor barrier or a floating floor typically built of pressure treated 1x4-inch sleepers. Carpet makers such as FLOR make high-recycled-content material that is much more moisture resistant that traditional carpet. Since this flooring comes in small 18x18-inch squares, you can easily replaced one if ruined by a wine spill (though this type of carpet is also remarkably easier to clean than the roll-out variety). These qualities make FLOR carpet a great choice for flooring in a basement. Any below-grade sheetrock should be moisture resistant, separated from contact where it could wick moisture, including any masonry, concrete or dirt. Sheetrock is installed at least ½ an inch above basement finished flooring to avoid direct contact with water.

Basements and crawl spaces were designed to offer accessible space for utilities. Storage and utility basements were not designed with the intent of future finishing. This makes obstructions — such as sprawling plumbing, HVAC and electrical systems — commonplace. Utilities may need to be moved, and ductwork habitually encroaches onto headroom.

While utilities obstruct finished space, finished space also obstructs utilities. Thus, before burying important systems behind walls, consider what sort of maintenance needs to be done on them and how often. Upgrade any systems before concealing them, and be cognizant of what would have to be done to finishes if service access were needed in the future. Proper planning minimizes the risk of a major demolition later.

Wherever possible, plan on keeping utilities exposed for future access or perhaps dedicate a smaller room in the basement for this sole purpose.

House Jacking

Fixing the foundation, or rebuilding it entirely, requires the temporary transfer of the house's loads above in order to perform the work. *Holding* the house consists of temporarily lifting the load-bearing girders or sills on a portion of the house just enough to remove failed members. One-half inch is usually enough. *Raising* the house consists of lifting the entire house at once. One foot elevation to an entire story is typical. Raising strategies might be considered when a usable basement is desired in tandem with major foundation reconstruction. The house may be raised as much as eight to ten feet to allow for the addition of a new floor below.

The merits of permanently raising a house is an ongoing debate in the preservation community. An argument that the house must be raised to ensure its longevity as a healthy structure makes a stronger case than arguing it must be raised because the owner wants a game room. Generally speaking, lifting the house significantly disrupts the streetscape by creating an unusually tall structure, particularly so if raising more than a few feet. In New Orleans, of course, it's argued that raising houses is necessary now to survive potential future flooding, so the debate continues.

It also is impossible to raise a house without reconstruction of chimneys, since the practice will throw all your hearths off elevation. Floors are raised while chimneys are not. Balloon-framed homes can be more difficult to jack than platform-framed structures. Since a balloon-framed floor may be tacked onto the studs with nothing more than a few nails, jacking up the floor may lift only the floor system, while not lifting the walls. To correct this, jacking may be required from the inside and out, and sometimes a temporary wall between floors is needed to ensure the whole structure rises in tandem.

Fig. 9.14-15: *Left, the house is held by steel beams while the foundation is reconstructed; a pier and curtain wall foundation is replaced by a more stable 12-inch-thick CMU block and brick veneer wall. Right, house jacks, typically 20-ton, do the heavy lifting.*

New Foundation Construction

Once the house is lifted, a new foundation wall can be built. Often a pier and curtain wall will be replaced by a continuous masonry wall made of either brick, CMU block or both. Wood wicks water from masonry, which is why building codes now specify that any wood in contact with masonry now must be pressure-treated. If a new foundation wall is supporting an existing non-treated sill, termite protection should be installed — either pressure-treated wood or a termite flashing made of 20 gauge aluminum. Be sure to install sleeves for utilities. Short PVC stubs suffice for electric, water and HVAC lines.

As with all exterior features, try to match any foundation detailing. If the piers protruded beyond the curtain wall on the exterior, or had some masonry corbelling for example, it would be good to restore that detail. I've found preservation boards to be reasonably flexible so long as the old foundation wasn't extremely distinctive.

Framing

Modern framing in the US represents the third generation of this evolving trade. Timber framing dominated Colonial construction, then balloon framing from the mid-19th century through the mid-20th. Nearly all homes have been platform-framed since.

Timber-framed (1600-1850) homes in the North tended to be based around a massive center chimney that heated the home and around which all activity revolved. In the South, chimneys were more commonly found on exterior walls. In both regions, timbers often rested on chimneys made of logs and plaster (not allowed today because of fire concerns). Corners of each room were made from timbers six to eight inches square, each laboriously formed by a hand chisel. Colonial times saw timber posts anchored in earth, with walls made of branches and mud. These construction materials made houses into tinder boxes, waiting to ignite.

Homes were built by the families that lived in them, with help as needed by

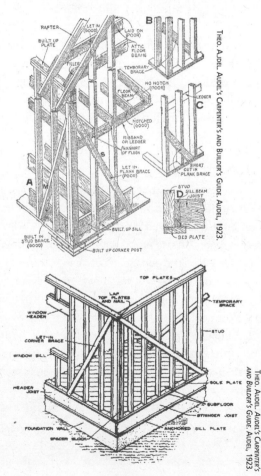

Fig. 9.16-17: *Top, balloon frames feature studs running continuous from foundation sill to roof rafter, with joists tacked onto the sides. Bottom, platform-framed houses have studs serving a single floor, with each additional floor built as a platform over the studs.*

THEO. AUDEL'S CARPENTER'S AND BUILDER'S GUIDE. AUDEL, 1923.

THEO. AUDEL'S CARPENTER'S AND BUILDER'S GUIDE. AUDEL, 1923.

extended family and friends. But as agriculture generated wealth, owners could afford skilled craftspeople to build houses framed with timber beams. The multi-year process consisted of timbering trees, then hewing the logs, then forming the beams and finally constructing the home. Specialists did the framing while families still tended to build the sides and roof. Soon after, heating stoves and furnaces negated the need for a central chimney, and the expensive, select, heavy hardwood trees that timber framing relied on gave way to spruce and fir, which were more plentiful, lighter and easier to work with.

Invented in Chicago in 1832, *balloon framing* (1832-1945) used manufactured dimensional lumber generated from production sawmills, with a method that built the exterior envelope first (the balloon), followed by the interior floors and walls. The growth of railroad transportation played a large role in the demand for balloon framing. Wood was readily shipped from timber forests to manufacturing centers to treeless plains, and homes were assembled with also-mass-produced nails. Studs, sometimes 30 feet long, ran continuously from sill to rafter top plate. Each floor was hung from the continuous studs. Joists were face nailed to studs, where they were (hopefully) supported by a let in plate. Since balloon framing used relatively smaller lumber, diagonal sheathing was added to give the whole frame structural strength. However, some carpenters incorrectly installed sheathing horizontally, which made balloon framing more likely to rack. Unlike timber framing, balloon framing was easy and quick to install, which led to the first production-built neighbor-

Framing Members

A *girder* is a structural member that bears directly on the foundation. Girders tend to be large beams in old homes, and built-up sistered 2x lumber or Laminated Veneer Lumber (LVLs) in new construction. Girder sizing is determined by the open span between foundation points and the loads it carries above.

A *joist* carries floor load and bears directly on girders. 2x10s 16 inches on center is a common joist sizing, though framing can be as shallow as 2x6 and as large as 30-inch trusses.

A *sill beam* is similar to a girder but rests on the exterior foundation wall. Today's construction typically uses continuous foundation walls, and large sill beams have been replaced with sill plates and rim joists.

A *stud* is the vertical member used for wall framing, typically 2x4s 16 inches on center.

A *header* is a structural member placed over a window or door void to distribute loads above around the opening. Headers are generally required over doors on any load-bearing wall. Header sizing is determined by the opening size and loads transferred from above.

A *rafter* is a sloped framing member designed to support the roof deck. Stick-built rafters are often replaced by engineered trusses on new construction.

Sistering involves installing an additional framing member adjacent and parallel to a similar framing member. It is typically done to reinforce floor and ceiling joists.

hoods. Its flexibility in design allowed for the great architectural detailing of the Victorian era.

In *platform framing* (1945-) each story is built on its own platform. Around 1955, plywood replaced diagonal sheathing, adding further rigidity to the frame. A platform-framed house is simpler to build, more resistant to fire and for the most part does not require abnormally long lumber. Platform framing represents nearly all construction today.

Understanding Your Framing

Before performing any structural repair or modifications, you must first figure out how your house is framed and how its concentrated loads are carried to earth. Timber frame houses carry larger loads directly to piers; its sills are solely for bracing and do not bear any direct weight. Both balloon and platform framing distribute smaller loads across the entire foundation, with studs bearing directly on the sills. The greater

Fig. 9.18-19: *Top, diagonal sheathing gave balloon frames greater sheer strength. Bottom, a Victorian has no sheathing, making it less structurally stable.*

The Sears Catalogue[2]

The stick framing industry created abundant business opportunities. From 1908-1940, Sears Roebuck and Co. sold over 75,000 homes through their mail-order Modern Homes catalogue. Four hundred and forty-seven different designs ranged from elaborate to simple, Colonial to Craftsman, Tudor to Spanish revival. Such production led to catalogue designs, such as the Sears homes, which were packaged and shipped by rail and truck to the construction site to be put together like a modern prefab cabinet. Everything from nails to stain was included. Because of the lowered costs of distribution and less material waste, Sears homes were wildly popular with budget-conscious buyers who still demanded style. Sears estimated their homes took 352 carpenter hours of assembly as opposed to 583 hours for custom-cut homes. Sears also offered loans for their houses, from five to 15 years. Unfortunately, credit extension proved problematic. Fifty percent of their sales were financed, and the Great Depression caused leveraged losses that doomed their program. Perhaps Sears was the subprime lender of the 1920s!

spread of load allows a small portion of the bearing plates to be removed for a time without the structure collapsing, which is not possible in timber framing. That's why structural repair is much easier in stick-framed homes.

You can document joist spacing in the crawl space and attic. Spacing is often referred to as *on center, so 16 on center* (16 o.c.), means that joist centers are 16 inches apart. Whatever your exposed joist spacing is in the crawl space or basement, it is usually the

Up In Smoke

The continuous studs on balloon-framed houses make them far greater fire hazards than platform houses. Balloon framing lacks fire blocking, horizontal pieces of wood placed in stud cavities to slow the spread of a fire. A fire originating in the basement, from a furnace for example, can quickly travel up a stud cavity and set the roof on fire. A large Victorian can ignite and burn to the ground in little more than ten minutes. In platform framing the platform itself serves as the fire block, making rapid fire spread in a modern house far less of a risk. If you're gutting a house, fire blocking may be required. Even if it is not required, installing it is a good idea. Acknowledge what a fire risk old homes can be, and take into consideration fireplaces, gas appliances, smoke detectors and fire alert systems.

Fig. 9-20: *A deteriorated stud. Sometimes partial sistering (called fish plating) can correct this problem. Other times an entirely new stud is warranted.*

Frame Sizing and Materials

Framing in stick-framed (balloon and platform) homes is mostly of 2x lumber — that means varying depths (four, six, eight, ten or 12 inch) of two-inch wood. One-by (1x) generally refers to non-structural trim material such as baseboards, though many balloon-framed let in ledger boards are actually 1x wood. Old girders and sills were huge timbers of 6x6, 8x8 or 6x10. Such large timbers are almost never used today.

Note, importantly, that old carpenters generally used actual dimension lumber, meaning a 2x4 was actually 2 inches by 4 inches. All lumber today is in *nominal dimension lumber*, where a 2x4 is actually 1.5 inches by 3.5 inches. Nominal 6 inches = 5.5, eight inches = 7¼, ten inches = 9¼ and 12 inches = 11¼. Nominal 1 inch is actually ¾.

Engineered structural members that are not prescribed by the building code require an engineer to design. Laminated veneer lumber (LVL) is common where dimensional lumber is not large or strong enough for a span. Steel can be used for even larger spans. An engineer's stamp would be required for the use of either.

same on the finished floors. Where framing is not exposed, you can still make a logical guess at sizing: Take a measurement from finished floor height to plaster on the ceiling below, subtract 2 inches (for the plaster, lath subfloor and finish flooring) and that's approximately the depth of your floor framing. Cross-reference this data with the span table (IRC 502.3), and you can judge whether your floors are over or underframed. You can also use common sense. If you jump and the floors don't feel stable, they probably aren't.

Fig. 9.21-22: *Termites love a good, wet sill beam. Bottom, termites are attracted to beams saturated by water not from the ground, but from a leaky radiator. Inside, the girder, sillbeam and floorboards all show clear termite tunnels and stalactites.*

What is a load-bearing wall?

A load-bearing wall is a wall that transfers weight from a structure other than itself, such as floor or roof. A non-load-bearing wall carries only its own weight. Confusion arises because load-bearing and non-load-bearing walls all look the same when finished. Inspection via the attic and basement helps to determine which is which. All exterior walls are load-bearing, carrying at least minimum roof load. Where ceiling joists run perpendicular into a beam, that beam is supported by a load-bearing wall. Where the joists run parallel, that wall is likely non-load-bearing. In stacked, two-story houses, it's likely that framing runs the same direction on each floor, though random and non-logical changes in joist direction are more common in old homes than new.

A stud detector can help indicate which way joists are going. Plaster lath, which forms a near continuous wood surface, confuses cheaper stud detectors, so be sure to do your homework before knocking out what is presumed to be a non-load-bearing wall. Sometimes good old fashioned exploratory demolition is warranted.

Removing a load-bearing wall is not rocket science. It requires the construction of a temporary wall, often called a false wall, to support any joists bearing on the wall you intend to remove. Once these joists are supported, you can remove the wall, install new supports, connect the old joists and remove the temporary walls.

Wall removal can cause preservation problems — particularly in public spaces like between the kitchen and dining room — so if pursuing a tax credit project always check with your SHPO before proceeding.

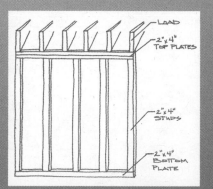

Fig. 9.23: *A load-bearing wall carries floor load above it. A non-load-bearing wall carries only its own weight.*

By code, there should be a minimum of six inches between the sill and earth. Practically speaking, it's ideal to have more than that. Water easily wicks into large sill beams, and they are the most common target of rot and insect damage on an old house. The further away from water, the better. Review the lowest layer of siding (or skirtboard), as its condition indicates the probable state of the sills. If rot is evident, remove layers to discover the extent of the damage.

Penetration and Notching Allowances

Old and new joists alike will have penetrations through them and notches at their edges. Some are installed properly, others, well, not so much. Plumbers are notorious for drilling a toilet waste line from above and taking out whatever may happen to be in their way beneath. If they have over-notched a major girder, you'll eventually see it by way of floor or wall sag. When joists are penetrated incorrectly, they can loose their ability to carry loads properly, and they bend or deflect. Notches and penetrations must not exceed the tolerances described below.

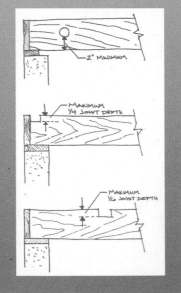

Fig. 9-24: *Above, the edges of a hole penetrated through framing lumber must be at least two inches from its edge. Center, a notch at the end of a joist may be ¼ its depth. Below, a notch in the middle of a joist may be ¹/₁₆th of its depth.*

Framing Fixes

Major sill beam issues are fixed by total or partial replacement. Some repair jobs can be performed with epoxy, which bonds to wood and takes on some of its structural characteristics. If replacing, the house is lifted or held, old wood removed, new wood installed and the house dropped back down.

When pests are present, treatment should always be performed before major carpentry. Termites and powderpost beetles love any wood in a moist crawl space. When joists are partially rotted, sistered joists can

Fig. 9.25-26: *Sill repair starts with jacking the home, done here by simultaneously lifting the joists from under the home and lifting the studs from the outside. The rotted sill was removed and replaced by a built-up 2x girder.*

be hung with hangers to sill beams and girders. If joists are heavily damaged, it's better to replace than to sister.

Girders are particularly laborious to fix, because they have dozens of joists hanging directly from them or on top of them. False walls are required to temporarily hold the floor joists, then each joist must be disconnected and the girder cut out, typically in pieces. New girders are ordinarily built-up, meaning they comprise two, three or four sistered 2x stock, or LVLs. Span tables in the IRC outline sizing: 2x10 is the modern standard for floor joists, though 2x8s and 2x12s are also common, depending on span and spacing.

Sagging joists can be supported by a mid-span girder, which simply cuts the span in half. Mid-span girders are common where floor joists are underframed and overspanned. They're too commonly a handyman or DIY fix; maybe 98% of the mid-span girders I see lack a proper footing. At the first freeze/thaw cycle, these assemblies fall slightly and lose their purpose. For every ten mid-span girders I see, nine have failed for lack of proper footing.

Sustainability and Preservation

Longevity is an important principal of sustainability. If you want the house to last, as

Fig. 9.29: *A structural letter by a professional engineer (PE) offers either a prescriptive solution or approval for a framing design. Stamped (sealed) letters are required for many alterations to balloon-framed structures.*

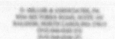

Fig. 9.27-28: Top, *laminated veneer lumbers (LVLs) allow for spans longer than dimensional lumber. One is seen here with spruce joists bearing. Bottom, proper headers rarely exist in old homes and must be installed if you are altering a wall or adding loads above them.*

June 12, 2008

Re.: Engineering Services – Framing modifications

Dear

D. Miller & Associates, PA has analyzed the following structural conditions associated with the above referenced project:

 1) New beam in left rear room ceiling.

The following modifications to the building framing are recommended. For the purpose of this letter, the orientation used (e.g. front, rear, right, left) reflects a person standing such that they are facing the front of the house.

 1) A (4)1.75x9.25 LVL, solid blocked to the foundation wall at the rear and to the foundation pier at the front, is required to support the wall and attic ceiling joists above.

If you have any additional questions, please contact us.

Sincerely,

JHL/0829-10041
P13/350/050

the cliché goes, you must build on a strong foundation. In an attempt to get an extra long lasting, extra strong structure, however, some intentionally overbuild their structures, which is a waste of material and money and contradictory to other sustainable principles. Instead, it's best to follow span tables and load charts or hire a professional to size structural members appropriately.

When dealing with old material, consideration of material reuse and environmental footprints is paramount. Even when replacing and repairing, keep whatever materials you have and try to recondition them for a future use. Old lumber doesn't have a structural stamp, which is required for any load-bearing purpose, but old lumber can be reused for non-structural purposes.

Any material that can be reused saves both dump fees and purchase money; dem-

olition and dumpster costs can be large on a major historic rehabilitation. The smaller portions of wood deemed unusable can be used as fuel. However, be sure never to burn pine indoors, as its tar produces a thick, toxic by-product. The same goes for painted wood or wood with nails: under the pressure of heat, nails can shoot out of a fire.

Lastly, foundation repair carries obvious associated risks. Holding a house on temporary supports while you work underneath carries significant risk to people and property. Make sure you completely understand load paths and ensure that any house held in the air is supported at multiple independent points. Then, if one support fails, nothing catastrophic occurs. On houses that are known to be in particularly poor structural shape, one should never work alone. Life, after all, is just as important to preserve.

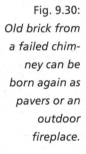

Fig. 9.30:
Old brick from a failed chimney can be born again as pavers or an outdoor fireplace.

Fig. 9.31-32:
Safety first when working on foundations. Bottom left, a house is supported two independent ways. Bottom right, an excavator digs out a basement underneath a temporary steel beam.

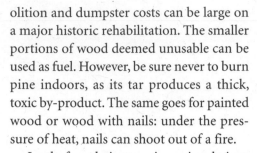

ENVELOPE

Preservationists must accept the need to improve the energy performance of the existing building stock. We simply cannot ignore the fact that the electrical power that runs our buildings contributes substantially to global warming and climate change …. let's be clear that meeting sustainable energy targets will require substantially improving building envelope performance ….

— Carl Elefante, *The Greenest Building Is The One That's Already Built*

Homeowners doing research into greening their historic homes will sooner or later realize that insulation and the thermal envelope are their number one concern. After all, most homes in the US built prior to World War II have little, if any, insulation. Residents may feel like they live outside in the winter and imagine they are the gas company's favorite customer. Corrective measures can address leaky envelopes, moisture management and insulation shortcomings. A sustainable rehabilitation should address all three.

The *envelope* is the shell that defines the home. It is defined as the building envelope (structure), as differentiated from the thermal envelope (heated space). *Moisture* is water, in liquid and gaseous state, and is readily present in and around any home. Moisture management aims to keep water from reaching dangerous levels. Finally, *insulation* resists heat transfer, allowing a home to operate comfortably and efficiently.

Questions to Ask

- What is my thermal envelope?
- Are the attic and crawl space properly sealed or properly ventilated?
- Are my heating or cooling bills abnormally high — and why?
- Are ductwork, mechanicals and plumbing located inside or outside the thermal envelope?
- Is air infiltrating my home? Where?

153

- If I tighten my envelope, how will I furnish fresh air?

- Is the basement or crawl space chronically wet?

- How will I allow moisture to escape an insulated wall cavity?

- Where does condensation most frequently occur in my home?

- Will I ever use my basement or attic as living space?

- What type of insulation do I have, how thick is it and how well is it performing?

Solutions often start with insulation, which raises a passionate debate in the preservation community. Some question the value of insulation relative to the destruction of materials, primarily plaster, required in retrofitting installation. Preservationists ask *why destroy original trim and plaster for wall insulation before you've air-sealed or insulated the attic?* Others are concerned about the permanence and non-reversibility of high performance insulators like spray foam.

But insulation alone will not make a home more livable and efficient. Yes, efficient structures must slow heat transfer. But healthy structures must also stay dry, and insulation cannot work if wet. Nor does insulation serve its purpose if air is allowed to pass around its barrier unhindered.

Of particular importance with older homes are leaks through the building envelope. While new homes are built to hold a comfortable temperature range of +/- 72°F,

leaky old houses operate at more extreme temperatures that force them to expand and contract more. Across the board, results from tightening the envelope of an historic home are almost entirely positive, creating a more comfortable environment, more constant temperature with lower humidity and lower operating costs. But with such gains come challenges and responsibilities. Old leaky homes have few air quality problems because they so frequently exchange internal with external air. Properly stifling air infiltration changes the equation, requiring a source of fresh air. Mechanical means to supply fresh air are generally installed in tandem with any envelope tightening.

The thermal envelope must be continuous. A break in the envelope is the equivalent of leaving a nice winter jacket unzipped on a -10°F day. The insulating qualities of the jacket are negated, and you'll still be cold. A healthy thermal envelope must comprise

1. A thermal boundary with insulation

2. An air boundary

3. A method for exfiltrating moisture

This is a tricky trifecta: traditional insulation alone does not stop air flow, and air boundaries do not slow heat transfer. Either can trap moisture. Installed improperly, envelope tightening can create an environment hospitable for mold. Notably, old leaky homes almost never have mold, since the fungi require a moisture-absorbing substance to grow and expand. Because plaster isn't paper-faced and old wall cavities lack moisture-absorbing insulation, the scrapping of these characteristics in favor of fiberglass batt insulation and paper-faced sheetrock introduces the potential for a hazard that was previously never a risk.

Homes undergoing gut restorations have a once-a-century opportunity to get it right. I'll define the thermal envelope, the important distinctions between air infiltration and insulation and discuss different approaches to envelope tightening and moisture management.

The Thermal Envelope

Moisture, air and heat move constantly through your home. To understand how they do so, keep these few simple rules of thermodynamics in mind.

- Hot air rises and cold air falls.
- Hot air carries more moisture than cold.
- Air is subject to laws of mass flow and fluid dynamics, making hot humid air prone to condense on colder surfaces.
- Temperature differentials cause condensation.

History of Insulation and the Envelope

Arguably, insulation dates to Mediterranean cultures using the bark of cork trees to provide insulation for pipes and roofs. Most, though, consider thermal insulation to be a more modern phenomenon, less than 100 years old, rooted in the industrial revolution.

In the late 1800s, steam power and boilers required a covering to keep pipes hot and workers safe. Fibers from stone (otherwise known as asbestos) found in abundance in Canada, Russia and South Africa demonstrated the excellent malleable and insulative qualities desired.

In 1910, at the request of refrigeration engineers, the US National Bureau of Statistics first provided data pertaining to heat transmission and insulation for design purposes, formalizing the building science of the thermal envelope.

After World War I, the business of wall cavity insulation boomed, with asbestos, rock wool and diatomaceous silica products all holding major market shares. In the 1930s, glass manufacturers sold glass foam and glass fiber insulations, still in use today. After World War II, rock wool dominated the

market while cotton, wood fiber and aluminum products were all typically manufactured and distributed according to the supply specific to geographical areas.

Building codes from the US Federal Housing Administration in the 1920s and 1930s made recommendations for venting crawl spaces and letting outside air in. Despite failures in their model, during World War II the FHA made it a requirement to vent all crawl spaces with outside air.

By the 1940s and 1950s, plastic foams were being developed in Europe, primarily for use in cold storage. The first attempts at foam insulations, starting in the 1950s through the 1970s, suffered from corrosion, structural and dimensional stability issues. In the 1970s, asbestos was found to cause cancer and banned from the market.

Today, there are sustainable insulation products such as post-consumer jeans and soy-based spray foams. Technologies continue to evolve, with an emphasis on performance, air quality and longevity.

- In winter, warm air rises via *stack effect*, promoting cold air infiltration at the base of a building.
- In summer, hot air collects at the roof, promoting heat retention in a building.

This basic understanding of heat transfer yields some obvious conclusions.

Fig. 10.1: *Left, a historic home has little or no insulation. Center, a traditional thermal envelope leaves uninsulated voids in the crawl space and attic. Right, the thermal envelope equals the building envelope, a strategy increasingly seen as better building science.*

- If we seal the top of the envelope, heat cannot be lost through it in winter.
- If we seal the bottom of the envelope, cold air cannot be sucked in through it in winter.
- If we seal both, we dramatically stop air flow by eliminating the stack effect.
- If we minimize temperature differentials around ductwork and cold water pipes, condensation is less likely to form on their surfaces and cause moisture problems. Thus, these systems should be placed inside the conditioned thermal envelope where condensation will not form on them.

Using such logic, some owners of two-story houses with dual zone HVAC use concepts of thermal mass flow and inverse stratification by running only the second floor air conditioning in winter and first floor heat in summer. Mass flow allows for heat to dissipate through the home in the desired direction.

A building science paradigm shift is currently altering envelope strategy. Ever since insulation became the norm about 60 years ago, architects and contractors believed they should only insulate occupied space, installing insulation below first floor joists and above the top floor's ceiling. This left uninsulated voids in the crawl space and attic. The thermal envelope, the conditioned area heated and cooled, did not match the building envelope, the entire structure. Now, building scientists are rejecting this idea and arguing that the structure is improved by expanding the thermal envelope to match the building envelope.

Air Sealing

A tight house is more important than a well-insulated house, a commonly misunderstood fact. Air infiltration, the uncontrolled flow of air into the envelope, is a much bigger problem than thermal transfer, and it requires more attention. Ventilation is controlled infiltration, while uncontrolled infiltration results from mixing the forces of nature with a leaky envelope. Old houses have so many aggregate leaks, it's equivalent to leaving the front door wide open all day in a modern house.

Complete changeover of interior air every three to four hours is a healthy bench mark, equaling six to eight changes per day or .25-.33 air changes per hour (ACH). This

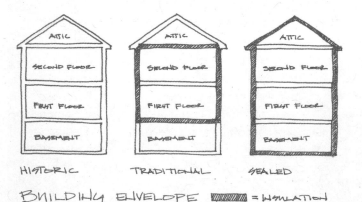

HISTORIC   TRADITIONAL   SEALED

BUILDING ENVELOPE ▨▨▨ = INSULATION

Heat Transfer, and Why R-Value Ain't The Whole Story

R-value is the measure of resistance to heat flow. Insulation increases resistance and slows heat transfer, so insulations are rated by their respective R-values. But there is more to the story.

Heat moves through structures in four different ways: conduction, convection, radiation and air infiltration. *Conduction* is the transfer of heat energy through matter, such as insulation. *Convection* is the transfer of heat in a gas or liquid by movement of currents, such as the stack effect or pressure imbalances. *Radiation* is the transfer of energy through electromagnetic waves, such as those produced by the sun. *Air infiltration* describes leaks in a structure through which air has unobstructed freedom of movement.

R-value only measures resistance to conduction. Additionally, R-value is tested in a lab under ideal conditions that most certainly do not exist in your home. The other ways heat moves through structures must all be addressed to create an efficient home. Proper air sealing limits air infiltration and in turn, convection. low-e, low SHGC windows[1] or window treatments limit radiation.

Fig. 10.2:
An FLIR Camera indicates the best and least insulated parts of the home.

amount of fresh air allows for gases and odors to exit frequently enough to be pleasant, but not so much as to be inefficient. Super tight new construction can operate as low as .1 ACH, requiring fresh air to be supplied mechanically and more frequently. Old houses average one to two ACH, four to eight times more than ideal and ten to 20 times leakier than modern green homes. Envelope-wise, in leaky old historic homes we're essentially camping.

Leaks cause a variety of problems. Lowered air pressure from aggregate leaks can result in backdrafts through flues, which can cause carbon monoxide poisoning. Large holes like chimneys and attic hatches can push so much air outside that they start to pull in air from smaller gaps.

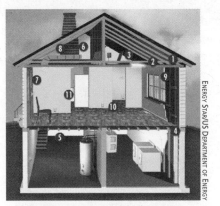

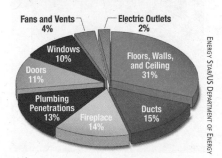

Sources of Air Leaks in Your Home

Areas that leak air into and out of your home cost you lots of money. Check the areas listed below.

1 Dropped ceiling
2 Recessed light
3 Attic entrance
4 Sill plates
5 Water and furnace flues
6 All ducts
7 Door frames
8 Chimney flashing
9 Window frames
10 Electrical outlets and switches
11 Plumbing and utility access

Fig. 10.3-4: *Top, the sources of air infiltration. Bottom, a graph of the most common culprits.*

A Professional Blower Door

US DEPARTMENT OF ENERGY

Diagnostic Tools
Testing the airtightness of a home using a special fan called a blower door can help to ensure that air sealing work is effective. Often, energy efficiency incentive programs, such as the DOE/EPA ENERGY STAR Program, require a blower door test (usually performed in less than and hour) to confirm the tightness of the house.

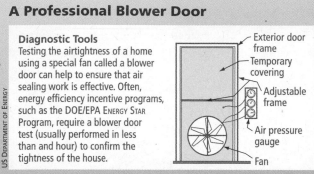

Exterior door frame
Temporary covering
Adjustable frame
Air pressure gauge
Fan

Fig. 10.5

To perform a blower door test, a professional installs a high-speed fan in an exterior window or door, closes all other windows, doors, dampers and vents, then turns the fan on to force air either in or out of the structure. The result is an artificially high pressurization (or depressurization) that allows leaks to be indicated by a smoke pencil used along baseboard, sockets, windows, doors, light penetrations and so forth. The test will also determine the volume of air leakage and the corresponding air changes per hour (ACH). Once major air infiltrations are caulked or otherwise sealed, it's good to run the test again and note improvements. A second test is often not performed in the interest of cost concerns, since a professional blower door test costs about $300. The professional testing is a standard part of Energy Star certification.

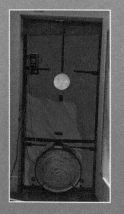

Fig. 10.6-7: *A blower door, operated by a building scientist at Southern Energy Management, depressurizes the home.*

Correcting a Leaky Envelope

An envelope is analyzed through a variety of tests then sealed by carpentry repair, air barriers and caulks. The first step is to find the leaks, done through a visual and tactile inspection, looking and feeling for obvious air gaps. Often visible light will be shining through. If you can see light, air can most certainly get through. Touch is the next step. Drafts can be felt around doors and windows. Shove a piece of paper in window and door openings. If you can shut them and still pull the paper out, air can get through. A blower door test (professional or makeshift, see sidebar) can do a more thorough job.

Poor Folks' Blower Door

Testing for leaks does not require a professional. A poor folks' blower door test can be performed with a window fan and incense. Install the fan in a window and seal with sheets, rags or clothes and tape tightly. A tight seal is critical. Because a window fan will not be as powerful as the professional rig, and depressurization is usually easiest to achieve, it's best to set the fan to blow air out of the house. This will a create a vacuum, allowing any leak to suck air into the house and distort the smoke from lighted incense. While this blower door test doesn't quantify air leakage or meet Energy Star certification standards, it does provide the necessary data for air sealing, the primary point of the test.

After locating points of air infiltration, the next step is sealing them. There are a variety of tools available, from socket gaskets to storm windows. Weatherstripping and caulks handle most of the small work. Don't fool yourself — there's a whole lot of sealing to do on historic homes.

Crawl Spaces and Attics

Crawl spaces and attics can be the greatest contributor to a leaky envelope, being subjected to extreme natural and human-made pressures. Humans fill crawl spaces with heat-producing equipment and stored random junk that often absorbs moisture. As many as 100 gallons of water can enter the building envelope every day through a crawl space. If it is not directed outside, it will cause issues with air quality and structural integrity. Termites love heat and moisture, and both are common problems in traditional crawl spaces. All these problems can contribute to structural failures.

Caulk — Your #1 Air Sealing Weapon

Buy high quality caulk and use a high quality caulk gun. The cheap stuff doesn't last long and is difficult to work with. Keep water and a rag handy. Painters and carpenters use their pointer finger to tool a concave joint. Latex and silicones come in many varieties, application specific.

- *Acrylic latex is* a paintable all-purpose caulk, easy to clean up and available in many colors. It does not expand or move as well as others, so is inappropriate for caulking two dissimilar materials. Cheaper grades are not appropriate for exterior work.

- *Silicone* is the most flexible of all caulks, durable, longer lasting than latex and costs roughly two to three times as much. It's better than latex for exterior work, though many silicones are not paintable — so be sure to choose a paintable silicone before you go sealing all the siding.

- *Polyurethane expanding foam* is essentially the same as open cell foam insulation, available in small pressurized cans. It's ideal for sealing all the small penetrations and gaps in the thermal envelope. Low-expanding is best for old homes, as high-expanding varieties risk damaging old finishes.

- *Acrylic copolymer* is a sticky, clear, flexible caulk, ideal for sealing dissimilar materials such as wood to window sashes.

- *Butyl rubber* is a sticky caulk best used in sealing glazing to substrate such as in an aquarium or roof shingles to flashings. It's very messy to use.

Fig. 10.8-9: *There are dozens of different caulk options, each with a specific application. Above, premium Kevlar caulks are so strong and pliable they are difficult to pull apart from even dissimilar materials, making it less likely to split as a house settles and moves seasonally.*

Vented crawl and attic spaces feature intentionally installed vents that allow free air to flow underneath and over the home. The vents allow moist air out, but also let it in.

Over the last 30 years scientific research has shown vented crawl spaces to cause or contribute to moisture problems. Science aside, anyone who has suffered through a commando scoot into their musty, wet, cricket-infested crawl space can conclude something isn't right. And, if you've been in a 140°F vented attic on a 100°F day, you'd draw the same conclusion.

Further, vented attics can produce terrible operating environments for mechanical equipment. Why pay to cool air in the summer, use it and then return it to a 140°F environment for cooling? This has a huge negative effect on efficiency.

Now, the sustainable building trend is to match a home's thermal envelope with its building envelope, which is done by sealing both crawl space and attic. Even though you may not occupy these areas while entertaining, thermally speaking they become part of your house. Once sealed, they will operate with more consistent temperatures and relative humidity and can be used for storage without fear of moisture damage. Insects and moisture are then kept out of the house, air quality is correspondingly improved and the house lives a longer, healthier life.

Non-vented crawl spaces (also referred to as sealed crawl spaces or closed crawl spaces) annex the crawl space area into the conditioned thermal envelope, keeping moisture and exterior air from flowing under the home.

Non-vented crawl spaces were new in the 2006 code, under IRC408.3. Some US states impose further requirements (examples outlined in parentheses).

Weatherstripping Types and Application

Weatherstripping is a material designed to prevent air infiltration at transition points. It's intelligent to have weatherstripping at any window, door or opening and wholly necessary for problematic transitions and established points of air infiltration. Adhesive foams are the cheapest options, but their longevity is certain to disappoint. I've seen some fail in a matter of weeks. Any plastic that requires a spring to function (shaped in a V form) will also not be long lasting. Spring metal, tubular gaskets, rubber and metal-backed felt are all more durable.

Fig. 10.10

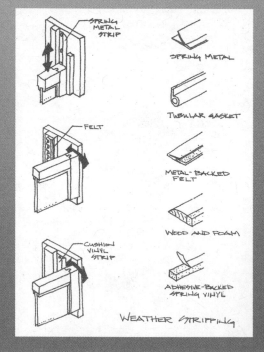

1. Exposed earth must be covered by continuous vapor retarder (North Carolina requires minimum 6 mil).

2. Joints must be lapped six inches and sealed with tape (North Carolina requires a 12-inch lap).

3. Edges must go a minimum of six inches up exterior walls.

4. Conditioned air must be supplied exceeding 1cfm/50 square feet, with a backflow damper to ensure crawl space air does not enter the occupied living space.

5. Exterior walls must be insulated.

6. The floor of the crawl space must be graded to one or more low spots and a drain to daylight or sump pump installed at each low spot. The drain must be separate from roof or foundation drain, and include a backflow valve to ensure water from the exterior does not enter the crawl space (This provision is specific to North Carolina code but a good idea regardless).

7. If exterior grade is higher than interior, dampproofing is required.

8. Gas water heaters and furnaces must be *two-pipe*, sealed-combustion.

9. Foam plastic insulation must be covered by an approved ignition barrier if in the same area of a combustible appliance.

Interestingly, many old houses feature non-vented crawl spaces, closer to modern design than homes built from 1940 through today. These old houses have no venting, just solid brick masonry walls. Since they do

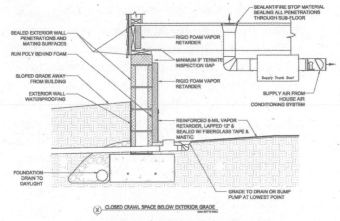

MODIFIED FROM *ADVANCED ENERGY'S QUICK REFERENCE ON CLOSED CRAWL SPACES*[2]

Fig. 10.11: *Sealed Crawl Space Diagram.*

Fig. 10.12-14: *Unlike a traditional crawl space, a sealed crawl space can be used for storage. Books, boxes and papers would normally all be ruined by water in a traditional crawl. Here, it's no different than putting them on a basement bookshelf. Bottom left, a close-up reveals the spray foam-insulated walls and polyethylene membrane on the floor.*

not feature a method for sealing against groundwater on the earthen floor, they are not fully closed, but their resistance to outside air can help limit temperature extremes under the home. Such designs fall short of modern standards for sealed crawl spaces with their continuous vapor barriers and supply air, but still can perform better than their consciously vented modern counterparts.

Fig. 10.15: Sealed Attic Detail.

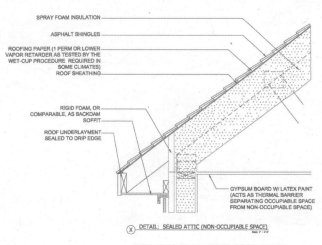

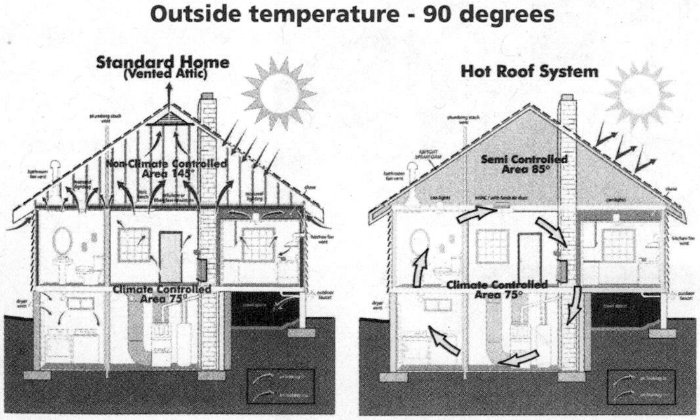

Outside temperature - 90 degrees

Fig. 10.16

Sealed Attics

Attics, like crawl spaces, are also being sealed; their prescriptive installation details are outlined in IRC 806.4,[3] and the same concepts apply. Attics differ from crawl spaces in that they are subject to different pressures. Crawl spaces involve earth, groundwater and hydrostatic pressure, while attics contend with heat gain from the sun and snow loads.

Sealed attics dramatically slow heat loss. This keeps your heating bills from going, quite literally, through the roof. In the summer, sealed attics stop heat transfer from the sun into the attic, blocking heat transfer to the living space, creating a far superior operating environment for HVAC and humans. In winter, roofs depend on heat from the home to melt snow off the shingles. Since a sealed attic stops such transfer, snow stays on the roof longer and can theoretically shorten shingle life. Some shingle manufacturers use this as a reason to disallow sealed attics or shorten their warranties. Sealed attics do not require soffit vents, ridge vents or attic fans, all costs that can be spared. Some old houses have decorative vents, in which case it's best to keep their decorative elements while sealing their venting function.

Moisture

Moisture causes the majority of problems in old homes. Ask yourself where moisture is coming from.

- Is rainwater getting into the envelope?
- is groundwater entering into the basement or crawl space?

- Is humid air getting into the house from outside through gaps in the siding?
- Are you generating excessive amounts of moisture by cooking or bathing?
- Do your bathrooms and kitchens lack venting?

Water comes from four primary sources.

1. Rainwater and groundwater
2. Plumbing
3. Vapor
4. Humidity

Each must be dealt with properly to keep a home healthy and dry.

Rainwater and *groundwater* must stay out of the house, and you can check for leaks by inspecting the roof for deterioration and exterior trim for tightly caulked seams. Have either wide eaves or functional gutters, making sure gutter downspouts discharge water far from the foundation. Use drought resistant plants adjacent to the foundation; any plant that requires artificial watering would be better placed elsewhere in the yard. Finally, to prevent groundwater from entering the envelope through the earth, install a polyethylene vapor barrier on the crawl space floor and consider sealing the crawl space.

Plumbing must not leak. Leaks can go on for years without being noticed, adding dollars to bills and moisture to the home. The simple test is to shut off all water valves and see if the meter moves overnight. Also periodically check the crawl space or basement for pools of water.

Vapor, airborne water in a gaseous state, is the most often-overlooked problem. It comes from some everyday pleasures: hot showers and baths, tea kettles, plants, firewood and laundry. Properly sized and operated venting at the bath and kitchen dump such vapors outside the home where they belong. Ductwork and plumbing located outside the thermal envelope cause condensation problems: water that is brought in as air vapor is turned back into water when its temperature and relative humidity reach their dewpoint. Placement of such systems inside the thermal envelope solves this problem.

Humidity is the measure of water vapor present in the air. *Relative humidity* (RH) is the ratio of the amount of water vapor present relative to the maximum amount the air can hold at a given temperature. Hot air can hold much more water than cold, which is why summers are more humid and winters are more dry. As temperatures drop, water vapor reaches a dewpoint where it condenses into water or ice. Outside, we call this moisture fog, rain, snow; inside, we call it trouble.

Take an example from building engineers Cyrus Dastur and Bruce Davis' 2003 crawl space study.

The average dew point of the outside air at Princeville during the summer of 2003 was 73°F. This corresponds to relatively moderate conditions of 88°F and 60% RH. When that air goes into the crawlspace and encounters any object that is cooler than 73°F, the RH peaks at 100% and the water vapor in the air will condense on that object just as it would on a cool drink set out on the porch railing. Supply ducts (55-65°F), water pipes and tanks (55-65°F), and even the floor of the crawlspace (65-70°F), and the wood framing above (70-78°F) can experience this condensation, especially if the owner likes to condition the house to temperatures below 72°F.[4]

In their study, vented crawl spaces exceeded the dangerously wet threshold of 70% RH for the vast majority of the summer, while sealed crawl spaces did so less than 5% of the time. The study concluded that the moisture extremes caused by vented crawl spaces cause material shrinking and swelling and even trim carpentry nails to pop. Thus, sealed crawl spaces keep hazardous moisture out and contribute to the longevity of the structure.

Humans feel most comfortable with relative humidity between about 30 and 40%. Above 50% RH, we feel sticky. Below 20% RH we feel dry and desire moisturizers or humidifiers. With low humidity we get sinus headaches, itch and scratch and generate static electricity. Structurally, low humidity can cause plaster and finishes to shrink and crack.

Though minimizing humid air *infiltration* is crucial, relative humidity in the home

---

Mold is a microscopic fungus and a common problem in overly wet homes. Some molds are extremely harmful to humans. Most, however, are not. According to building scientist Arnie Katz, mold requires exactly five criteria to survive. Eliminate any of the five and you'll eliminate mold growth.

1. Mold spores — any organic matter such as decaying trees or kids' clothing
2. Mold food — any carbon-based material including wood, drywall paper, paint or carpet
3. Oxygen
4. Temperatures from 40-100°F
5. Relative humidity in excess of 70%[5]

Since mold spores and food are everywhere, and humans consider oxygenless spaces with temperature ranges below 40 and above 100oF to be rather inhospitable, that leaves relative humidity as the obvious variable within control. Relative humidity is controlled through HVAC, dehumidifiers and envelope tightening.

Of note for preservationists, plaster and uninsulated wall cavities offer no mold food, so mold is extremely rare in historic homes. In the South, mold is a near given on unkempt homes built from 1950 on, but I've never seen it on even the most dilapidated of homes built between 1900-1920. For old home purists, this shows the huge environmental benefit of plaster.

Any old house project introducing insulation and sheetrock must manage moisture and humidity appropriately. These new building materials create a far more hospitable environment for fungi to feed and thrive. If you do install sheetrock in moisture-prone areas, be sure to keep the base at least ½ of an inch above the floor where it cannot wick standing water. Never use water-resistant greenboard sheetrock for tile base. It is inferior in a wet environment and subject to mold growth. Use concrete backerboard instead.

is largely dictated by human behavior. Breathing alone produces ¼ cup of water per hour, while cooking pasta produces five pints. Your average shower puts ½ pint of water into the air. This is significant because introducing only ten pints of water into a 2,000-square-foot house can cause its relative humidity to jump from 15 to 60%. Then there's a need to dehumidify or push humid air out of the house.

Houses are dehumidified by air conditioners, bath vents and kitchen vents. Many modern green homes set bath fans to automatically run to expel stale air from the home at fixed times during each day.

Wall Assembly

Excessive moisture in the wall cavity will shorten the life of the home. It can get there two ways: diffusion through assemblies or carried via unobstructed air. Air carries a massive amount of water and can distribute up to 100 times more water into wall cavities through leaks than is distributed through diffusion. It's one of the most underappreciated reasons why air sealing a newly insulated house is so important.

The traditional design of a wall section specifies a vapor barrier (typically 4 mil polyethylene) to be installed on the warm side of the wall. The *warm side* is the interior side of insulation in cold climates and the exterior in warm. Theoretically, the vapor barrier will keep the moisture and condensation from the warm air out of the wall cavity. Unfortunately, theory is synonymous with lab work, and you most certainly do not live in a controlled lab. Many variables punch holes in the belief: oil paint, for instance, does not allow vapor to pass through it and can serve as a second vapor barrier effectively trapping moisture in the wall. Penetrations through a vapor barrier for sockets and lighting allow humid air to flow freely in the wall cavity where it can condense. In mixed climates, the warm side switches with the seasons. Because of such variables, builders are now shying away from installing vinyl in wall assemblies. I don't recommend using polyethylene vapor barriers in the walls of old homes, and spray foams negate the need for it anyway.

Insulation

Insulation creates resistance to heat flow. It keeps heat where you want it: out during summer and in during winter. R-value is the measure of thermal resistance, the higher the number the better. Each region of the US prescribes a minimum R-value that new construction must meet, and old homes fall far below these standards. In cold climates, naturally, more insulation is required.

Old homes often have literally no insulation, yielding a huge opportunity for operational improvement. Because of existing obstructions or access issues, it may not be possible to retrofit these recommended amounts of insulation during a rehabilitation. In this case, use the US Department of Energy's recommendations as a guideline and goal, and upgrade the best you reasonably can.

Superinsulated homes exceed the DOE's recommended values though insulation over

Fig. 10.17-18:
Recommended Total R-Values for New Wood-Framed Houses.

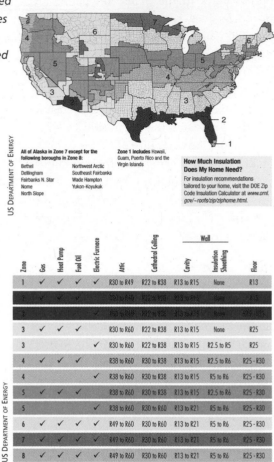

U.S. Department of Energy Recommended* Total R-Values for New Wood-Framed Houses

All of Alaska in Zone 7 except for the following boroughs in Zone 8:

Bethel
Dellingham
Fairbanks N. Star
Nome
North Slope

Northwest Arctic
Southeast Fairbanks
Wade Hampton
Yukon-Koyukuk

Zone 1 includes Hawaii, Guam, Puerto Rico and the Virgin Islands

How Much Insulation Does My Home Need?
For insulation recommendations tailored to your home, visit the DOE Zip Code Insulation Calculator at *www.ornl. gov/~roofs/zip/ziphome.html.*

US DEPARTMENT OF ENERGY

Zone	Gas	Heat Pump	Fuel Oil	Electric Furnace	Attic	Cathedral Ceiling	Wall Cavity	Wall Insulation Sheathing	Floor
1	✓	✓	✓	✓	R30 to R49	R22 to R38	R13 to R15	None	R13
2	✓	✓	✓		R30 to R60	R22 to R38	R13 to R15	None	R13
2				✓	R30 to R60	R22 to R38	R13 to R15	None	R25-R30
3	✓	✓	✓		R30 to R60	R22 to R38	R13 to R15	None	R25
3				✓	R30 to R60	R22 to R38	R13 to R15	R2.5 to R5	R25
4	✓	✓	✓		R38 to R60	R30 to R38	R13 to R15	R2.5 to R6	R25 - R30
4				✓	R38 to R60	R30 to R38	R13 to R15	R5 to R6	R25 - R30
5	✓	✓	✓		R38 to R60	R30 to R38	R13 to R15	R2.5 to R6	R25 - R30
5				✓	R38 to R60	R30 to R60	R13 to R21	R5 to R6	R25 - R30
6	✓	✓	✓	✓	R49 to R60	R30 to R60	R13 to R21	R5 to R6	R25 - R30
7	✓	✓	✓	✓	R49 to R60	R30 to R60	R13 to R21	R5 to R6	R25 - R30
8	✓	✓	✓	✓	R49 to R60	R30 to R60	R13 to R21	R5 to R6	R25 - R30

US DEPARTMENT OF ENERGY

R-values and Efficiency Ratings

The efficiency rating (ER) of an insulation accounts for the blockage of drafts and moisture. How well does the material perform with one inch of application? Where fiberglass, cellulose and open cell foam all have ERs below 44%, closed cell foam has an efficiency rating of 92%. According to national energy laboratories at the Department of Energy, even though two inches of closed cell equals only R-14 it feels like R-40.

and above the recommended amount quickly reaches a point of diminishing returns. Some sustainable builders take a contrarian view, arguing that as long as you're installing you might as well add a little extra.

Remember, R-value does not consider air infiltration, and thus not all insulations are created equal. This is the core reason spray foam insulations offer such superior performance. By their nature, spray foams insulate *and* air seal. And, unlike nearly every other insulation, they are resistant to moisture absorption. An inch and a half of spray foam can prevent more heat loss than batt insulation up to eight inches thick. It can yield heating and cooling costs ½ that of other insulations and ¼ the operating costs relative to having no insulation.

Modern insulation comes in four forms.

1. Blankets, including fiberglass batts, blue jeans
2. Blown-in, including dense-packed and loose-packed cellulose and rock wool, vermiculite and perlite
3. Foam, including expanded polystyrene (EPS), extruded polystyrene (XPS) and open and closed cell polyurethane spray foam (SPF)
4. Reflective films, including foil-faced polyisocyanurate

The market today is dominated by batts for basic construction and spray foam for higher end construction. Batts are the cheapest and most common cavity-fill insulation. Blown-in materials are common for horizontal applications and some wall retrofits.

But open cell and closed cell spray foam insulation are the best available products on the market, particularly for sealing historic homes.

Foil-faced products are designed for radiant reflectivity and only work if they have between a ½ and one-inch gap between the foil and adjacent surface. Products that are

Fig. 10.19: *Comparing Modern Insulation.*

INSULATION	R Value per inch	Cost	Installed	Ease of Retrofit	Life Cycle Toxicity	Sealing Ability
Fiberglass	3.2	$	Stapled between studs, joists and rafters, paper facing warm side	Requires open stud cavity or gut job. Sizes are 16 o.c. or 19.2, other widths require precise cutting. DIY.	Some is high VOC, some not	**
Rock wool	3.2	$	Poured into attic bays, blown in into walls through 4" holes	Easy in attic, walls require a 4" hole cut and repair. Exploratory holes must be cut to ensure complete coverage. FLIR cameras also test for coverage. No longer used.	Excellent	*
Blow in / loose-fill cellulose	3.2	$	Blown in or machine sprayed	Common retrofit, machines available for rental at big box stores. DIY, great for tight areas and around obstructions.	Some is high VOC, some not	*
Closed Cell Spray Foam	7	$$$$$	Sprayed in place by professionals	Requires open stud cavity. Some slow rising foams can be used for injection behind existing plaster or sheetrock, but are cost prohibitive	Highly toxic when sprayed, inert within seconds./ toxic if burned	*****
Open Cell Spray Foam	3.5	$$$$	Sprayed in place by professionals	Requires open stud cavity	Highly Toxic when sprayed, inert within seconds./ toxic if burned	****
Extruded Polystyrene (XPS)	5	$$	4x8 boards glued in place (basement slabs, foundations)	Cut to size, typically used as sheathing & not used in stud cavities	Inert, toxic if burned	***
Expanded Polystyrene (EPS)	4	$	Same as Extruded Polystyrene	Cut to size, typically used as sheathing & not used in stud cavities	Inert, toxic if burned	***
Polyisocyanurate (Polyiso)	7.5	$$$$	Foil faced boards meet flame spread requirements where other foams do not. Use in sealed crawlspaces, wall sheathing	Cut to size, typically used as sheathing & not used in stud cavities	Less harmful manufacturing than other plastics, still toxic if burned	****
Perlite, Vermiculite	2.5	$	Loose fill, poured in place, often used in concrete block walls	Rarely used any longer. Old materials may contain asbestos. still used in lightweight insulating concrete asbestos material)	Excellent (except for asbestos material)	*

only foil aren't really insulation, they just have a comparable effect by resisting the sun's radiant energy.

I try to talk clients out of batt insulation, because batts are specifically made for 16-inch o.c. stud cavities. Old houses are filled with irregularly sized stud and joist cavities (17, 18 or 23 inches for example). In these cases, the installer must cut batt insulation to size. Unless the installer is a pro (and many are not), you'll end up with voids or over-packed insulation, and insulation does not perform when it is compressed beyond its recommended depth.

The Superiority of Spray Foam

Spray foam is accepted as the best available insulation for its superior air sealing and its equal or better thermal values compared to traditional batts. Air sealing is particularly important in historic homes, which are exceedingly drafty. It is important that contractors and homeowners understand and take measures to address the ways houses were built differently 70+ years ago.

Fig. 10.20: *Spray foam insulation fills cavities, simultaneously insulating and air sealing.*

Understanding how each foam deals with water and old house wall assemblies is imperative to evaluating its real costs and benefits, and this understanding is the primary reason for my preference of closed cell foams on old houses.

There are two types of foam: open cell and closed cell. Open cell, or ½-pound foam, is light and has a spongy texture. It resists moisture absorption but can retain water and does allow water vapor to pass through. Closed cell, or two-pound foam, is a rigid structural product that does not retain water or allow water vapor to pass through. Either product is applied in the same way, shot through a compressed air system into a stud or roof cavity. Within seconds it expands to 150 times its original size (50 times for closed cell) and closes all draft pockets.

Unfortunately, designers, architects and contractors have been specifying insulation into historic retrofits without carefully considering the consequences to water management. This is often overlooked for three reasons.

1. Lacking in any insulation, stud cavities in older homes have a very high drying potential, so moisture entering the wall cavity quickly evaporates leaving little evidence of a problem.

2. Historic homes feature plaster, which has less moisture-absorbing capacity than paper-faced sheetrock.

3. Building teams simply fail to recognize that the building wrap or moisture drainage plane installed behind the sid-

ing on modern homes is typically either absent or damaged.

A wall cavity with moist insulation and a low drying potential is one of the leading causes of mold and termite activity common in post-war housing. To avoid water in the wall, most builders install a building wrap or vapor barrier. The building wrap keeps air-driven moisture out, but has a permeability rating that allows for vapors trapped in the cavity to escape. The vapor barrier, installed between sheetrock and studs in cold climates, keeps moisture from entering the house.

Historic homes often have no building wrap or other type of weather barrier, and thus there is no barrier between outside moisture (such as rain and snow) and the stud cavity. Wind-driven rain and moisture from infiltration and condensation have an easy path into the cavity where it can wreak havoc on any moisture-absorbing insulation. Water-saturated insulation has a

greatly reduced thermal value and is a playground for mold, insects and other undesirables.

My logic is simple: all insulations absorb water except one — closed cell spray foam. Thus, closed cell the best choice for historic retrofits.

The installation of the closed and open cell foams is relatively similar, though each requires different preparations and cleanup. Since it can absorb moisture, open cell requires a building wrap or other moisture barrier to protect it. Closed cell requires no such barrier. Open cell is oversprayed beyond the stud cavity and the overage trimmed off with a hand saw after spraying, while closed cell is sprayed to 2 to 2.5-inch depths and requires no such cleanup.

As an added and often overlooked benefit, closed cell adds structural rigidity to the home. Remember, historic homes were built prior to the emergence of the structural engineering profession, so many old houses are underframed. Closed cell foam

	Batts	Open Cell Foam	Closed Cell Foam
R-Value per inch	3	3.5	7
Efficiency Rating	32%	44%	92%
Typical Wall Insulation Depth	3.5"	3.5"	2"
Air Barrier (draft stoppage)	No	Yes	Yes
Fits irregular Stud Cavities	No	Yes	Yes
Structural Stability	No	No	Yes
Moisture Barrier	No	No	Yes
Applicator Availability	Common	Specialty	Specialty/Rare
Other Requirements	Building Wrap	Building Wrap	
Other Requirements		Shaving Excess	
HVAC ft^2 per ton	400-600	800-1200	800-1200

Fig. 10.21: *Comparison of Insulation Characteristics.*

is a structural product that will actually provide sheer and tensile strength to existing walls by locking studs and rafters in place.

Preservation

Generally speaking, an historic home's envelope is an aesthetic shell, failing in many ways to meet modern system standards of efficiency, control and comfort. Old houses' envelopes, like modern, are designed to shed water with overlapping materials flashing each other like scales on a fish. It's worth noting that many old houses do this better than their newer counterparts: wide eaves shed water better than shallow ones and often do so without the need of a guttering system. Plaster forms a solid wall surface while being resistant to moisture absorption. These systems are superior to modern alternatives, and if they exist, should be kept or replicated wherever possible.

Still, historic character should not be sacrificed in the name of envelope tightening. Demolishing plaster in order to insulate is one of the great debates between preservationists, who question its benefits, and environmentalists, who champion it. There's little value in trashing old trim, mantles, plaster, flooring and exterior details in favor of insulating properly. Let's not throw the baby out with the bathwater.

Ultimately, improving the thermal envelope lowers operating costs, which makes old homes more affordable. As more buyers can afford to buy and maintain older homes, the more older cities will be rebuilt. The preservation of all that embodied energy is sustainable, in and of itself.

Sustainability

Rectifying a leaky envelope is often the most sustainable thing you can do to your home. It lowers your operating costs, shrinks your environmental footprint and makes the home affordable for the 21st century. Along with HVAC and windows, it is one of the three critical pillars of making an historic house more sustainable. Address all three, and the house will perform well for years to come.

These old homes were built to deal with nature, well, naturally. Wide overhangs successfully kept water away from foundations without the use of gutters. Windows managed air flow and light by their size and operability, not artificial mechanization and lightbulbs. Such superior characteristics should be kept, rehabilitated and duplicated on any addition or accessory building.

Insulation is a sustainability catch-22, because the products that perform the best do not have an overwhelmingly green life cycle. Spray foam offers vastly superior performance, but it has a harmful manufacturing process and is toxic when being sprayed (though it becomes inert ten seconds after installation), creates a fair amount of waste and is not biodegradable. I'd argue the significant lowering of operating costs and fossil fuel demand for the life span of the insulation outweighs the downsides. Such contradictions are typical sustainable building quandaries.

WINDOWS

Sustainability looks even better through a restored window.

— Walter Sedovic and Jill H. Gotthelf,
What Replacement Windows Can't Replace:
The Real Cost of Removing Historic Windows

Questions to Ask

- Are the house windows original?
- What style are the windows?
- What condition are the windows in?
- Are they operable?
- Are storm windows present?
- Are there decorative windows that are more distinctive than others?
- Do any old windows present breakage safety hazards on stairs, bathrooms or near doors?
- If I'm reconfiguring the exterior or adding on, are salvage windows or new windows best?

Window preservation and rehabilitation are near the top of the agenda for historic home professionals. Original windows are the third rail of preservation, vital to the spirit of an historic home. Preservationists argue that irreplaceable craftsmanship trumps any effort to marginally lower utility bills. Each window's uniqueness is treasured, and its replacement a cause for sadness. Nothing evokes more emotion in the preservationist.

Ironically, for the energy efficiency-minded sustainable green builder, window replacement is near the top of the priority list. The window replacement versus rehabilitation debate is hands down the greatest conflict between the two movements. Builders argue that they can't properly tighten the envelope when leaky single pane windows are present. Recently, the pace of window technology inventions has accelerated. Improvements such as low-e, triple panes,

Fig. 11.1

lamination and argon-filled insulated glass have made new windows more efficient than in the past. It's no wonder window replacement is all the rage in our technology-obsessed society. On top of the advantages of the new materials, window salespeople tell us original windows are old, outdated and leaky, so they *must* be replaced. The

Fig. 11.2-5: *Unique windows display unparalleled architectural character. Clockwise from Center left, nine-lite casement windows with interior screens complement the detail of the French door and transom. A table can be positioned to enjoy a view through a two-over-two wavy-glass window. Dramatic doorways can be grand in style or sizing: an entryway with side lites and stained glass transom is indicative of pre-1900 Victorian style.*

pressure to replace windows comes from all sources. Salespeople, energy auditors, builders and family all tell us to chuck the things. Additionally, while attics, basements and systems penetrations all cause air infiltration, windows are the most visible culprit. Thus, windows are disproportionately targeted over less in-your-face but more pressing problems, such as the thermal envelope.

Not only are the assumptions of both movements incorrect, they miss the point. At the end of the day both movements have the same aim: to conserve. A proper window rehabilitation simultaneously conserves human and natural resources.

Sustainability is also about more than monthly energy bills. Social, economic and environmental considerations should be weighed alongside craftsmanship, authenticity and historic value. The rehabilitation of original windows saves manufacturing material, production energy and dump fees, while offering a show-stopping 100-year-old hand-crafted piece of woodwork that is mechanically operational and energy-efficient. Old windows' authenticity shows in unique molding profiles, ripples, graining and flaws in the blown glass. Replacement of such materials leaves behind a sterile, uniform look. With a replacement approach, authenticity is lost forever. Despite arguments to the contrary, the greenest thing you can do to your old window is fix it.

Preservation ethic and financial incentive probably require you to repair the window anyway. In historic districts, original windows help tie individual buildings together, allowing the story of the district to be told. Thus, tax credits are very often contingent on windows being kept in place.

Types of Windows

Windows are either *operable or fixed*. Operable windows can be opened, fixed windows cannot. Operable windows are obligatory for *egress* (the ability to exit during an emergency). Egress from any bedroom is required by most building codes. Non-operable windows are most common in commercial applications and specialty windows.

A Brief History of American Windows

In the Colonial days (1700s), where windows were installed they tended to be single hung, featuring a fixed top sash and an operable bottom sash supported by a peg or notched piece of wood. Double hung windows were first installed in 1750, around the same time the counterweight system was patented.

By the 19th century, American glass became world renowned, with production centering around Pittsburgh, where coal and sand were mined in abundance. As glass technology progressed, so did the size of glass panes. The latter half of the 19th century was marked by huge single panes as large as 36x36 inches. The six-over-one Colonial was a popular design and still is today. Multi-glazed windows spread in the 1970s, with first double and then triple pane glass. Single pane windows are now a custom order, hard to locate and may not be allowed by local building officials on new construction.

After World War II, obsession with mechanical heating and cooling led designers to specify fixed (non-operable) windows. Today, the obsession with non-operable efficiency has partially given way back to operability, as more homeowners demand fresh air via the window.

Windows can also be defined by the way they operate. Turn and tilt sashes anchor in the middle of a jamb. Sliders are a double hung window on its side. Casement windows hinge on the side, awnings on the top and hopper windows on the bottom. Double hung windows have dominated American architecture for nearly two centuries; they are simple and traditional, and allow both sashes to operate.

The Parts of a Window

The *casing* is the finished, often decorative framework around a window.

The *rails* and *stile* form the sash frame. The bottom rail is subject to rot due to its position on the sill, which sheds water. Make sure all rails and stiles are tight. If they are not, remove the sash and tighten with screws, glue or epoxy.

The *bottom (inner) sash* is the generally operable lower half of a double hung window.

The *top (outer)* sash is the upper half of a double hung window and is sometimes operable, sometimes not (the latter would make it a *single hung* window).

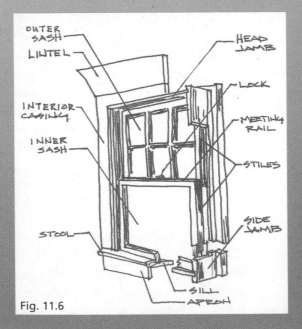

Fig. 11.6

OUTER SASH
LINTEL
INTERIOR CASING
INNER SASH
STOOL
HEAD JAMB
LOCK
MEETING RAIL
STILES
SIDE JAMB
SILL
APRON

Often the top sash is fixed in place intentionally to avoid random sash drop or to add additional insulation in the top sash (rear) counterweight pocket.

The *muntins* divide the glazing within a sash; they vary in size and detail. Because they are small they can be frail, reglazing and careful carpentry repair may be needed.

The *meeting rail* is where the top and bottom sash meet and the latching mechanism sits. It's the first and most obvious place to look for air leaks. Look for a tight fit between the meeting rails. If one does not exist, you can adjust the stops or add heavy duty weatherstripping suitable for an operable function.

The *pane* is the glass; each individual pane of glass (glazing) is a *lite*. Old windows are truly divided, so that there are seven individual panes in a six-over-one window. Newer windows (called double paned) would have only two real panes with a fake divider. Each lite needs to be rehabilitated individually. To restore, replace broken panes and reglaze transitions.

The *jamb* houses the window and is the outermost frame installed in the rough opening (typically with one inch smaller dimensions than the rough opening).

The *stop* guides the sashes in their upward and downward movement, keeping them from falling inward or outward. The stop must be removed before removing the sash.

The *stool* is the interior shelf-like board at the bottom of a window against which the bottom rail of the sash rests.

Historic homes are likely to have a mix of window types, with a single type dominant and diversity showcased in off-the-beaten-path rooms. As an example, a house may have 25 double hung windows, plus a fixed oval window in the gable and a casement over the kitchen sink. When modifying and adding windows, take cues from what's already on the home; this will ensure design cohesion throughout original and new construction.

Replacement Windows

Replacement windows are quite simply not the silver bullet solution they are presented to be. Of course, when all you have is a hammer everything looks like a nail, and when all you sell is a replacement window every window looks like it needs to be replaced. Why is replacement presented as the only available solution? Is it even a good one? And what other options are there?

Why Replacement Windows Are Bad

Would you believe that up to a third of windows being replaced are maintenance free windows less than ten years old?[1] Why?

The answer is as straightforward as the old window, really. Old windows are simple. New windows are complex. Old windows have few parts; new windows are an assembly of many interdependent parts. Each of these parts has different life spans. When any one of those small parts on the new window fail, the entire window fails.

Here's the big difference: on an historic window, wood, glazing or glass failure is a simple carpentry fix. On a new window, the

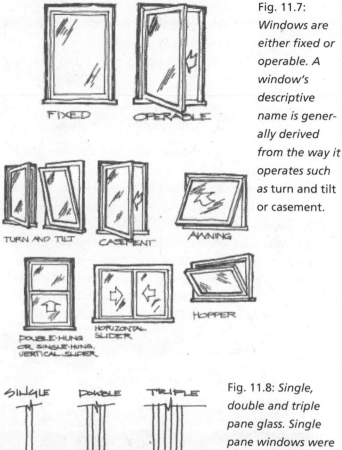

Fig. 11.7: *Windows are either fixed or operable. A window's descriptive name is generally derived from the way it operates such as* turn and tilt *or* casement.

Fig. 11.8: *Single, double and triple pane glass. Single pane windows were the norm until the 1970s. Today, double pane is most common, with triple paning widely available and installed in up-market designs. Multiple panes leave odd shadowlines and reflections between the panes, making imposters of old windows easy to spot..*

repair is complex or requires hard-to-acquire parts, so the whole unit is more frequently replaced.

- Did the gasket break? Trash the window and replace.
- Perhaps the vinyl sash cracked in the sun? Trash the window and replace.

Fig. 11.9-11: *Vinyl replacement would have been bad enough, but these replacements also don't match the size of the windows they're replacing. Left and center, new windows are half the size of the originals. Right, a vainly fake-muntin arched transom window, typical of modern McMansions, is installed on the second floor. Often in these cases, the cheapest available window is bought prior to sizing, then the opening is framed to the smaller unit. It often ends up costing more than rehabbing or buying a window of the proper size.*

- Did the seal between the two panes of glass fail? Trash the window and replace.

Illinois SHPO Chief Architect Mike Jackson summarized it beautifully, *If they tell you it's maintenance free, all that means is that it can't be repaired.*

Plus, many new windows are made from vinyl, a petroleum product that is non-renewable — or aluminum which has a harsh, off-gassing manufacturing process. Vinyl or aluminum conduct heat more than wood, so they make poor insulators (though many artificial sashes are insulated).

Advertised new window warranties range from as little as two to 20 years. Of course, many historic windows are operating fine after 100 years with maintenance little more than paint. Aside from potential tax credits for energy efficiency, replacement windows make poor green solutions for three reasons.

1. Double pane glass is separated by a sealed layer of gas that reduces heat transfer. This seal is prone to failure, requiring complete window replacement. Though double pane insulated glass provides better energy efficiency, the seal breaks down

as the windows expand and contract, allowing moisture to enter the glass.

2. Vinyl sashes are prone to cracking, requiring a total window replacement.

3. The disposal and life cycle costs are huge for replacement windows and negligible for rehabilitation.

Lastly, some more established historic districts are now seeing replacement windows actually lower property values. A growing body of preservationists are demanding that any prospective house they purchase have its original windows. If you replace your windows, you'll lose all those potential buyers.

Why Old Windows Are Good

Unlike replacement windows, old windows are easily repaired. Ninety percent of repairs use wood putty, glazing, caulk and paint. This is relatively unskilled work that can be performed by the average homeowner. More complex repairs involve counterweight repair, epoxy reconstructions, embedded weather-stripping and glass replacement, each of which is simple work for a skilled carpenter. Basic maintenance and minor repairs will pull your windows through another decade or two. A complete refurbishing, which most windows have never undergone, will set them up for another century.

Old wood is of generally better quality than new since it was harvested from dimensionally stable old-growth trees. So old wood sashes are expected to last longer than their newer knockoffs (our window salesperson brags of the extra long 20-year warranty on his new wood window product line). Wood

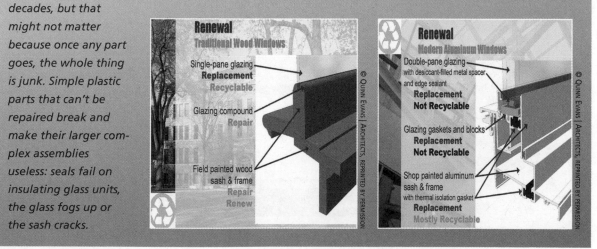

Differential Durability

Fig. 11.12-13: *Architect Carl Elefante discusses the concept of differential durability.[2] He argues that parts of a replacement window may last for decades, but that might not matter because once any part goes, the whole thing is junk. Simple plastic parts that can't be repaired break and make their larger complex assemblies useless: seals fail on insulating glass units, the glass fogs up or the sash cracks.*

Alternatively, original wood windows have lasted a century or more and with minimal effort and expense, they can last another.

Renewal
Traditional Wood Windows

Single-pane glazing
Replacement
Recyclable

Glazing compound
Repair

Field painted wood
sash & frame
Repair
Renew

© QUINN EVANS | ARCHITECTS, REPRINTED BY PERMISSION

Renewal
Modern Aluminum Windows

Double-pane glazing
with desiccant-filled metal spacer
and edge sealant
Replacement
Not Recyclable

Glazing gaskets and blocks
Replacement
Not Recyclable

Shop painted aluminum
sash & frame
with thermal isolation gasket
Replacement
Mostly Recyclable

© QUINN EVANS | ARCHITECTS, REPRINTED BY PERMISSION

Government At Its Finest

The US Department of the Interior says in one of its Preservation Briefs, "windows should be considered significant to a building if they 1) are original, 2) reflect the original design intent of the building, 3) reflect period or regional styles of building practices, 4) reflect changes to the building resulting from major periods or events, or 5) are examples of exceptional craftsmanship or design." The report goes on to recommend "the retention and repair of original windows wherever possible."[3]

The US Department of Energy, in its *Consumers Guide to Energy Efficiency and Renewable Energy*, says, "If you have old windows in your home, the best way to improve your home's energy efficient is to replace them with new, energy efficient windows."[4]

The Department of Energy tells us to replace our windows while the Department of the Interior tells us to keep them. This conflicting advice is indicative of the larger problem.

has one of the highest embodied energy values, and the manufacture of wood products is less damaging to the environment than metal or plastics. Wood lasts longer as sash material, and when retired, will break down and return to earth many centuries faster than synthetics.

Window Options

Over time, historic windows will require maintenance. Weights and ropes sag or disconnect; gaps form between jambs; sashes and stops rot or fall out of place; air leaks through the assembly. Here's a short maintenance checklist.

Fig. 11.14-17: *Rails and sashes are cleaned of paint debris to ensure easy operability. A new counterweight rope is installed, which will hold the bottom sash up when in an open position.*

Fig. 11.18-19: *When exterior window glazing falls into disrepair, reglazing is required. The old glazing is removed, the new glazing installed and a doughy putty is applied and cut at an angle to minimize the profile. Glazing is being installed at left, and new glazing is completed at right.*

1. Keep all exterior surfaces painted or otherwise sealed. Horizontal surfaces catch and retain water, so take particular care.

2. Replace glazing compound once it dries out or cracks, otherwise it contributes to air leaks. Paint the compound only after it's cured.

3. Ensure that the window's lock functions and is set properly, as it holds the sashes in place. The sashes must be properly positioned, so that when closed the tight fit reduces air infiltration.

4. Install or replace worn weatherstripping. Use durable, long lasting material. The cheapest thing will never last.

5. Keep rails clean to ensure operability. Five or ten coats of paint on rails and jambs will increase friction. When so many layers of finish are present, paint stripping would be a good start. Generally speaking, don't paint or caulk the sashes shut. Though in specific cases, such as a very tall window, a fixed top sash may be desirable.

6. Replace broken glass, which is not safe and leaks air.

7. Test for air leaks with a blower door test, incense or candles.

8. Watch for condensation and water. After a heavy dew, check to ensure water is not pooling. Ensure all storms have tight seals. They should be screwed, caulked or weatherstripped.

9. Ensure windows yield proper egress. Ensure at least one window per bedroom meets modern egress requirements of

5.7 square feet of operable space, and 20x24-inch minimum dimensions. Consider egress requirements prior to sealing any sash permanently.

10. Fix counterweights which allow for operability of moveable sashes.

Storm Windows

Storm windows are an additional window mounted inline with an existing window, on the interior or exterior, with the intent of increasing thermal efficiencies, reducing noise or offering protection from inclement weather. In many climates, storm windows were historically swapped with screens through the seasons. In winter, the storm offered extra thermal insulation, but in spring a screen was preferred to allow for fresh air. When no air conditioning existed, screens were also used in the summer. Where air conditioning is used today, we'd

Fig. 11.20:
Storm Window
Options.

typically use storm windows in winter and summer.

Properly installed storm windows create an air barrier between the primary window and outside elements, creating a retrofitted double-pane assembly, thermally comparable to newer windows. The Lawrence Berkeley National Laboratory showed that an historic window with a low-e pane of glass on a storm window yields the same efficiency as a replacement window. Preservation Brief #3 argues that this design exceeds the R-value of a typical window by 5-6%.[5]

There are three storm window options, each with varying costs, effectiveness, historical accuracy and availability. *Interior storms* are ideal when exterior installation is difficult, or you want to keep the view of window's exterior unobstructed. *Triple-track storm* windows are highly operable, allowing for storms and screens to be easily swapped,

	Cost	Aesthetics / Preservation	Sustainability	Availability	Conclusion
Interior Storm	$$$	Excellent, less obstruction from outside, more from inside. Good option when protecting the view from the streetscape is crucial, or when installing exterior storms is difficult or impossible.	Excellent	Custom	Great option to protect exterior aesthetics.
Triple Track Storm	$	Large profile is deemed a negative by some preservationists.	Aluminum conducts more heat than wood, and is a poor insulator.	Stock	Best inexpensive option.
Traditional Storm/ Screen	$$$$$	Historically accurate solution, made with low profile wood frames, typically hinged at the top and swapable with screen frames through the seasons.	Great insulator. Custom work allows for the installation of energy efficient storms including double panes and low-e films.	Custom	Best option if operability and aesthetics, historic accuracy and swappable operability are priorities.

but they are not aesthetically pleasing. Traditional *fixed storms* and screens are more historically accurate, but generally non-operable.

Some Window Case Studies

The Webb-Thompson House

This two-story transitional Craftsman sat abandoned for years before our rehabilitation began. We were lucky to meet some of its previous residents, who confirmed the house had worst-month heating bills in excess of $500 per month, astronomical for a 2,000-square-foot home in a North Carolina winter. Part of the problem was the home's windows — gorgeous four-over-one windows, 42 in all, each averaging 18 square feet of glass (756 square feet of glass total). A modern tract home of the same size might have 20 windows averaging 10 square feet of glass (only 200 square feet glass total). The daylight the windows provided was certainly a major plus, but that's nearly four times more glass than a modern home — and all that glass was single pane.

The solution? First, repair the windows sashes and reglaze. The sashes and counter-weights were repaired to a level of tightness where additional weatherstripping was not necessary. Second, triple track aluminum storm windows were installed. While the frame covered some of the window detailing, operability was preferred by the client and thus a triple track window was suggested. The character of the windows is unobstructed from the interior. Combined with insulation and HVAC upgrades, utility costs were cut 60-70%.

The Bussel House

This client requested that their window assemblies be as airtight as possible and their storm windows be inconspicuous. Further, they did not frequently open and close their windows, so the windows did not need to be operable. Lastly, the client had grown up in a home that had uncommonly drafty counterweight pockets, so she wanted this issue addressed, too. The solution was twofold. First, we insulated the rear counterweight pocket, locking the stop sash in place. This stopped all air infiltration through the counterweight cavities, an often-overlooked void. Second, custom low

Fig. 11.21-23: Webb-Thompson House. *Triple track storms are viewable from the exterior, but barely noticeable from the interior.*

profile storm windows were installed, less noticeable and more energy-efficient than aluminum, but not operable. The client got rid of the drafts, and the home looks great from the street.

The Cranford House

In this case, the client wanted energy efficiency but didn't like the look of triple track storms. Challenging us for a solution, she wanted to be sure her windows were operable

Fig. 11.24-25: Bussel House interior/ exterior. Top right, the addition of a non-descript 2nd pane of glass to each individual sash is almost completely unnoticeable from either side of the window.

Fig. 11.26: Cranford House. Center, the counterweight cavity is opened, insulated, reinstalled and caulked airtight.

Fig. 11.27: Cranford House. Bottom left, original window without custom low profile storm windows, during installation.

Fig. 11.28: Bottom right, a top-hinged storm is made operable by retractable metal brackets.

SARA DAVIS LACHENMAN
SARA DAVIS LACHENMAN

to enjoy North Carolina's mild seasons. So neither triple track nor fixed storm windows were a viable option. In working with a local building scientist we authored a solution — install an additional pane of glass over the existing pane, adding an effective double pane to the window. We installed small weep holes to allow for condensation draining, if needed. Custom weatherstripping from Conservation Technologies tightened the design. The windows look great, and are fully operational all seasons of the year.

Where To Use Specialty Glass

Specialty glass is either required or preferred in certain applications. Tempered glass may be required by code, laminate glass has benefits for security or sound and decorative glasses may be used in showers, transoms or nonfunctional window art. Sometimes it's worth replicating an old glass detail when restoring an important street façade. Original old wavy glass is not easily replicated, and though some manufacturers have tried, few pull off an authentically old look.

Tempered glass is processed to increase strength over normal glass. It will shatter into small fragments instead of sharp shards and is required by modern building codes in stairways, doors, windows adjacent to showers and baths and all windows less than 18 inches above finished floor.

Laminate glass is a thin film placed between two panes of glass, used for security or soundproofing purposes. It holds together when shattered and produces a spiderweb when broken. The laminate blocks nearly all UV light and is a great application for soundproofing an infant's nursery or music room.

Some historic glass can be laminated, and it's been argued by preservationists that this is aesthetically preferable to replacing an original 1/8-inch single pane glass with a heavy-shadow line 1/4-inch double pane. As an added bonus, the lamination offers a thermal break, limiting condensation transfer through the window.

Frosted glass is decorative glass made by etching or sand blasting. It creates a

Fig. 11.29-31:
Left, tempered glass is required in any new door, adjacent to any shower and in all stairwell windows. Center, storm windows are constructed of laminate glass, dramatically reducing exterior noise pollution into the baby nursery. Right, textured frosted glass serves as an architectural detail and a privacy barrier.

translucent, opaque finish, transferring light but blurring images.

Beveled glass is a common detail on old windows made by taking a ¼-inch piece of glass and beveling the outer inch. The bevel becomes a prism that creates interesting

Fig. 11.32-34: *Stained glass is customized to a homeowner's liking. Sometimes, stained glass is hung from the meeting rail of a bathroom window to provide decorative privacy screening over the lower sash. Right, frosted glass is common in bathroom windows and shower doors.*

light, bringing a full spectrum of colors into the house.

Finishes

Traditional windows will be constructed from either wood or metal. Wood can be painted or stained; metal is typically painted. Most wood has been painted previously, so any virgin stain-grade wood is a real find that should be protected. Windows and casings are most likely white and glossy, meaning they are expected to have, at one point, been painted with lead. Since they are also operable, they are also liable to have

Fig. 11.35-36: *Bottom left, replication wavy glass, inspired by handblown glass of historic windows. Bottom right, beveled glass, common on original windows, doors and mirrors.*

CLEAR VUE GLASS

flaking paint. Be sure to know what you are working with prior to rehabilitating.

Window hardware and treatments are opportunities to enhance an already grand window. Period hardware is readily available from suppliers such as Restoration Hardware and Van Dyke's Restorers. Simple locks and pulls are available from big box stores in a range of finishes like bronze, stainless steel, brushed nickel and white. It's always nice to coordinate finishes in a room; little looks more amateur than random finishes on the door knobs, hinges, window locks, window latches, electrical plates and light fixtures. A mix of material can be tastefully done, but a good balance is only achieved with proper planning and forethought. Additionally, treatments such as blinds and curtains add

How to Read a New Window Label

While preservationists shun replacement windows, additions and modifications generally require new windows. While architectural salvage yards may have some old windows worth considering, their stock is often limited because so few people buy old windows anymore. So one is left to buy new windows. In such a case, it's important to know how to read a new window label.

U-Factor — measures heat loss through conduction (U value moves inversely to R-value, which represents the thermal resistance that slows heat loss. Specifically U is the inverse of R, U = 1/R). The smaller the U-factor the better. Energy efficiency tax credits are available for windows with U-factors under .3. U-factor measures the heat loss through the pane, but does not consider heat loss around the pane, including gaps from the meeting rail, stiles and stops.

Solar Heat Gain Co-efficient (SHGC) — measures the amount of direct solar radiant heat that gets through the windows. Lower SHCG values reduce cooling needs but limit passive solar heat gain in winter.

Visible Light Transmittance (VT) — measures the amount of visible light that gets through. Low VT reduces glare and limits nighttime viewability. Multiple panes lower VT, so single panes offer the least obstructed view, triple panes the most.

What is *Low Emissivity* (low-e)? When someone refers to low-e, they are talking about a microscopically thin layer of film that helps reflect radiant heat, resisting its transfer through the glass. The presence of a low-e barrier helps lower the SHGC by reducing or eliminating long wave radiation through the glass. Some local codes now require low-e glass on all new construction.

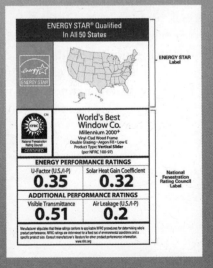

Fig. 11.37

security and style and resist heat transfer. They can reduce radiant and thermal loss through a window by 30% or more. Due to modern HVAC, most have forgotten how to operate blinds for the purpose of temperature management. Amory Lovins calls this the *lost Victorian art of actually operating the Venetian blinds.*

Preservation and Sustainability

Windows are a major tax credit issue, one of the first things a SHPO reviewer will consider in your project. If you propose to retain and rehabilitate, you're golden. If you wish to replace, you're dead in the water. Windows must be retained at all cost to be in compliance with the Secretary of the Interior's Standards and SHPO guidelines. There's simply little, if any, wiggle room there.

Oddly, we've worked on projects that had windows previously replaced and caused no issue (other than huffing disappointment). Our local SHPO was flexible to look past windows in these cases, allowing rehabilitation of the rest of the house as a qualifying project. A different SHPO or stringent local district may not offer such flexibility. A similar protocol exists for windows on the street façade, typically deemed more important because of their role in design cohesion. Moving, altering or changing windows in the back of a house may be acceptable, but this is unheard of on the front.

On an addition or modified portion of the house, try to replicate style or take cues from the home. The devil is in the details, though, as there are a lot of faux products that fail to replicate old character. A one-over-one double hung with a six-lite pop-in mullion is not the same as a six divided lite sash. The shadow line difference between true divided lite and faux divided lite is extraordinarily noticeable.

Finally, each window is different so consider each window's need individually. You might carefully restore the house's front windows and add interior air panels seasonally, add weatherstripping and exterior storms to side windows and replace the rotting windows out back during a kitchen remodel. Some windows may need no work at all.

Old windows are in so many ways better than their more recent descendants. They last, are repairable, demand few new resources, cause no waste, can be as efficient as new windows and are works of art. Clearly, historic windows serve both preservation and sustainability well.

PLUMBING

The house of the future is likely to be a house that evokes memories of our roots. The technology of the future needs to be integrated gracefully, not worn like a badge.

— Sarah Susanka, *The Not So Big House*

Perhaps no modern luxury is as under-appreciated as indoor plumbing. It brings us cold potable water for drinking, hot water for cleansing and removes human waste from the house efficiently, effortlessly and safely. No longer do we have to waddle to a cold lean-to and hole in the ground on a 10°F January night. Who remembers that, in just our grandparent's generation, indoor plumbing was the new snazzy technology? Amazingly, as recently as 1921 99% of buildings in the US lacked either electricity or plumbing.

The plumbing system consists of three types of piping: supply, waste and vents. Water is furnished by supply lines, waste is removed through waste lines and sewer gases are removed from the home by vent stacks. These basic components have comprised the basic plumbing system for almost a century and a half.

Old systems are typically upgraded, retired or fail every 25-40 years, so a century-old home may be on its third or fourth plumbing system. A plumbing system's poor longevity is the result of a variety of assaults: water, pressure, bacteria, weight and time. Luckily, today's systems are designed to last 50 years or longer, and there are a plethora of sustainable options to put less load on water demands, recycle water for multiple uses, lessen energy usage and get hot water faster. A major rehabilitation or partial remodel presents the homeowner the opportune moment to improve the efficiency, ease of use and longevity of a plumbing system.

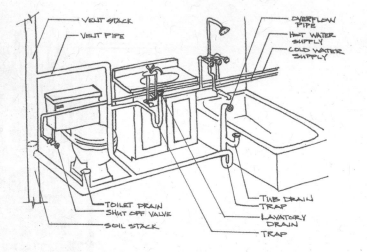

Labels in figure:
VENT STACK
VENT PIPE
OVERFLOW PIPE
HOT WATER SUPPLY
COLD WATER SUPPLY
TOILET DRAIN
SHUT OFF VALVE
SOIL STACK
TUB DRAIN TRAP
LAVATORY DRAIN TRAP

Fig. 12.1:

Plumbing systems have supply lines, waste and vents. Plumbing fixtures are the bridge between supply and waste.

Questions to Ask

- Does the house have original plumbing fixtures?
- How old are the waste lines?
- How old are the supply lines?
- What type of piping does the home have?
- How efficient is the water heating system?
- How close is the water heater to the kitchen sink and primary shower?
- How efficient are the fixtures?
- How can I use multiple water lines?

As for inspections, some localities require all new plumbing work to be performed under a licensed plumbing professional. Other states do not care. Some states allow an owner occupant to perform unlicensed work as long as it's limited to their own residence. Either way, nearly all plumbing work is supposed to be permitted, putting it under the review of code enforcement officials. Until these officials are convinced that work meets applicable codes, a certificate of occupancy will not be forthcoming.

A Brief History of Plumbing

Early plumbing systems, such as chamber pots and exterior wells, required manual labor to transport water to and from a home. Water has long been collected and stored in ponds, cisterns and wells located as close as possible to the home they served: the first reservoirs date to 3000 BC in Gimar, India, where dry climate and water scarcity led to water management experimentation. Artificial lakes in Greece date to 500 BC.

Romans build advanced civil engineering projects not all that different from modern sewer systems. Yet the earliest waste systems in North America were nothing more complex than ditches or outhouses, separated from the house to ensure sanitary conditions. Early settlements in the US used daisy-chained hollowed logs for waste piping, and it wasn't until the late 1700s that cast iron allowed for more formal systems. Hollowed wood waste pipes sealed together with animal fat were being used in Montreal and Boston even in the 1800s. Through the 19th century most sewage simply drained untreated into stream or lakes and in turn contaminated drinking water.

Modern reservoirs came to being in the 1800s in England, storing large amounts of water in an urban setting for municipal use. Thames river water was stored underground and contained by thick brick walls. In 1909 the Honor Oak reservoir was the largest such underground reservoir. Its roof was and is still used as a London golf course.

The 1840s-1860s saw the first attempts at municipal water supply installations. Generally, the supply lines served an exterior yard faucet. Even sinks of this era had no waste piping, having to be drained by hand. By 1860, indoor plumbing was catching on. Soon after, the first hot water systems were created by adding a heating coil and water tank to the rear of large stoves.

Elevated cisterns captured roof runoff and supplied houses via gravity feed, negating the need for a pump. Eventually, dense city settings put huge demands on plumbing systems. Taller buildings were extremely difficult to engineer, often struggling to get water above the fourth floor. Pumps and hydraulic jams of the early 1800s helped lift water into holding tanks at the top of buildings. Supply lines were first pressurized with steam pumps during the industrial revolution. Then electric pumps took over that function in the late 19th century.

Non-plumbed portable metal tubs for bathing gave way to plumbed clawfoots in the 1880s. Shortly after, the interior bath gained popularity, and soon after entire rooms were designed strictly for the bath (hence the room name we still use today). Since the plumbing was already routed to the bath room, the predecessor of modern day toilet — the water closet — was also installed there. Water closets were first mass-produced in the 1840s. From nearly a full century leading up to World War II, inventors tripped over themselves applying

for patents for better toilets.

In 1890, the first complete sewer system moved waste from the house with minimal human effort. Still, with all the progress, in 1900, only 15% of American homes had a complete bathroom as we know it today, and in 1940, only 55% of American homes had one.

Beginning around 1900, inconsistent plumbing codes began being enforced by local officials. These efforts were consolidated into the US National Plumbing Code in 1947, which turned into the International Plumbing Code (IPC), the governing code in use today.

The 1960s and 1970s saw conservation movements spawn dual flush toilets, low flow showerheads and create (well, bring back) water reuse systems. The conservation movement caused expedited retirement of many historic fixtures, their aesthetic value forgone for their inefficiencies. Old water closets typically use over five gallons per flush, while modern toilets use 1.6 gallons per flush or less. Since 30% of home water usage is tied to toilet flushing, that's a huge savings.

Today there is a general renaissance in the water conservation movement. At the beginning of 2007, Water — Use It Wisely introduced a water-saving designation standard the equivalent to Energy Star rating.[1]

Only in the last generation have polymer products (primarily plastics) become the main material in plumbing applications. PCV, PB and PEX have all made plumbing inexpensive, easier and accessible to the do it-yourselfer. PEX and PVC have done for plumbing what latex paint did for painting: they have simplified the use of materials and made plumbing accessible to the amateur.

How Plumbing Works

Plumbing is best thought of as two separate systems, each requiring separate rough-ins: one system brings water in (supply), the other takes wastewater out (waste). The *supply system* works under pressure of enough force to lift potable water around bends and up flights of stairs. The *waste system* works by gravity, with drainage pipes sloped at a downward grade.

Conventional wisdom concludes that supply and wastewater must never mix. Similarly to hot and neutral currents in electrical systems, serious health problems can arise from the seepage of one plumbing system into the other (electrocution or cholera, respectively). Plumbing fixtures bridge the supply and waste systems, drawing in fresh water and discharging wastewater. All of these fixtures are designed to keep the supply and drainage systems strictly separate. However, without proper system design, engineering and installation, wastewater can be a serious private and public health threat. The separation of potable water and wastewater is a good general concept to follow and consistent with codes, though I will address times when certain wastewater can be recycled for reuse.

The Supply System

The supply system starts at the meter or well and delivers cold water to the house via the water main, typically a $5/8$ to one-inch diameter pipe. A main shut-off is located at the meter, vital in case of a burst pipe or other emergency. Traditionally, the cold water main branches to the water heater to create a hot supply. The hot water heater is controlled by a thermostat, which is normally set between 140 and 160°F. From here, cold and hot water run parallel to each other, serving kitchens, baths and laundry. Each line terminates at a fixture, most of which have independent shut-off valves. Supply lines are typically ½-inch pipe or tubing. Three-eighth-inch lines, in some situations, can supply sinks, toilets and some showers; ½-inch lines are needed for most baths, washers and hose bibs.

You'll find a variety of piping in your crawl space, basement and walls, but in new installations and remodels PEX is the dominant supply tubing.

Supply Pipe Material

Cross-Linked Polyethylene (PEX) is relatively new to North American markets, but has been in use in Europe for 50 years as supply and radiant piping. It's readily available in

---

The Two Phases of a Plumbing Installation

Rough-in plumbing consists of the installation of supply lines, waste lines, flanges, vents, water heaters and manifolds. Finish plumbing is the installation of the fixtures.

3/8 to 1-inch diameters and is able to stand wider temperature ranges than other plastic pipes. PEX has all but displaced copper as the primary choice for radiant heating. It's popular in today's marketplace due to its extreme flexibility, low cost, ease of installation and need for fewer joints. PEX can be turned 90° either by flex or an adapter, where its competitors all require a fitting. This allows for *home run installations,* direct shots from a distribution point to fixture without any joints, a core principle in the manifold systems discussed later. Though PEX fittings do cost more, it is always less costly to install PEX than copper, as the pipe and labor is much less expensive.

Copper was the leading supply pipe for most of the 20th century. It is still very common to find it in existing houses. It is strong, does not corrode and withstands heat very well. Copper pipes are available in 10-foot lengths and are joined by fittings, which are sweated in place, but the material is not flexible so labor costs are greater than when working with PEX. Copper prices have been extremely volatile of late, adding to material costs. Unfortunately, scrap metal prices have also been high, and copper pipe theft is a concern in many urban settings. Some plumbers and developers will no longer use copper solely because they suffered significant losses from theft.

For centuries, *lead pipe* was the primary material used to supply water, due to its malleability. On rainy days, plumbers would role pipe from lead sheets, stored for future use. The word plumbing itself is derived

Fig. 12.2-3: *Top, colored PEX with yellow gas line; bottom, copper.*

from the Latin word for lead, *plumbum.* Today we're lucky enough to know the hazards of ingesting lead and thankfully, lead pipe is now rare. If you do find active lead piping, it needs to be replaced.

Polyethylene (PE, or black plastic pipe) is commonly used as a supply pipe from water meters as the water main. PE pipe is popular because it's cheap and is unlikely to burst. It can be purchased in rolls up to 1,000 feet (which eliminates the need for buried joints), and minerals do not adhere to plastic like they do galvanized pipe or lead. PE pipe is prohibited beyond the main supply because the material breaks down above 120°F, and domestic hot water runs at least that hot. PE also has a tendency to fail at joints. If you see PE beyond the water main, that's a sure sign of amateur fix-it work.

Polybutylene is a rigid plastic pipe that has a sad history in the US. Polybutylene was installed in over six million homes from 1970s through 1995, but the material oxidized when put under extreme hot or cold temperatures and would crack longitudinally, causing major flooding. Its failure happened when exposed to the elements, often in a vented crawl space or uninsulated attic, or if the house has been shut down in the winter and no one bothered to turn off the water main and drain the system. Though still popular in Europe and Asia because of recent improvements, a billion dollar class action law suit ended its use in the US. If your polybutylene pipe was installed between January 1, 1978 and July 31, 1995 you may have the pipe replaced for free, as part of that class action lawsuit.

Fig. 12.4: *Standard Trap Sizing by Fixture Served.*

Fixture	Minimum trap size
Bar sink	1½ inch
Bathtub with shower	1½ inch (2 inches beyond trap under UPC code)
Bidet	1¼ inch
Kitchen sink, disposal and dishwasher	1½ inch (2 inches beyond trap under UPC code)
Laundry sink	1½ inch
Lavatory (bathroom sink)	1¼ inch
Shower	2 inch
Toilet	3 inch
Washing machine	2 inch

The Waste System

Waste pipes carry used water and waste to the sewer by utilizing gravity drains. While supply lines are under constant pressure and use, waste lines only have water in them when a fixture is in use. Pipes must be sloped at a minimum of ⅛ of an inch per foot of run, enough to allow gravity and water to move waste. Diameters increase as water flows downstream and carries more aggregate waste, the sewer main being a larger diameter than branch lines. A four-inch sewer main must be sloped ¼ of an inch fall per foot. Large jobs can require complex load calculations for pipe sizing, which is why it's advised to work with a professional.

As water leaves a plumbing fixture, it immediately goes through a trap that is engineered to always hold water. Human waste decomposes into hydrogen sulfide, methane and carbon monoxide; traps keep such poisonous vapors from migrating into living space. Special traps are designed to prevent certain drains from clogging. *Drum traps* are often used on tubs to collect hair and dirt, and some kitchen sinks have *grease traps. S-traps,* for example, were made illegal because they have a tendency to siphon away the water that is supposed to stay trapped and block sewage gases. Toilets are self trapped and do not require additional trap plumbing.

Any new waste system requires good design, particularly when undergoing design reconfigurations. Whenever possible, design waste lines to run parallel with joists. There are major limitations in cutting waste lines through the joists, and the depth of many old house floor joists is actually too shallow to penetrate with a waste line. Sometimes the plumber must have the carpenter reorient the floor joist system by adding headers and trimmers to create a runway for the waste line. A false floor or ceiling can also hide waste lines, though they can cause preservation issues if they alter historic living space.

Vent pipe can be slightly smaller than the drains and waste they vent and traditionally are piped through the roof or an exterior wall. Aesthetically, it looks nicer to run them through walls and hide them behind sheetrock so they are only visible above the roof line.

Air Admittance Valves (AAVs) (otherwise known as Studor vents after one of the primary manufacturers) are one-way mechanical vents that negate the need for a conventional vent through the roof. They're easy to install, durable and great for remodels where a roof vent would cause excessive destruction, labor and refinishing costs.

Waste Pipe Material

Polyvinyl Chloride (PVC) is the dominant waste pipe now in use, with 1½, 2, 3, 4 and 6-inch diameters most common in residential construction. It is also commonly called Schedule 40, a reference to its wall thickness. Grey PVC is UV-stabilized and commonly used where pipe is exposed to the weather or underground, or as conduit for other materials. PVC can split when frozen or exposed to sunlight and emits toxic fumes

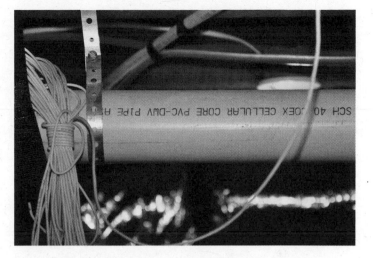

when ignited. There's also a PVC foam core product that minimizes drain noise, a great product on vertical drops through living spaces where you do not want to hear each flush.

Acrylonitrile Butadiene Styrene (ABS) is comparable to PVC, less toxic in retirement and offers more sound insulation than PVC. It has a tendency to split longitudinally and will wilt if exposed to sun. In some jurisdictions, ABS is required for waste pipe. Most regions of the country are dominated by either PVC or ABS; rarely is a plumber familiar with both materials.

Cast iron absorbs sound better than plastic pipe and is by far the most dimensionally stable pipe. It expands and contracts eight times less than plastic, so less anchoring is required to keep it from moving out of alignment. Cast iron is more difficult to work with than plastic, however, as it's much heavier and fittings are three times the cost.

Fig. 12.5: *PVC waste — the most commonly used residential pipe.*

What You'll Find Wrong
Lead Piping

Lead was once used for piping, packaging and joint sealing. It was popular because its malleability was so useful in fishing and bending pipe through difficult spaces. Such ease of use made it yesterday's PEX. Cities commonly used lead supply lines, most of which have been replaced. Because of its low melting temperature, lead was considered the ideal material for sealing joints in metal piping, too. The hazards of ingesting lead, which include stillbirths and high rates of infant mortality, were misunderstood until recently. Lead pipes were still being installed in the 1900s, and though rare, can still be found in use today. Such pipes should always be replaced.

Metal Corrosion

Corrosion results from the inherent pipe contact with air and water and is accelerated in the presence in high-pH water. Galvanic action, where two dissimilar metals touch, is another cause of corrosion. Corrosion clogs pipes like cholesterol clogs arteries. Materials collect at the edges, the passable area of the

Fig. 12.6: *Lead piping — a rare but serious concern.*

pipe's diameter shrinks, increasing friction for passing liquids and eventually blocking passage. Some corrosion can be addressed with chemicals or snakes. If the pipe is cracked, it generally must be replaced.

Clogged Waste and Sewer Lines

Waste lines clog from poor slope, improper pipe sizing and toilet and sink debris. Hair and grease are common culprits. Old sewer mains were built out of clay tile which had joints every 12 inches or so making them subject to assaults from tree roots. Cast iron sewer mains, though they have fewer joints, can be subject to the same problems; blockage in cast iron is often a sign of corrosion. Any buried pipe that fails structurally may simply collapse. Once clogged or collapsed, a blockage can cause sewage to backup into the house. Some insurance polices offer specific coverage for this. Vents may become dysfunctional due to poor installation, cracked piping, termination in an attic or animal nests. Clogged vents will cause slow drainage. The first step is generally a clean out with a snake. If that doesn't work, plumbers' cameras may spot a problem. If the sewer main is completely broken, an excavation and installation of new sewer main is required.

Busted Pipes

Water expands as it freezes causing pressurized pipes to burst. Some types of pipe are more prone to bursting than others. PEX has enough flex to withstand minor freezes; polybutylene does not. Unoccupied houses or houses under renovation should be winterized by turning off the water supply and opening the lowest valve in the house, typically an exterior hosebib. Occupied houses should detach exterior hoses in winter. Owners should be cautious with uninsulated piping in exposed crawl spaces that are most exposed to freezing. On extremely cold nights some keep the water on with a slight drip that keeps water moving just enough to avoid freezing. A better solution is insulated pipe, a sealed crawl space or both.

Structural Failure Due to Plumber

Plumbers tend to put their pipes where they need to go, irrespective of structural framing. Plumbers notch joists and girders to the point where they no longer offer structural support. Unfortunately, this is really common. 100-year old houses have been plumbed multiple times, increasing the likelihood of such snafus. Another common problem is a structural framing under a tub. Filled tubs can weigh up to a ton and often require additional framing support. A 60-inch whirlpool in an attic might seem like a good idea until you find out the hard way that 2x6s, 24 inches on center can't take such weight. Someone who knows how to read a span table is required for such a renovation or repair, and a structural engineer is advised when unusually heavy fixtures are involved.

Sustainability

Sustainability in plumbing can best be achieved by considering water sourcing, transfer and use. In areas where fresh water has always been bountiful, water conservation has been an afterthought, though conservation practices are an everyday part of life in drought-wrought regions of the US. California has a huge population and equally huge fresh water resources, but they are located nowhere near each other. The transfer of such water required one of humanity's largest ever engineering projects and involved a massive amount of energy to construct and operate. In the Virgin Islands, on the other hand, rainwater harvesting systems are required alongside any new construction, maximizing point-of-use principles. Obviously, each region brings different challenges and each house offers different opportunities, so homeowners may be motivated by one application more than others.

Fig. 12.7: *A plumber installed a waste line directly through a primary structural girder, compromising the structural integrity of half the house. A heavy clawfoot tub, weighing nearly a ton when filled, lay directly above. Inadequate support for such weight can lead to serious structural failure.*

Sourcing Water

Essential to any sustainable plumbing system is an efficient, reliable reservoir of water. Consider the water's original source, how it is accessed, what contaminants it contains, how much it costs and how it can be reused.

It is already predicted that access to water will be central to many 21st-century conflicts. Droughts cause reservoirs to run dry, and in many areas of the US municipalities have to pump water across great distances and purchase water from neighboring states. Indeed, in the West rural agricultural interests have already been at odds with urban residential users. These fights are certain to intensify.

Some systems (including some groundwater well systems) have excessive amounts of lead or other contaminants. Improper water chemistry can cause lead to leach from old plumbing fixtures and pipe solder. Check with your local water source to see if any basic testing has ever been performed. The US *Safe Drinking Water Act* is the primary federal law that ensures the quality of drinking water. Within it, the Environmental Protection Agency set standards for drinking water quality and oversees states, localities and water suppliers responsible for implementing the standards.

Water Recycling

Nearly all municipal systems deliver clean and drinkable water to homes, even though drinkable water is not required for tasks such as laundry, toilets or landscaping. These tasks can use recycled water, allowing the use of the same gallon of water two or more times putting less stress on reservoirs, sewers and stormwater systems. Water reuse also saves the energy required to pressurize

Fig. 12.8-10: *Left to right: 1) A rain barrel for use with minor drip irrigation, 2) multi cistern storage holds water for pool and pressurized irrigation and 3) a filter and cistern system used primarily for flushing toilets.*

and transfer water. Water recycling saves huge amounts of municipal energy.

There is some debate over the terms for recycled water, adding to confusion in specification and fastidious code enforcement. Some call all recycled water gray water, while others refer to a specific type of recycled water as gray water, as I do here.

Black water is the dirtiest wastewater. The term is typically reserved for toilet water, highly regulated for the obvious health risks associated with reuse. Water from kitchen sinks is also considered black water, as the kitchen sink hosts bacteria and debris that is far more organic and active than that common to bath sinks. There are some rare, specialized and expensive septic systems that allow for black water to be used as garden fertilizer. In general, black water should go straight to the sewer or septic system.

Gray water is relatively clean water from interior plumbing sources: baths, showers, laundry and bathroom sinks. Each source tends to have some soapy water, helping cleanse a gray water reservoir. Gray water can be used for toilets, laundry, cleaning and landscaping.

Rainwater is clean but not treated water, typically collected from exterior sources such as roof runoff via gutters. Rainwater can be used for toilets, laundry, cleaning, landscaping and pools.

All water reuse systems involve dedicated waste piping, a reservoir and supply pipe. Waste piping is a separate PVC pipe or gutter that leads to a reservoir, either a rain barrel or cistern. Water is then supplied from the reservoir to toilets or landscaping by gravity or a pump.

Gray Water

Gray water is covered in Appendix C of the International Plumbing Code (IPC). However, in reading there that "gray water recycling systems shall only receive the waste discharge of bathtubs, showers, lavatories, clothes washers and laundry sinks"[2] some enforcement officials interpret this code to specifically exclude rainwater. The omission has caused all sorts of interpretation problems, particularly when trying to recycle rainwater for use inside the house. The 2009 IPC for the first time defined rainwater as "water collected from roof areas and other approved areas."[3] By code, it requires filtration prior to reaching a reservoir. If there is a city water valve to refill the reservoir, a backflow preventer must be installed. And, when water is used inside the house it requires disinfecting and either blue or green coloring. Color can be injected in a variety of ways, most typically through a mechanical injection tank or color pellets.

Systems that source water from interior plumbing fixtures capture less water than rainwater-sourced systems, but they function better in an extreme drought. Since interior-source systems collect water from baths and showers, they continue to function regardless of rainfall (presuming the occupants are still showering) where a rainwater system would eventually run dry. A gray water system can be engineered entirely within the building's envelope. It's effectively

a separate system, plumbed parallel to wastewater lines. In a bathroom, the toilet will be plumbed to the sewer, while the sink, shower and bath all run to the gray water reservoir. Each requires a separate waste line, and some code officials require separate venting, thus gray water will cause more roof penetrations.

A typical occupant uses 10-20 gallons per daily shower, roughly the same amount they'll use flushing the toilets. This basic ratio of 1:1 water use is why gray water systems require less storage, sometimes as small as 100 gallons.

Nonpotable pipe and fixtures must be labeled by code. All gray water piping must be yellow and display a *NONPOTABLE, NOT FOR DRINKING* sticker every 18 inches. This ensures that a future remodeler would not confuse a gray water line for a sink supply. Yellow pipe is not commonly available, so spray paint is often used. The costs of the extra plumbing can be excessive, not to mention code enforcement hassles, which is a main reason people scrap pursuit of gray water in favor of simpler, cheaper and larger rainwater collection systems.

Rainwater

Rainwater harvesting systems offer the largest volume potential, and in normal operation capture far more water than gray water alternatives. Simple roof runoff calculations can estimate how much water you can claim and help calculate how large a cistern is appropriate. Fifteen hundred to

Fig. 12.11-13: *A 100-gallon gray water system and associated plumbing.*

2,500 gallon residential systems are typical and can fill up in a single medium-to-large storm. Rainwater-to-landscaping systems capture the greatest amount of water and use it where water demand is highest. In most applications rainwater systems are the best option for recycling water, lowering water bills and insuring against water use regulations associated with droughts.

I've had an odd bird-poop argument posed by inspectors — the claim that rainwater is also gray water as it is contaminated with substances on the roof. This is a bit of a stretch, since neither rainwater nor gray water is drinkable. Still, a first-flush system solves most of this problem by keeping the first bit of rain from a dirty roof out of the reservoir through a system of pulleys and tipping gutter. This is particularly useful during pollen season. A filter can yield similar results.

Cisterns

Cisterns are basic receptacles for holding water. They are the core component of any rainwater harvesting system. In residential applications, cisterns are made of plastic or concrete, with heavy plastic being dominant. While some cisterns operate on gravity, most urban settings require a pump to pressurize water for use. A complete rainwater system features a supply line, filter, cistern, access hole, venting, pump and controller and overflow discharge.

Cisterns generally get water from gutter downspouts. Rainwater passes through a filter, which captures debris such as leaves and

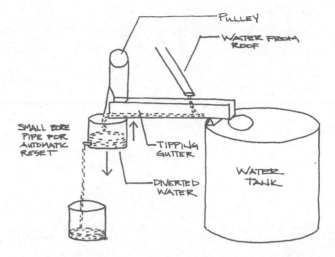

Fig. 12-14: *A first-flush system directs the first rains away from a reservoir.*

dirt and allows clean water to pass into the tank. The cistern holds the water and a submersible pump. The pump is most useful when linked with a controller (the pump's *brain* so to speak), which senses pressure from the opening of a valve and kicks the pump on. Without the controller, the pump requires a switch to turn on manually.

Fig. 12.15: *A filter box catches debris before it enters the cistern.*

Fig. 12.16:
*A typical
underground
cistern
installation.*

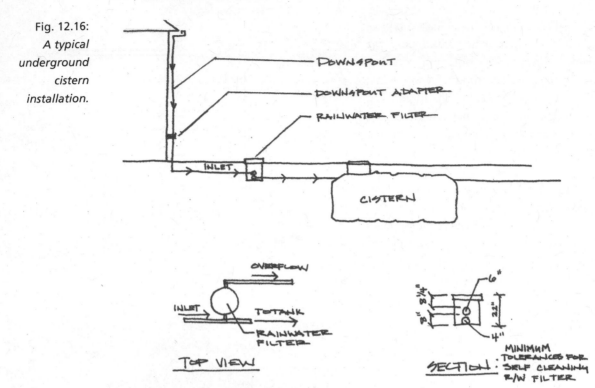

DOWNSPOUT

DOWNSPOUT ADAPTER

RAINWATER FILTER

INLET

CISTERN

OVERFLOW

INLET

TO TANK

RAINWATER FILTER

TOP VIEW

SECTION

6"

3¾"

3"

2.2"

4"

MINIMUM TOLERANCES FOR SELF CLEANING R/W FILTER

A cistern pump must be properly sized. The cheapest ½-horsepower (hp) pumps will be disappointing, a ¾-hp is good and if you have a large area to irrigate on pressure a 1-hp pump is best. Use a large 1-inch line to a hosebib which allows for plenty of pressure and flow. You can always step down to a smaller diameter downline, but you can't step up.

Some less expensive cisterns have a thin-walled body that is subject to collapse. Cheap versions are often modified septic tanks that require a $1/3$ of the tank to be continuously filled with water to avoid a cave-in. This makes a 1,500 gallon tank effectively a 1,000 gallon tank. Any such cis-

tern isn't worth it, as it won't last long. It's best to buy a tank that's made for cistern use and can be fully drained.

There are above ground and below ground tanks. Each has its ideal application. Above ground tanks are less expensive to purchase and install and can be run off of gravity. Below ground cisterns require excavation and earth finishing, but do not take up large portions of the yard. Cisterns come in a variety of shapes and sizes to match roof runoff volume, demand needs and site placement requirements.

When a site has large landscaping demands a cistern is a no-brainer decision with quick payback. Landscaping typically demands more water than any other task, sometimes 2/3 of a home's water use. The cistern can be easily tied to drip or spray irrigation to automatically water an otherwise labor-intensive yard.

One of the most overlooked considerations of cisterns is the insurance they provide against drought. While installation costs can be $3,000-6,000 for an above ground system or double for a below ground, the costs of losing expensive landscaping due to draught or water restrictions could be much greater. Cisterns insure against such risk. Even under drought restrictions, many cities allow for watering of lawns via drip efficient systems or via cisterns.

Hot Water Delivery

Cold water transfer is pretty straightforward. It doesn't make much difference if it's delivered in small or large pipes, via a manifold or conventional system, or through PEX or copper. Hot water, however, requires considerable energy. Conventional water heating can account for 14-25% of the energy consumed in your home, so the efficient creation, storage and transfer of hot water is the focus of many sustainable solutions.

There are a fleet of interesting technologies for heating water. Conventional water heaters still dominate the market because of their low installation costs. Tankless heaters have long been the norm in Europe and are quickly becoming the norm in high-end projects or green-built homes in the US. Solar hot water heaters are a niche product that can be an obvious choice in certain

Storage water heater

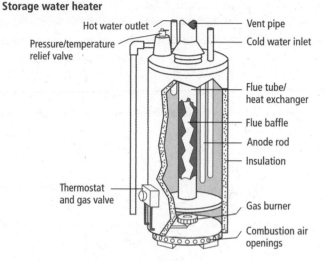

Electric Demand Water Heater

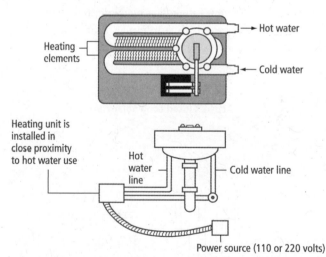

applications, especially when stacking historic and energy tax credits.

Conventional (tanked) water heaters heat and store 20-80 gallons of water for use when demanded. When a hot water valve is

Fig. 12.17-18: *A typical conventional and tankless water heater.*

opened, hot water leaves the tank and is replaced by cold water which is then heated. The cold water takes some time to heat, which is why long showers eventually run cold. Conventional heaters are fueled by either electricity or gas.

Hot water heater manufacturers set their thermostats to 140°F to avoid complaints that their systems aren't producing enough heat (the same reason HVAC subcontractors oversize their units). A temperature of 120°F is adequate for nearly all uses and is more economical. Not to mention that 140°F is scalding and a safety hazard, particularly to children.

Operating at 120°F slows breakdown of the water heater, pipes and fittings, making the system longer lasting. Note that dishwashers are the only appliances that require 140°F water, and some offer onboard temperature boosters to add the additional 20°F. Check your dishwasher specifications before lowering the water heater's dial.

Standby heat loss occurs when heat and energy are lost even though no hot water valve is open. It's the whole reason tanked heaters are less efficient than tankless alternatives. Simply lowering the set temperature to 120°F can save 6-10% of your utility bills. The best tanked water heaters have between R-12 and R-25 insulation. Further, when on vacation, turning off the hot water completely will save energy costs.

On-demand (tankless) water heaters have no tank and therefore no standby heat loss. They create hot water only as it is needed. On-demand systems deliver a constant, never ending supply of hot water, which ironically can lead to wastefully long showers: a local green builder, frustrated with his teenage daughter taking never-ending tankless-heater-supplied hot showers, joked that the most energy-efficient thing he ever did for his house was send her to college.

While demand is continuous, a tankless heater's *flow rate* is limited, meaning it can only heat so much water per period of time. Flow rate is not an issue with tanked heaters, since the water is already heated. Still, tankless flow rate is only an issue if an unusual number of fixtures are demanding hot water simultaneously. Typical systems provide 2-5 gallons of hot water per minute, plenty for normal operations.

Gas on-demand heaters are more efficient than electric, even with their constantly burning pilot light. Some heaters now have an intermittent ignition device that lights

Fig. 12.19:
A typical solar hot water heater.

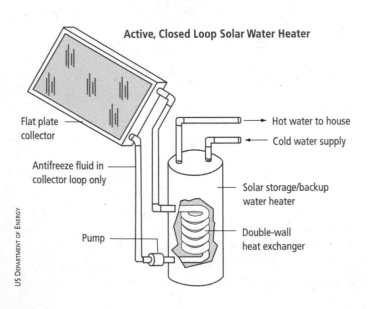

Active, Closed Loop Solar Water Heater

Flat plate collector

Antifreeze fluid in collector loop only

Pump

Hot water to house

Cold water supply

Solar storage/backup water heater

Double-wall heat exchanger

the pilot only when needed, similar to the spark device on a gas range.

On-demand systems offer the most utility savings for small families. If use is less than 40 gallons of hot water a day, they can have operating costs 35% less than tanked heaters. For larger families, exceeding 80 gallons a day, it's closer to 15%. Tankless water heaters are also great for houses that have long vacancies and standby times, such as vacation homes or accessory dwellings.

Solar water heaters use the sun's energy to heat water. Radiant heat is captured through solar collectors and transferred directly or via exchanger to a tanked water heater. Since solar systems can be subject to seasonal efficiency fluctuations, cloudy days and spikes in demand, they are often installed as a pre-heater to a conventional tanked heater. Solar water heaters are extremely efficient and convenient add-ons for pool heating and radiant floors. Though standby heat loss is still a factor, it's relatively inconsequential since the sun, *um*, charges lower rates than a utility company.

Solar hot water systems are involved installations, and they require a solar specialist to perform a site analysis to conclude how much sun hits the proposed site and how efficient the system will be. Installations can be expensive, though in many states 65% of the costs are rebated through energy efficiency tax credits. Where available, historic tax credits can cover a good part of the remainder. Placement of solar panels is of particular concern to preservationists, however, and placement on roofs viewable from the

streetscape should be avoided. Poor placement can cause an entire tax credit project to be disqualified, though there is recent evidence of SHPOs bending on this point.

Hot water insulation can be installed at the tanked water heater and on hot water pipes.

If your water heater has below R-12 insulation, adding insulation can reduce standby heat loss by up to 45%, saving as much as 10% in water heating costs. If R-value info is not available, the touch test is very simple: if the water heater is warm to the touch, it needs additional insulation. Blankets are very inexpensive and easy to install, though you should never cover instructions, warnings, controls or pressure valves.

Insulating hot water pipes costs very little and can raise the temperature 4°F over uninsulated pipes, and reduce heat loss between morning showers. It's particularly

Fig. 12.20:
Hot water pipe insulation is an inexpensive and simple upgrade.

beneficial to insulate the pipes closest to the hot water heater, including the cold water inlet. Pipe sleeves made of foam are most common and readily available.

Hot Water Delay

Another energy and water waste occurs every morning when we turn on the hot water for the shower. We wait 20-30 seconds for the stagnant cold water to purge from the lines before hot water starts to flow. The practice wastes an average of a gallon of water per shower, in addition to the energy spent to heat the water that went cold in the first place. There are two solutions to the problem: recirculating systems and manifold (home run) systems.

Recirculating systems deliver hot water with minimal delay, using a pump to circulate water to and from the water heater. The pump can be activated on demand, by thermostat or motion sensor. It essentially extends the water heater to the hot water piping downstream. As water temperature drops below a certain point (often 100°F), the water circulates back to the heater for reheating. Recirculating systems are best installed during gut jobs or when all supply plumbing is exposed.

Critics of recirculating systems complain that

1. The pump consumes energy.
2. The water heater has to work harder to keep water hot outside its insulated heater.
3. Recirculating systems are difficult to retrofit.

In defense of recirculation, the pump consumes minimal energy, so it's considered a marginal factor. The water heater does have to work harder, but for on-demand or solar systems, it's only a small amount. Systems can be retrofitted by installing a crossover valve at the fixture farthest from the heater and a pump on the cold water heater supply. This retrofit uses the cold supply line as a return. Thus, if you turn on the cold water line at the same time the recirculating pump is on, you'll get hot water from the cold tap. Still, recirculation is an economical way to get hot water instantly in the morning.

Manifold systems (aka home run systems) run individual lines from a source manifold directly to each individual fixture. Manifold systems function much like a breaker box in an electrical system: each fixture has its own dedicated line. Manifolds yield a couple of benefits. First, there are no joints between the manifold and fixture, meaning no possible leaks behind walls and a longer lasting, easier to repair system. Second, no joints result in less pressure drop, which means lower flow fixtures can use smaller diameter pipe. Where ½-inch PEX is common for traditionally plumbed residential installations, with a manifold system ³/₈-inch lines are sufficient for all lines except washers, baths and hosebibs. These smaller diameter lines actually carry 50% of the volume of ½-inch lines, so hot water gets to the fixture in half the time. Thus, the morning shower happens with less delay and waste. Of course a shower and bath sink are on different supply lines, so when you get out of the morning shower and demand hot water from the sink, it actually takes longer than it would in a traditional system. Most people do not use a lot of hot water in the bath sink, so it's not generally a major sticking point. Third, manifolds allow for easy long-term maintenance, as you can shut off individual fixtures or whole rooms at the manifold. This makes future remodeling a breeze and is an important consideration if trying to build a system to last 50 years or more. Manifold systems have been popular in Europe for years and just now are becoming more common in the US.

Human Control

Even with all the efficient systems and finishes one can plumb, human demand will always be the biggest variable in sustainability. Only so much can be pre-engineered and automated. If you still love 90-minute showers, your energy and water usage will still be huge. If you install leaky 3/8-inch supply lines, they do not save you any water just as a cracked sewer line doesn't adequately remove waste from the house. Humans must take care to ensure systems are installed, maintained and operated with conservation and longevity in mind.

Lastly, build for 50 years. In your design and systems implementation, plan for additions, assume leaks will happen and acknowledge that fixtures will one day be replaced. Keep plumbing easily accessible and unobstructed where possible and build

access panels for maintenance behind tubs and shower valves. Minimize joints and allow for work on other systems without having to do major disconnection or demolition. Make all walls that carry waste lines, now or in the future, out of 2x6 studs (wide enough to plumb toilet waste lines) and stub future lines appropriately.

Preservation

Historically, plumbing systems last 25-40 years before failure, major remodeling or replacement. Old houses often have remnants of three or four systems. Abandoned piping isn't a total waste because it may serve as a ghostmark indicating where bathrooms and kitchens were once located.

However, there's little reason to save an old rough plumbing system just for preservation's sake, and such systems generally fall outside the realm of preservation review. As far as the preservation world is concerned, there

Fig. 12.21:
A manifold plumbing system — 3/8-inch supply lines mean hot water gets there faster.

is no reason to save cast iron waste pipes just for the sake of saving them.

Preservation and plumbing *fixtures* are a different story: fixtures have varied with tastes and time, ranging from ordinary to ornate, depending on their use, the class of the home and location. Even within a single home, a bathroom pedestal sink may show elaborate detail, while a kitchen sink in the same house might have been quite basic. Still, some old fixtures can offer inferior flow rates, and old toilets can be particularly wasteful. A plumber can help address potential fixes to such problems.

Preservation concerns arise over the extent of demolition required to replace rough systems, and the potential obstructions or protrusions into living space new upgrades can cause. While the cast iron and lead pipes can go, try to take careful measures not to destroy original tile or plaster in getting to it. Replacing or even adding a second floor bathroom may be effortlessly approved by preservation officials, but if the waste line causes a drop soffit through the middle of the historic entry foyer, it may be a point of contention. Meeting required waste line slope in tight spots is tricky so, to

be alliterative, proper planning with the plumber prevents poor protrusions and preservation problems.

There is a rule in general contracting that the tradesperson requiring a penetration is responsible for making that penetration, but when working with historic homes tradespeople are reluctant to do so. They may be afraid of the consequences of ruining historic material, or a plumber might just see plaster as not his problem. The intensive nature of replumbing is reason enough to try to design plumbing in localized areas or on back-to-back walls where they can share supply lines, wastes and vents.

Finish fixtures are another matter entirely. The preservation, reuse, rehabilitation or replication of finish plumbing fixtures is highly encouraged and can be a rewarding process to boot. Kitchens and bathrooms are the most frequently remodeled rooms and the location of most plumbing fixtures. Because of this relatively short service life and their propensity to be remodeled, it's rare to find original fixtures. When you do find historical fixtures, consider yourself lucky and mull over potential ways to rehabilitate them for continued use.

HVAC

Mechanical and electrical equipment often is grossly oversized. Engineers, fearful of losing their jobs or being sued for underestimating a building's particular needs, are likely to "round up" when in doubt… The best designs often require an investment of time for learning new methods or seeking out whole-system solutions. Only truly integrated design can yield projects that are both ecologically and economically green.

— Amory Lovins, "Institutional Inefficiency: Guidelines for overcoming the market failure that is now causing widespread energy waste"

No system of the house has changed more in 100 years than the Heating, Venting and Air Conditioning systems, most commonly referred to as *HVAC*. Houses were once heated with coal or wood, air conditioning was unheard of and venting was accomplished by opening a window. Now such operations are done mechanically, which is why the systems are often referred to as the mechanical system.

Heating warms the air and allows humans to live in frigid temperatures. Cooling makes hot and humid regions in the southern US bearable for habitation. Ventilation moves air to where we want it, ensuring good indoor air quality. These components comprise all the elements of the mechanical system.

Old HVAC finishes, such as decorative radiators, add architectural character to the home. But modern HVAC is intentionally hidden from view, purely functional and offering little artistic value, so most mechanical upgrades have little effect on the historic character of the home. There are some notable exceptions, such as decorative radiators and grilles. Since HVAC equipment and ductwork is so bulky, careful consideration must be given to placement, chasework and the extent of demolition required for installation. Designs that obstruct the character-defining parts of the home are highly discouraged.

The thermal envelope (see chapter 10) and HVAC must be considered a complete

207

system. While HVAC creates desired temperatures, the thermal envelope preserves it. Planning one while ignoring the other is one of the most common mistakes in rehabilitations. At best, poor coordination can lead to an inefficient house and wasted investment. At worst, it can cause moisture problems resulting in material and structural failure. With leaky buildings, properly designed and installed HVAC and insulation can yield huge benefits. Because of their interlinked nature, I often address the two simultaneously.

HVAC consists of mechanized or natural systems, each designed to create (or capture) and distribute hot or cold air. HVAC efficiency is measured by *Seasonal Energy Efficiency Ratio (SEER)*, *HSPF rating* when using heat pumps and an *Annual Fuel Utilization Efficiency* rating (AFUE) when using furnaces and boilers. Insulation efficiency is measured by an R-Value, a measure of thermal resistance. For both, the higher the number, the better. In other words, the HVAC efficiency rating addresses how efficiently the system moves heat. The insulation efficiency dictates how often a mechanical system has to run to achieve and hold desired temperatures.

Modernizing HVAC and the thermal envelope are crucial to preparing old homes for the new century.

Questions to Ask

- Are there any architectural details in the old HVAC system worth rehabilitating?
- Will my new system cause any awkward alterations to core living spaces, such as visible chases?
- Is a central system the best option for my house, or are other alternatives worth considering?
- Are any of the roof planes, not viewable from the street, ideal for the use of a solar heater?
- How much would the most efficient system cost, and how many years would it take to pay back the premium?
- Does anyone in my house have breathing problems, and if so, what options are out there to increase fresh air intake and air changes per hour (ACH)?
- What months am I likely to run a mechanical system?

The Weakest Link

Your HVAC and envelope design is only as strong as its weakest link.

- HVAC is sized to heat and cool a specific area with a defined insulation value. HVAC sized for an uninsulated house will be oversized after a major envelope tightening.
- An old HVAC system used in tandem with a tight envelope will still cost a substantial amount to run.
- A new HVAC system plus envelope tightening only works if windows are rehabilitated and storm panes are installed.
- A new, super efficient HVAC system installed in an uninsulated, unsealed home will remain inefficient. A very leaky home is thermally equivalent to camping. No matter how efficient the unit may be, it will be heating the entire neighborhood.

- What indoor temperatures do I prefer?
- What have my past utility bills been, and based on standard ratios, how much do I spend on heating and cooling?
- Do I typically spend more on heating or cooling?
- Are there ways I can use more natural heating and cooling methods, such as wood fireplaces, window operability, fans and shades?

A Brief History of HVAC

Before lightweight framing became the norm, heavier wall systems of stone, masonry and logs, as well as natural features like snow, maintained thermal mass and helped to heat or cool the home. Occupants emphasized natural means, with strategies that encompassed fire, sunlight and ventilation through operable windows, awnings and clerestories. Passive designs (mistakenly referred to as *new* design strategy) often allowed buildings to be heated and cooled naturally, without mechanical assistance or power. Where central systems are absent in the world, daily life remains driven by seasons and weather. Midday siestas are still a part of everyday life in scorching regions where there is no mechanical cooling. The development of mechanical systems allowed humans to conduct lives not dictated by temperature extremes.

Occupants have long controlled temperature by operating windows by hand. While window operability requires no electricity, it does require human effort to function,

Fig. 13.1-2: *Coal fireplaces were common in homes from the 1880s to 1920s. Some coal remains in use in New England, but the fuel is mostly retired because of its significantly negative impact on air quality. Still, many old decorative fireplaces remain and are easily retrofitted with gas logs (top) or gas coal baskets (bottom) by routing a gas line to the unit and purchasing stock kits. Coal baskets tend to look more authentic.*

and windows can be difficult or awkward to open and close in extreme weather.

The process of circulating air through buildings is nothing new. Romans left exposed areas beneath their bathing rooms to allow for hot air circulation from their furnaces. This was more than likely the first vented distribution design. King Charles of England passed the first ventilation code in 1631, which stated that you had to have windows that were taller than they were wide to facilitate hot air flow and allow in light. The central fireplaces common to 1600s New England Colonial houses evolved into central heating systems by the simple addition of a fan and ductwork, though that didn't evolve for another three centuries.

The British Count Rumford wrote in 1796 that fireplaces had to be of a certain depth and required chimneys to vent them. That document is widely credited as the first prescriptive fireplace code and guidelines. The fireplaces we have today essentially use Rumford's design. Chimney design became more complex in the Victorian era when multiple flues shared a single structure (flues today cannot cross or be shared because of carbon monoxide and backdraft concerns). Coal and gas fireplaces allowed for shallower fireboxes, which could be installed in tighter spaces.

The technological focus quickly shifted from fireplaces to furnaces. In the early 20th century, furnaces were ducted to a single large register in a central location serving the entire home. The invention of the electrical fan in the late 19th century allowed for forced-air distribution via ductwork. This technology is the grandfather of the central systems that dominate the market today. It wasn't until after World War II that it became common to run ductwork to each individual room, creating a more balanced environment. By then, ducted forced-air central systems displaced fireplaces as the primary source of heat. Correspondingly, many

Digital Thermostat

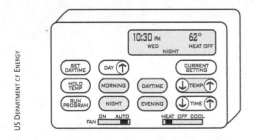

Fig. 13.3-4: *Programmable thermostats monitor mechanical equipment and direct it to meet specific, predefined user bench marks. A programmable thermostat allows for daily temperature planning, lowering loads on the system when people leave or go to sleep and raising them during times of activity.*

homes of this era lacked, for the first time, any fireplace.

The energy crisis of the 1970s sparked the first major movements towards energy efficiency in the US. Savvy automation entered the market with the invention of programmable thermostats, mechanized air flow and humidity control.

Today, variable speed air handlers and condensers are super-efficient units that move heat at a fraction of the cost of units just ten years older. As of January 1, 2006, the US Department of Energy (DOE) set stricter efficiency standards, legislating minimum efficiency ratings on all air conditioning units. According to the DOE, the higher standards are forecast to save 4.2 quadrillion Btus over 25 years, equivalent to the energy consumed by 26 million Americans each year, and save one billion dollars over the same period.

Rough Systems

Like plumbing and electrical, HVAC installations happen in two phases, rough-in and finish. A typical forced-air *HVAC rough-in* consists of a heat producing unit or heat pump, ductwork, boots, venting and gas lines. *Finish HVAC* consists of grates, returns and often the placement of exterior condensers. Systems that are not forced-air have different rough-in requirements, such a radiant piping.

Since residential mechanical work is less regulated and engineered than commercial, it's all too common for contractors to base their estimate of system sizing on gut feeling.

Of course, installers don't want a client complaining in the middle of the winter that the system is not producing enough heat, so the tendency is for HVAC installers to drastically oversize a system. Unfortunately, oversized systems cycle on and off more frequently, which sucks energy and can lead to stagnant moisture and its associated problems. In historic homes, it is very common that systems are not sized properly. Installers often make errant assumptions about how leaky and underinsulated the structure is, or simply conduct flawed system sizing calculations.

Manual J is a prescriptive checklist designed by the Air Conditioning Contractors of America that requires the HVAC designer to address local climate, size, shape and orientation of the house, as well as insulation levels, window area, location and type, air infiltration rates, the number of occupants, occupant comfort preferences, the types and efficiency of light and major home appliances. A Manual J analysis will indicate how many *British Thermal Units* (Btus) you'll need to heat your space (12,000 Btus per hour = one ton). The unit ton measures heat absorption, and is a reference to the old days of refrigeration that consisted of blowing a fan over a block of ice. *One ton* was used to describe the equivalent heat absorption of the typical one ton block of ice. Specifically, it's the amount of heat required to melt a cubic ton of ice in 24 hours. Typical residential systems range from 1.5 tons up to five tons, and large or multi-story houses require multiple systems. It's industry standard (and a code requirement in many places) that installers conduct a formal sizing analysis. Yet many still don't, particularly if you don't ask, so always insist that your HVAC installer provide a Manual J analysis.

One ton per 400-500 square feet is a pretty common calculation for a typical uninsulated house. Extremely tight and well-insulated houses can demand as little as one ton per 1,200 square feet. Manual Js on historic houses (including storm windows and spray foam insulation) typically yield estimates of one ton per 800-1,000 square feet. That's less equipment to buy, and savings that can be used elsewhere in the project.

Good HVAC units feature variable speed fans at the condenser, air handler or both.

Variable speeds allow for systems to ramp up to speed gradually and run at lower speeds, as opposed to just on or just off. Getting efficient performance out of a system with no variable speed functions is like trying to get good gas mileage out of a car when your only options are no gas or pedal to the metal. Though it seems counterintuitive, efficient units actually run *more* frequently than oversized behemoths. It's their small size and variable speed that allow small units to run more cheaply than their obese siblings.

Thermodynamically speaking, heat exists and cold does not. In fact, cold is most accurately defined as the absence of heat. Heat pumps move heat, while boilers and furnaces create heat. Other heat sources include radiant heat, fireplaces and passive solar designs. Still, in most scenarios, forced-air central systems are most cost-effective and appropriate. There are a variety of considerations to ensure the system is efficient, is easy to operate and yields good indoor air quality. I'll walk through the basic technology options and their pros and cons.

The Heat Pump

Heat pumps move heat from one area to another. In the winter, they take heat out of

Fig. 13.5:
Although different types of fuels are available to heat homes in the US, over half of us use natural gas.

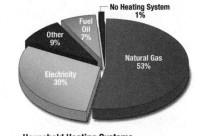

Household Heating Systems
Although several different types of fuels are available to heat our homes, more than half of us use natural gas.

US Department of Energy

Fig. 13.6-7   **A Split-system Heat Pump Heating Cycle**

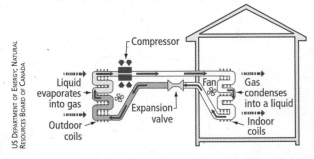

US Department of Energy; Natural Resources Board of Canada

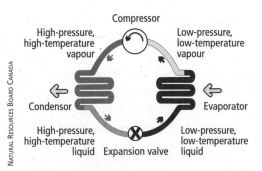

Natural Resources Board Canada

the exterior air and pump it inside. In the air conditioned summer months, they reverse the cycle and actually take heat from the interior of the house and pump it outside.

A heat pump system consists of two coils, each serving a basic function in the refrigeration cycle — expansion (through an *evaporator coil*) and condensation (in the *condenser coil*). The compression and expansion of fluid allows the transfer (or *pumping*) of heat inside or out. Since heat pumps move heat but don't actually create it, they can supply up to four times the amount of energy they consume.

Heat pump efficiency is measured by SEER ratio. SEER is the Btu output divided by its electric energy input. The less energy required, the higher the SEER. Today, heat pumps and air conditioners must be a minimum of 13 SEER. A 13 SEER system is 30% cheaper to run than a 9 SEER system.

A variety of SEER-rated systems are available. For many applications a minimum 13 SEER unit is an appropriate upgrade, but if the user will have a long mechanical season, is subject to high electricity costs or will be in the house for many years, incrementally higher SEER units are justified for their easy-to-calculate return on investment. The cost to upgrade from a 13 SEER system to 14, 15 or 16 SEER is usually marginal and worth considering. At the top end of the spectrum, residential systems of up to 23 SEER are now available but at substantial cost premiums over the standard units, but they tend to offer only air conditioning without heat. High efficiency units

dehumidify well and yield better comfort at higher real temperatures. Current heat-and-cool systems max out at about 19 SEER. Engineers predict the SEER limit will continue to be pushed, as they are yet to reach the limits of the technology.

It's not uncommon to find old houses with no physical insulation and old HVAC with a rating of 8 SEER or lower. These houses offer huge opportunities for improvements in comfort and operational costs. By addressing insulation and HVAC, some slash their utility costs by 70% or more. Remember, up to 50% of a homeowner's electric utility bill is spent on heating and cooling. Units installed between 1986-1991 typically have a SEER of 8, 1980-1985 a SEER of 7 and units before 1980 are typically SEER 6 or worse. Any system that old and inefficient is an obvious candidate for replacement.

Dual Fuel Heat Pumps

Heat pumps operate efficiently when the temperature is above 45°F, but struggle to pump heat from air colder than 45°F. For colder temperatures, they require backup electricity strips, energy hogs that create heat from electricity. Such backup heat is labeled *emergency heat* on the thermostat. That's a little dramatic, but no matter, electric strips are a horribly inefficient way to produce heat. Under 45°F, furnaces work better. Dual fuel systems use a heat pump at higher outside temperatures (above 35°F) and a gas furnace when it's below freezing, so the system runs most efficiently at all temperatures. In mixed climates, dual fuel is an excellent, sustainable option.

As for sustainability, heat pumps use electricity, so you should consider how your local utility produces their power. If it's coal, then you're burning coal to drive your heat pump. Also consider all the line loss in delivering power from the power plant to your home. If minimizing greenhouse gases is an important factor, it may be better for the environment to consider other heat sources. Natural gas produces heat at the source (maximizing efficiency, eliminating line loss) and though combusted it burns very cleanly. Operational costs vary greatly by region, including average temperatures and utility costs per unit. In the southern US, heat pumps are generally less expensive to run than gas furnaces, but natural gas prices are subject to wilder price fluctuations.

Finally, many heat pumps still use R-22 refrigerant, which is a major contributor to greenhouse gases. R-22 will be banned from use starting in 2010, but is still the cheapest option in most cases. Your installer may try to install it by default, so review other options with the HVAC technician, such as the greener $4/10$ refrigerant.

Two Variations on the Heat Pump

Mini splits, otherwise know as ductless systems, are forced-air systems minus the ductwork. They are great options for projects where ductwork cannot be installed. Flexible and small, they allow for zoning up

What Does Geothermal Cost?

While larger HVAC systems might cost $3,000-4,000 a ton, geothermal might be $6,000-10,000 per ton. The greatest cost is the drilling. On urban lots, a geothermal system requires wells dug 400-500 feet deep. On top of all the drilling, a conventional heat pump system and ductwork still has to be installed. On a 10-ton installation (a very large home), a geothermal system would cost $64,000 versus $47,000 for a traditional three-zone, high SEER system. On another job cost estimates for a basic two-zone system were $19,000 and for geothermal $40,000. Geothermal appears most worthwhile on larger projects, though one local architect installed geothermal on a 1,200-square-foot home for approximately $17,000, and his heating and cooling bills virtually disappeared. The technology is still spreading into the mainstream, so better cost data will be available in future.

Fig. 13.8: *Large drilling machine drills the well for a geothermal loop.*

Andy Shull

to four units per condenser, and since up to 30% energy is lost through ductwork, they operate much more efficiently than ducted systems. Ductless systems are mounted permanently on exterior walls and at seven inches deep aren't overly protruding. Some don't like the look of the units, and imprudent placement can certainly be a preservation issue. But wall-mounted units are safer than window-mounted units which are fall hazards and easy access points for burglars.

Geothermal systems use the ground temperature to heat and cool. A closed loop cycles refrigerant below the frost line, where the earth's temperature is a constant 50-55°F. The earth's temperature is transferred to the home through a heat exchanger, with a small heat pump boosting the extra few degrees required. On a 30°F winter day, you set your thermostat to 70°F. A geothermal pump will deliver 55°F fluid from the earth to the air handlers, allowing the heat pump to cover the additional 15°F differential to get to your thermostat setting. A traditional heat pump has to cover a 40°F differential. Since it requires much less energy for a heat pump to move smaller differentials of heat, geothermal systems are extremely efficient. Some systems claim to reach 35 SEER, which would be 1/3 the operational cost of most new HVAC systems. Geothermal systems put less demand on the system mechanics, making them last longer than other systems. The drilling required can be cost prohibitive, and the installation costs are what keep most people from taking the plunge (no pun intended).

Furnaces and Boilers

As the US population migrates south, heat pumps are gaining market share. Still, the majority of Americans live through frosty winters with heat from furnaces or boilers, which are more efficient in cold climates.

Furnaces combust fuel and work with forced-air blowers to distribute hot air through central ducts. They are rated by Annual Fuel Utilization Efficiency (AFUE), the ratio of heat output to total energy consumed. Thus, in a furnace with a 95% AFUE, 95% of the energy input is put to use heating the system. The remaining 5% is lost as exhaust, typically through a chimney. Seventy-eight percent through 100% AFUE products are on the market, and the US Federal Trade Commission requires AFUE information to be displayed on all furnace units. Sealed-combustion units, which conduct their fuel burning within a concealed unit, are at least 90% efficient. They're required for sealed crawl spaces or any

Fig. 13.9: *A high efficiency furnace.*

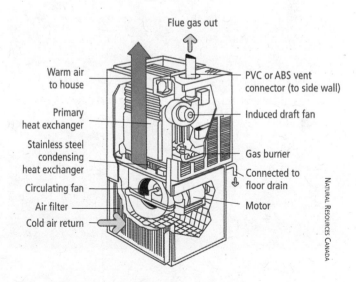

Flue gas out

Warm air to house

Primary heat exchanger

Stainless steel condensing heat exchanger

Circulating fan

Air filter

Cold air return

PVC or ABS vent connector (to side wall)

Induced draft fan

Gas burner

Connected to floor drain

Motor

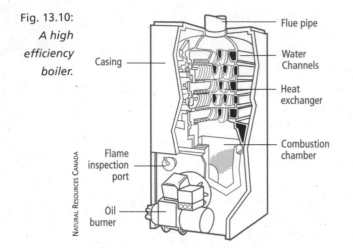

Fig. 13.10:
*A high
efficiency
boiler.*

Casing

Flame
inspection
port

Oil
burner

Flue pipe

Water
Channels

Heat
exchanger

Combustion
chamber

NATURAL RESOURCES CANADA

Furnace and boiler system efficiencies

Old, low-efficiency heating systems

• Natural draft that creates a flow of combustion gases

• Continuous pilot light

• Heavy heat exchanger

• 68%–72% AFUE

Mid-efficiency heating systems

• Exhaust fan controls the flow of combustion air and combustion gases more precisely

• Electronic ignition (no pilot light)

• Compact size and lighter weight to reduce cycling losses

• Small diameter flue pipe

• 80%–83% AFUE

High-efficiency heating systems

• Condensed flue gases in a second heat exchanger for extra efficiency

• Sealed combustion

• 90%–97% AFUE

placement inside a thermal envelope. For maximizing indoor air quality, sealed-combustion units are the only way to do a furnace —they also happen to be the most efficient.

Boilers heat water into either hot water or steam which is then distributed to terminal devices such as a radiator or fin-tube convector. *Steam boilers* require a higher operating temperature and are less efficient; *hot water boilers* are more common. Like furnaces, boilers are rated by AFUE, the minimum AFUE rating on a boiler being 75%, with some high-end units achieving 100% efficiency.

Both furnaces and boilers can use combustible material as a heat source. The burning of any fuel will create measurable emissions contributing to climate change. Some are worse than others: Fuel oil is essentially diesel, which is not clean burning and causes soot that can clog chimneys, flues and ductwork. Natural gas and propane are cleaner and are more common in newer systems. Ask local suppliers about their experience with operational costs, as they vary greatly by region.

Fireplaces

Historic fireplaces offer localized heat to a small area at a time. While such a heat source is an inefficient way to heat a large house, it's a perfectly fine solution for small families who may relax adjacent to the fireplace for long periods of the evening. Fireplaces provide natural heat, and some people gravitate to the emotive smell and feel of a wood-burning fire. Fireplaces in historic houses are generally surrounded by mantles and hearths with incredible detail. Their reincarnation as functional and decorative heat sources accentuates such architectural detail better than a retired firebox.

Old coal boxes are typically too shallow for burning wood, but can be retrofitted for gas logs. Gas logs are expensive to operate and not particularly efficient, but they create a great ambiance as well as local heat on demand. Gas logs are either vented or ventless. Ventless logs do not require venting to the exterior; venting is, however, recommended for indoor air quality, particularly in a very tight house. While venting causes additional heat loss through the chimney, it minimizes the risk of carbon monoxide poisoning.

Old woodstoves are the efficiency equivalent of an SUV, wasting lots of energy to get from A to B. Because newer wood-burning appliances are much more efficient, a new stove working through an old chimney may be an appealing and sustainable retrofit.

Excluding the sun, fireplaces and woodstoves are the original method of heating, and they are enjoying a recent comeback as primary heating sources. As energy prices rise, some prefer burning wood found on their own property. A similar trend happened in the 1970s, but old wood stoves emitted significant pollution into the environment, which led to the creation of more stringent air quality regulations. In 1988, the EPA restricted the amount of particulate matter wood-burning appliances could emit, and states followed suit in the 1990s with even stricter regulations. The market for wood equipment all but disappeared.

Luckily, recent advances in wood-burning technology are making heaters more efficient and less polluting. Models work as stand alone units, retrofitted into hearths as inserts, and some even double as cooking appliances. They are built from cast iron or masonry. The most efficient units are variations of Russian and Finnish masonry stoves which can heat a whole house for 24 hours on a few sticks of wood. They are, however, bulky and may be impossible to retrofit into historic living space; additions may be an exception.

According to the US Hearth, Patio and Barbecue Association, the average home uses 100 million Btu annually, equivalent to $3,245 in fuel oil or $1,550 in natural gas. The same 100 million Btu could be produced for $945 in wood with an efficient wood appliance.[1]

Wood-burning furnaces and boilers are specialized pieces of equipment that create problematic pollution and have low energy efficiency. And most wood is not sustainably harvested. Consider your source, particularly if purchasing a large amount for fuel. It may help to establish a relationship with a local tree service or landscaper where you can get wood, and they could save on dump fees.

Alternative Systems and Considerations

While most existing and proposed HVAC systems are forced-air or radiator oriented,

Fig. 13.11:
A radiant floor rough-in prior to slab pour.

a myriad of other systems offer options for any situation. Like all systems, careful attention must be paid to preservation principles. A radiant floor may be the most efficient option but is inappropriate if one has to tear up original wood floors to install such a system. Additionally, the average HVAC company will know about only some of these options, so pursuing them may require consulting a green building expert.

Once the primary system is chosen, there are a few additional technologies to consider. Most people don't realize that there are a host of HVAC add-on options that can easily increase comfort, lower energy costs or both. In tending towards cheapest bid, it's common for HVAC subcontractors to not present these options, so be sure to ask.

Radiant floors heat a thermal mass, usually a concrete floor, by piping hot water through it. Masses such as concrete and stone retain heat well and can stay warm for hours after being heated. Radiant floors are

a popular design choice in modern green buildings. They have the added benefits of creating a slightly more humid air, adding moisture in the winter and being less noisy than central systems. They do not filter air, however, so an additional air filtration system is recommended.

Unfortunately, radiant floors are difficult to retrofit, since most old homes already have their slabs in place or no slab at all. Pouring a slab over original floors would not be appropriate in an historic house. There are ways to install radiant floors under wood floors, either through a very expensive specialty subfloor or underneath existing wood floors. However wood doesn't hold heat well so neither option is overwhelmingly efficient. Insulation is required underneath any radiant floor to ensure that the heat is directed upward to warm you. When radiant slabs are installed in contact with the earth without insulation, they lose their heat to the earth through heat sink. Even when retrofitting over an existing slab, insulation must be installed for this reason. Clients up on their green building technology often inquire about retrofit radiant floors; it may not be a feasible option because the ideal situation that yields energy gains *without* tearing out architectural detail rarely presents itself.

Humidification makes air more moist, and is performed by a *humidifier*. Humidifiers put water into the air. The case for and against humidifiers varies by region. The argument for humidifiers is that a winter house is uncomfortable if too dry. Dry air can parch the skin and mucus membranes. Manufacturers argue that adding moisture to the house is a good thing and can keep plaster from cracking. I think the plaster argument is suspect, particularly in wet southern states where humidifiers have less appeal anyway. I struggle to justify the conscious effort of putting moisture into a building since most old house problems can be traced to the presence of moisture. Contrarily, restoration contractors in arid Denver and Phoenix might install humidifiers as stock technology.

Dehumidification is the process of taking moisture out of the air, intentionally making it dryer and lowering humidity. The process is performed by a *dehumidifier*. Air conditioners naturally dehumidify, and in many humid regions dehumidification is desirable. Dehumidifiers can extract up to 91% more water vapor than a standard AC unit, and studies show that occupants feel more comfortable at higher real temperatures with lower humidity. Thus, on a 100°F Texas day, a dehumidified 78°F can feel more comfortable than a wet 70°F. That's an energy saver. On the negative side, dehumidifiers add resistance to the HVAC system and can cause the blower to work harder, costing additional money to operate. It's often a worthwhile cost; in removing water, dehumidification ensures a home's structural integrity and overall health. Central HVAC will do the heavy lifting, so the addition of an add-on dehumidifier is largely an occupant comfort issue. Variable speed units dehumidify the best. Some central HVAC units have humidity settings, even without the installation of a dehumidifier.

A *desuperheater* is a high-efficiency heat pump that recovers waste warmth from the heat pump's cooling mode and uses it to heat water. A desuperheater heat pump can heat water two to three times more efficiently than typical electric water heaters.

ERV/HRV

Energy recovery ventilators (ERVs) and *heat recovery ventilators* (HRVs) minimize air temperature differential and energy loss in a fresh-air vented system. ERVs are used in hot climates, HRVs in warm. Consider a 95°F summer day. Cold 72°F conditioned air inside the home becomes stale, so we mechanically vent it out of the house. We replace it with fresh 95°F air from the outside. The ERV allows for the incoming and exiting air to mix through a heat exchanger, cooling the incoming air with the outgoing.

Fresh air is, in this sense, energy inefficient. It'd be cheaper to return and recirculate stale 72°F air without introducing fresh air. But it would be less healthy. We sacrifice

Fig. 13.12: *ERVs save energy by tempering incoming fresh air with stale conditioned air.*

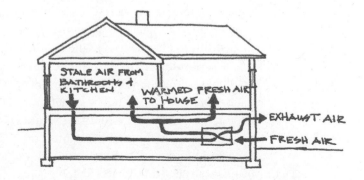

In 2003 ASHRAE 62.2 wrote the first residential ventilation standard that gives builders and designers guidelines for providing good indoor air while keeping costs low. It's not code, but may soon become so. In short, install

- 50 cubic feet per minute whole house mechanical ventilation
- 100 cubic feet per minute minimum vented range hood
- 50 cubic feet per minute minimum vented bath fan
- Fans that must not exceed maximum noise standards
- Airtight garage ducts to avoid carbon monoxide poisoning
- Filtration upstream from air handlers to filter particulate matter from the coil and blower, which would not be caught in a traditional grate return

energy to have high quality breathable air, and the ERV helps minimize additional energy loads.

Ventilation, Ductwork and Air Filtration

In old buildings, ventilation occurs inadvertently through old walls, penetrations, roofs, chimneys and the absence of insulation or air sealing. Preservationists have named this inadvertent ventilation *breathing*, a misleading term that implies it's a good thing. Building scientists, on the other hand, note that a leaky house is inefficient to run and subject to Mother Nature's wrath. In a tight house it's essential that fresh air is supplied. The burden of fresh air is thus transferred from accidental leaks to

a ventilated mechanical system, with fresh air delivered and stale air expelled through a system of vents and ducts. In addressing these concerns building scientist Max Sherman coined the mantra *if you build tight, you must ventilate right.*

In modern houses air is pressurized and pushed by an air handler with a blower fan. The air is circulated through the structure then returned to the air handler through a return, for reconditioning. Variable speed blowers are an important component of any efficient system. They keep air moving at a near constant velocity, minimize hot and cold between cycles and eradicate noise because the fan rarely runs at full speed. Lower speeds put less pressure on the system, which lowers costs and increases component operating life.

Forced-air systems have the added benefit of being able to filter away particulate matter from the air. The filter is typically located at the return(s) or at the air handler. Dust, pollen, mold and bacteria can all be captured in the air return cycle, enhancing indoor air quality. The cheapest filters do little more than keep the cat out of the ductwork. Pleated electrostatic filters catch pollen, mold spores and dust mite debris. Specialized filters with activated carbon and potassium permanganate can also remove gases from the home, effectively removing odors, smoke, ozone, cleaning chemicals, paint fumes and even formaldehyde.

Filter efficiencies are rated by their *Minimum Efficient Reporting Value* (MERV), ranging from 1-16. The higher the number the better, corresponding with a greater percentage of the particles captured in each pass through. Filters with rating MERV 8-13 are typically provided by local hardware stores. Contrarily, the higher MERV rating, the more resistance to air flow. Thus, as with an ERV, you can sacrifice energy efficiency in favor of air quality. If allergies are an issue in your household, high MERV filters are a wise investment. Filters must be replaced every few months and can be purchased in bulk online for about half the price of a big box home store. Changing air filters is the building equivalent of changing the oil in your car. It's common for this basic maintenance to be overlooked, which can make a very efficient system operate very poorly.

Ductwork carries tempered air into, through and out of a structure. The unit of measurement in duct design is *cubic feet per minute* (cfm). Bedrooms may require supply air of 100 cubic feet per minute, and a crawl space 50 cubic feet per minute. Bath fans exhaust 80-150 cubic feet per minute and are sized by the square footage of a bathroom.

Ductwork comes in four types; galvanized steel, pre-insulated aluminum, fiberglass non-metallic and flexible tubing. Galvanized steel is typically fabricated and then wrapped with exterior insulation to minimize heat loss during distribution, noise during transfer and condensation from cool air. Pre-insulated aluminum panels are manufactured off-site and fabricated in the field, then wrapped with aluminum. Fiberglass non-metallic duct board is similar to the pre-insulated aluminum, but closed with staples or metal-backed tape. Flexible tubing (flex) is thin plastic over a metal wire coil, covered in R-4 fiberglass insulation and another layer of plastic. Flex is quick and cheaper to install than metallic systems, but it yields higher pressure loss than other types of ducts and requires runs of less than 15 feet, minimal turns and elimination of kinks.

Old ductwork is probably uninsulated. If it is in good shape, it's possible to retrofit insulation with a duct wrap. This can sometimes be less expensive than replacing ductwork. Lawrence Berkley National Laboratory found that retrofitting between R-2 and R-4 to uninsulated ductwork reduced summer energy consumption 18-24%. Insulation above that level had diminishing returns.

Duct leakage is a huge and all-too-common problem. Air seeps through metal, insulation and plastic at transfer points between air handlers, registers and other ductwork, where it should be fully sealed with a mastic tape. Fly-by-night contractors will use only zip ties (which have virtually no air sealing qualities) to secure ducts because mastic and foil tape is more expensive. Ironically, despite its name duct tape is not allowed, as the adhesive dries and breaks the seal over time, making it not appropriate for any long-term construction use.

Building science engineers have documented that 25-30% of energy is lost through underinsulated or improperly installed ductwork. Leakage is almost always unknown to the building occupant. Plumbing or electrical system leaks can have catastrophic results. HVAC leakage rarely threatens building failure; it's simply paid for in incrementally higher utility bills. In fact, building inspections highly regulate and test for electric and plumbing system leakage, but require no similar testing on HVAC.

For a few hundred dollars, energy auditors will perform *duct blaster* tests which pressurize the ductwork by blowing colored air into the return and sealing the registers. Any excess air will blow through the leaks. Duct blaster tests measure how much air is leaking, allowing an expert to recommend necessary sealing measures to create maximum air flow and efficiency.

Manual D is a prescriptive instruction for properly designed and sized residential ductwork. It works in tandem with the Manual J, which qualifies proper equipment size. The Manual D sizes duct equipment

High velocity duct systems use two-inch ducts and force air up to ten times faster than traditional ducts. Ducts that small can theoretically be fished through existing walls. Outlets are about the size of a CD. Often seen in house museums, they're worth considering in homes where HVAC upgrades are a must but duct runs are problematic and walls cannot be demolished. Because their registers are a different size and shape, they're not great as a replacement option for most HVAC. They'd leave you having to patch up old register penetrations which would involve major wood floor weaving.

Fig. 13.13-15: *A duct blaster being performed: a high-powered fan is hooked to the return, and all supply ducts sealed. The engineer will measure and identify leakage.*

and factors in basic principles of blower efficiency, pressure loss, duct size, junction box resistance, duct leakage, envelope performance and noise control. When installing a new system or performing major upgrades, it's smart to ask your installer to perform a Manual D analysis or have it done by a third party energy auditor.

Venting is also required on dryers, bath fans, gas furnaces, gas water heaters and is not required but highly recommended on range fans. Most appliance venting is simple three to four-inch flex tubing, terminated through the roof, soffit or exterior wall. By code, mechanical venting is required in bathrooms that do not have three square feet of operable window space. Even with this low threshold, it's wise to install venting in all bathrooms, because it helps move stale air and helps pressure balance a tight home. Finally, while code does not require venting ranges to the exterior, it is no-brainer to do so. When burnt grilled cheese or bacon fill a house with smoke, simple mechanical ventilation moves the odor outside.

Whole house fans are installed in a building's ceiling and designed to force cool air into the house and hot air into the attic by accelerating the stack effect. Blowing air into the attic forces the extremely hot air out of the attic through the soffit, gable and ridge vent, which also cools the home. The fans are inexpensive to install and run, much less expensive than air conditioning. They're common retrofits in many historic houses and popular with those who have and use them, though their loud noise can

be objectionable. Whole house fans are a bit problematic to install in very tight houses, and their benefit is debatable when used in tandem with a sealed attic.

Sustainability

While this chapter focuses on the options to make mechanical systems most efficient, let us not forget that the least expensive method of heating, venting and cooling is to open the windows. It costs nothing to do so, and luckily, in our 100-year-old homes, the windows were designed for this exact purpose. Window operability, covered in chapter 11, is really an HVAC issue.

Coincidentally, old homes also might have the benefit of massive shade trees that shield the house from the direct heat gain of the summer sun. It is estimated that a large oak shadowing your entire roof is the

Running Gas Lines

HVAC contractors generally install all gas lines, even those that are not directly associated with heating or cooling. Gas lines can serve ranges, ovens, water heaters, dryers and fireplaces.

Black iron gas pipe is common in old homes; it was threaded in defined lengths and installed like copper pipe. It often does not meet modern code standards, and inspectors might balk at the expansion of such systems. Stainless steel flex pipe, usually seen in a corrugated yellow sleeve, is the modern standard — simple to run and installed more like electrical wire with fewer junctions. Gas line installation requires a professional in nearly all jurisdictions.

Since gas lines are not necessarily tied to a heat pump or furnace, it's common for do-it-yourselfers to overlook the cost and underestimate the budget for these items.

Fig. 13.16: *A massive oak tree shades the home in the summer. Its direct blockage of the sun in the summer dramatically lowers energy demands. Leaves fall off in the winter, and the sun heats the home.*

equivalent of running four tons of HVAC all summer. Consider your increased energy bills before removing any shade trees.

It's best to reconcile your climate with your comfortable temperature range and budget. If you live in Southern California where the temperature is always 60-80°F and you are comfortable with any temperature in that range, then an expensive, super efficient HVAC system is of little use to you. In North Carolina, some use their systems 12 months of the year, others five or six. Those that use mechanical systems more should dedicate more of their rehabilitation budget to high-quality systems.

Modern HVAC systems are complex, but their operation should be largely automated and simplified. Any central systems should be run by *a programmable thermostat* that automates predefined temperature settings when you wake, go to work, return home and go to bed. Since you will be automatically demanding less energy when no one is home, they pay for themselves in as little as a year. The best programmable thermostats allow for separate programs for weekdays and weekends. Most HVAC installers install non-programmable thermostats by default, so it's

Fig. 13.17-18: *Center, an asbestos-wrapped boiler pipe with deteriorated outer skin (evident by the non-smooth surface), a sign it is likely friable and needs to be addressed. Bottom, an underground storage tank (UST) is pumped empty and removed from the site to ensure against a fuel spill. Its metal shell is recycled as scrap.*

best to request an upgrade. Some thermostats also measure and control humidity and have onboard humidistats too. Though typically used in tandem with add-on dehumidifiers, some variable speed air handlers can adjust fan speed to meet humidity preferences.

All systems require a maintenance schedule, including filter replacement. At least once a year conduct a visual review, check for loose fans and duct connections and ensure that any condensers are free from landscaping overgrowth.

Old HVAC systems can feature environmental hazards. Asbestos-wrapped boiler piping is very common. When flaking and friable, it needs to be addressed as a priority. Where it is in good shape, it is usually best left alone and encapsulated to prevent future deterioration.

Preservation

HVAC systems mostly reside behind the scenes. During an upgrade, a subcontractor may have a tendency to throw out old devices, requiring a DIYer or general contractor to go out of their way to protect such old materials. Terminal devices such as returns, grates and radiators are subtle details in a home and during an HVAC upgrade are most at risk of damage or deletion. Systems come and go, but most old finishes can work with modern systems with little or no modification.

Residual architectural details from old HVAC that can be creatively reused should be reused. Sometimes owners will keep architectural radiators for their look, even

Fig. 13.19-21: *Top, old radiators are sometimes kept in place as decoration, even after they are made nonfunctional. Center, a ghostmark wood patch indicates the placement of an old radiator pipe. Bottom, a new central system return claims a former closet, which is then uniquely turned into a nook for art display.*

when functionally retiring them in favor of central systems. Fireplaces, their fireboxes, hearths and mantles should be retained. Firebox interiors often require rehabilitation with high- heat bricks or cement. While a firebox might undergo a total reconstruction, careful effort should be made to retain and rehabilitate its original hearth, mantle and tile detail.

When an architectural element is removed, there may be an opportunity to leave a ghostmark. Radiator piping requires sizable holes in wood floors. On one job, we patched these holes with wood that was intentionally differentiated from the surrounding wood, creating a ghostmark feature which showed off the old system.

Old chimneys can require major work to make them functional again. Often a decision is made to retire the chimney flue by sealing the damper penetration rather than repairing it. When this is done, care should be taken to ensure that the chimney could be rehabilitated at a future date. Above the roofline, brickwork often fails from years of exposure to the elements. Any chimney at risk of failure needs to be removed or rebuilt. Deletion of chimneys can be a major preservation sticking point, particularly if they are viewable from the streetscape.

Given how large and bulky HVAC systems can be, placement can be tricky. Access to furnaces and air handlers must meet code clearances and often requires new penetrations in basement or crawl space walls or attic stair drop downs. Sometimes there is no great place to install these new access holes, creating eyesores in otherwise historic quarters.

One of the major upgrade challenges is running ductwork to areas of a house that have never had service and were never designed for ductwork, returns and registers. Ductwork can be routed through utility spaces like attics and basements, but sometimes require chases. Chases are best limited to existing closets or secondary living spaces. Sometimes there is just no way around it and obstructions must be added to primary living spaces; check this with SHPOs to ensure it doesn't become a tax credit issue.

It's common for old systems to be abandoned in place, rather than removed. Many old boilers are too large, heavy and rusted to remove. If they are not in the way, there's no need to deal with the cost of demolition and removal. Historically, little effort has been made to preserve rough systems or the spaces they exist in, and they are not typically reviewed by SHPOs or subject to tax credit scrutiny.

Remember, historically nature was used to adjust the temperature. That's preservation and sustainability to a tee. Use of the window is still, and will always be, the most energy-efficient heating and cooling method.

ELECTRICAL

There are old electricians, and there are foolish electricians.
But there are no old foolish electricians.

— Trade Saying

14

Any remodel project comes with an opportunity to upgrade the electrical system. Over 40% of American homes were built before 1940, which means they were originally wired under an extremely outdated version of the National Electric Code, assuming they were wired with any code at all. In the 70 years since there's been no shortage of opportunity for material degradation, amateur wiring and technological obsolescence. Any project should clarify existing conditions, outline new demands and carefully plan what upgrades are necessary to meet modern safety standards.

Safety is the primary ingredient in electrical codes. Modern technology is efficient, practical and safe. A century ago today's safety mechanisms did not exist. Grounding, fault protection, varying wire gauges, 240V appliances and breakers were all yet to be invented. Modern systems in old homes operate everything from simple lightbulbs to powerful heat pumps, electric ranges and hair dryers, and these demands require net five to ten times the capacity of a typical house's original wiring.

While modern systems are great, old fixtures can be major, character-defining features of a home. Where original fixtures do not exist, period replication fixtures can become focal points of design. A good green restoration balances these factors, keeping the charm of the finishes while making the rough systems safe, simple and serviceable for years to come.

Questions to Ask

- How old is the electrical system?

- What sort of wiring was used, and is it safe?
- What amperage service does the home have?
- What upgrades can I do now that will allow for future work?
- Are there enough receptacles?
- Are any of the light fixtures original, and can they be salvaged?
- What lightbulbs are primarily used in the home?
- How can I get the light I need while minimizing energy usage?

Electrical Basics

Electricity functions a lot like water. Household water typically has a reservoir source, electricity a power generation station. Water flows through pipes, electricity flows between differences in potential, a charge between its source and the ground. Each has a continuous current flow. By design, an electrical charge must form a loop and return to its source. Along that path, electricity performs work. It turns on lights and computers, it runs fans and refrigerators. It can also electrocute humans should they choose to put themselves in the way.

Electricity originates at a generator, typically from a large, faraway power station, but sometimes it is microgenerated on-site. It travels via *alternating current* (AC), which is easily transmitted over long distances. Power in towns and cities is transferred via high voltage power lines to a step-down transformer outside the house. The transformer reduces the voltage pressure from a typical 7,000+V to 110V, a pressure home electronics can handle. Unlike *direct current* (DC), AC cycle changes polarity (+/-) every 60 seconds, called 60Hz. On quiet nights, you can actually hear the hum of the polarity cycle.

Electricity is brought from the transformer to a *weathermast* as three wires, two 110V hots and a single neutral. The two hots can be combined to provide power for 220V devices, such as electric ranges, dryers, water heaters and heat pumps. From the weathermast, power goes through a utility *meter*, to an *electrical* or *circuitry panel*

Fig. 14.1: *A comparison of systems.*

Problem	Plumbing	Electrical	HVAC
Minor Leak	irritating drip	minor shock/fire hazzard	typically unknown
Major Leak	flooding and eventual structural failure	electrocution/death	high utility bills, overstressed system
Pressure	pounds per square inch (psi)	volt (V)	pascals
Rate	gallons per minute (gpm)	ampere (A)	cubic feet per minute (cfm)
Friction/Resistance	poises	ohm (Ω)	resistance
Loss over Long Distance	pressure loss	voltage drop	air change per hour (ach)
Utility Meter	cubic foot	kilowatt hour (kWh)	non specific

where it is distributed to various circuits for lights, appliances and receptacles. Safety devices such as surge protectors and ground rods are added to protect property and life.

A disproportionate amount of the modern electrical codes deals with preventing injury. Leaks happen: wire becomes overheated, is disturbed by a remodel project, is eaten by rodents or is hit by a screw meant to hang a picture. During an electrical leak, current will run continuously from the leak unless a protective device shorts the circuit. The US National Electrical Code (NEC) now mandates this protection by requiring all electrical devices to be grounded. A bare copper wire is designed to take a current to ground more directly than to a human, ensuring circuits will break before catastrophic events occur. Safety mechanisms are designed to ensure the ground does not run through you. Remember: electrical current always wants to run to ground, and it will run through a dishwasher or a nervous system to get there. Old wiring lacks grounding, so this protection is generally absent from old circuits.

A *short* allows more current to flow through a wire than it is designed for, resulting in heat and eventually breakdown. A fuse or circuit breaker is designed to break the circuit before damage occurs. A *fuse* is a thin wire that is designed to break when overheated, cutting the circuit. A *circuit breaker* trips to the off position when heated and is reset easily by flipping in back to the on position. In the absence of such protective devices, the circuit is unsafe.

Fig. 14.2-3: *Electricity comes to the home through an elevated weathermast, through protective conduit to the meter and on to the circuitry panel. Generally speaking the homeowner is responsible for all maintenance beyond the meter, and the utility for everything on the other side.*

There are two types of shorts, both dangerous. *Low-resistance shorts* combine low resistance and high current. They cause electrocution and are most common in the presence of water, such as the fabled hairdryer or TV falling into the bathtub. A *ground fault circuit interrupters* (GFCI) is designed to protect against fatal electric shocks and is required by electrical codes in water-prone locations.

High-resistance shorts feature high resistance and low current. They come from corrosion and loose connections and cause arcs, which cause fires. An electrical arc forms when a current flows through a medium that is usually non-conductive, such as air or cloth. Arcs form a visual spark, usually acute. A good example is the subway car pickup cleat arcing with the third rail. Frayed electrical wire is a risk for arcing. Forty thousand fires are attributed to faulty wiring each year, many rooted in extension cords powering technology in living rooms and bedrooms. Each year fires from high-resistance shorts cause 350 deaths and 1,400 injuries, most of which could be avoided with simple *arc fault circuit interrupter* (AFCI) protection. AFCIs are required in bedrooms and living spaces, where arcing is most common.

Rough Electrical Systems

Historic homes on average are often on their second or third electrical system. Some may have remnants of four or more which may be in a failing condition or be working flawlessly. It's common to find a combination of issues from years of tinkering, localized repairs and remodels, amateur work and functional obsolescence. Each issue can be addressed as part of an upgrade strategy.

For the purposes of this book, the rough electrical system starts at the *electrical panel.* Currently, the NEC requires a minimum 100 ampere (A) service. Most homes need 200A, the practical default for any new service. Homes over 4,000 square feet may require 300A or even 400A service. That's a whole lot of current.

It's not uncommon for old homes to have an undersized 60A or even 30A service. If the home had few appliances and no air conditioning, that may have been enough

Fig. 14.4-5: *Top, a 30A panel is insufficient for modern living. Bottom, a modern 200A 40/40 panel offers plenty of room for expansion and modification.*

to get by. But it's usually way too small for modern life. Nearly all panels state their maximum service amperage on or inside the panel. Any service under 200A is a prime candidate for upgrade.

The panel should be placed where it is easily accessible. I prefer them to be inside the house, easily reachable during inclement weather. Be aware, electricians like to mount the panel on the exterior, often next to the utility meter, minimizing the length of expensive feeder cable. If replacing the panel, spend the extra money to get a large 200A 40/40 box, which allows for 40 spaces and 40 circuits. This leaves plenty of room for a clean installation, legible labeling and future upgrades. It might cost $20 extra.

On old electrical panels, breakers were sometimes added to fuse lines as overcurrent protection, and they can be 40 years old, past expected life span. Breakers do wear out over time and should be tested if believed to be decades old. Verifying that a breaker this old works is smart, and can be done by a specialty tool that intentionally shorts the circuit and measures the time between the short and the breaker trip. It can be cost prohibitive to replace some old

The Anatomy Of A Rewire

There are many different strategies for rewiring. If you are gutting, rewiring an old home is little different than new construction. If you are not, electrical work is more of a surgical procedure. Access is the problem, requiring exploratory work, strategic demolition and fishing. The baseboard approach consists of removing baseboards and using the exposed cavity as a chase. Run the wire, then reinstall baseboards.

Keep in mind that a cheap stud detector may be worthless in an old home because plaster lath forms a near continuous wood surface, and the tool can't differentiate between lath and studs. Pilot holes or exploration via crawl space, attic or baseboard may provide clues to stud placement and spacing. Sixteen inches on center is typical, though old homes have all kinds of weird patterns.

You can also run new wire by cutting a chase with circular saw. If you do so, be sure to set depth to match stud depth. Do not use jig or reciprocating saws, as you're guaranteed to cut something you don't want to slice.

Note that sawing or drilling holes in plaster will cause splits in the plaster. There is no paper face to hold back the gypsum, lime and sand material, and it quickly creates a mess that's difficult to patch.

Fig. 14.6: *Electrical work is easy where wiring is accessible in basements and attics. It is difficult where wire is hidden in walls and between finished floors.*

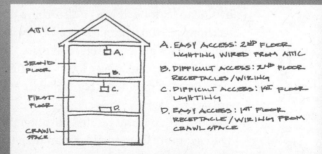

breakers, and the test can at least give you confidence that the safety mechanism is functioning properly.

Beyond the panel, you'll find a variety of *wire*. I've found when people upgrade electrical wiring, they tend to retire the existing wire in place, not bothering to remove it. This adds to confusion when tracing and trying to make sense of wiring in a crawl space or attic. Some will be active, some long-retired. A simple voltage detector pen is a useful tool to see what's active and what's not.

Although many things in old houses are better than their new counterparts — like plaster versus sheetrock — this is not true with electrical wire. New wire, of which there are a dozen or so common varieties, is vastly superior to the old stuff. That's not to say all old wire must be upgraded. Often a plan calls for wiring upgrades to offices, kitchens, bathrooms and selective electronics areas. Circuits that are functioning fine and carry minimal loads can be left alone.

Knob-and-tube wiring is still extremely common. There is nothing inherently dangerous about knob-and-tube wiring, provided you respect the limits of what it can and can't do. Where it's functioning and you are able to not disturb its surrounding, it's actually fine to let it be. If you're disturbing the area, however, you'll definitely need to rewire. If the insulating mesh is frayed, replace the wire. If you are insulating a knob-and-tube cavity or extending the circuit, replace the wire.

All sorts of hazards result from attempting to get more from an old circuit than it's designed for. Don't add *anything* to it and don't overload it. Old circuits may be designed to drive a couple of 1A lightbulbs, not an electric range. Don't upsize the fuse if it blows. A blown fuse is explicit evidence of overcurrent on the circuit, evidence that shouldn't be taken lightly or ignored.

A century ago, nearly all wiring was the same *gauge*. Today, we drive equipment with a wide variety of energy loads and corresponding wire sizing. Heavier gauges typically wire water heaters, dryers and heat pumps. The smaller the gauge number, the larger the wire. The first number of wire name indicates the gauge. 12-2 wire is adequate for most of the house, serving receptacles, lights and switches. 14-2 can handle lower voltage loads and is often substituted for 12-2 common wire to save the installer a few bucks on material. 14-3 wire is used for *three ways*, where two separate switches run a single light. Three way wire is a more expensive, premium wire and since lights require little amperage, 14 gauge wire is perfectly acceptable. Where a high schooler or older rock star wannabe plugs in a 750W bass guitar amplifier, however, it is not. To completely wire a typical 2,000-square-foot house requires 12 to 15 250-foot rolls of 12-2, four to six rolls of 14-2 and three rolls of 14-3.

Circuits terminate at *switches* and *receptacles*. Switches were once exclusively knob-and-tube push styles. Modern switches that match this style are available and growing in popularity for their retro feel. Faceplates offer more variety in finish styles, with options only limited by your imagination. Some homeowners match the switch plates to the furniture or electrical fixture, others might install a custom ceramic piece from a local art fair. Note that without specific instruction, an electrician will install basic white or almond switches, receptacles and faceplates. If you don't specify such finishes, expect basic default materials from the installer.

Structured wiring is a modern data transfer system that allows for nearly limitless high speed use and transfer of information. It's typically installed by an electrician or a specialist. Structured wiring replaces the common telephone *Bell* wire, which is fundamentally the same piece of communication technology on which Alexander Graham Bell called Watson in 1875. Traditionally wired with Category 5 (Cat 5) wire (and increasingly Cat 6) and often bundled with RG6 for high definition television, structured wiring consists of four twisted pairs of 23 gauge wire, each capable of carrying computer data, access to servers, intercoms, security camera, music, telephone, fax and internet at high speed. All terminate at a central panel that coordinates connections.

For homes that expect huge multimedia demands, *fiber optics* offer the most bandwidth and options and have recently been made affordable. A single fiber optic line can carry data equivalent to all the phone conversations going on in the US simultaneously. In a residential setting fiber optics are an unnecessary overkill right now, though it may be beneficial down the road. I wonder what sort of data demands my three-year-old will have when he's in high school.

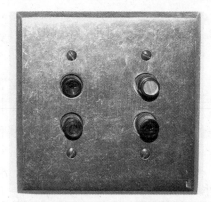

Fig. 14.7: *Retro knob-and-tube looking push buttons are available for about $20 per set, a great old house feel restoration feature.*

Structured wiring is a smart upgrade for any modern family. It's a particularly useful communication tool in large houses and for families, such as academics and researchers, who store or transfer significant amount of data for work. It is best installed during gut jobs as retrofit installations through finished walls can be four times the cost, or plaster walls even more. Always install structured wiring after rough electrical. The structured wiring must generally stay away from 110V and 220V lines which cause electromagnetic interference.

Wireless systems are a great data transfer alternative when walls must be kept in place. Wireless systems typically only service the internet and phone, though technology exists for television too. Still, wireless systems transfer only one 10 megabit datastream, 1,000 times slower than Cat 5. And, of course, there are more security issues with wireless data transmission.

Finishes

In 1900, electricity was a luxury reserved for the rich and urban. Most lighting came from table lamps serviced by long, heavy and dangerously fire-prone cords. As late as 1921, only eight million households in the US were wired; by 1926, the number had increased by 75%. By then, most fixtures were controlled by a switch, rather than a pull cord. In 1930s literature, lighting marketers pitch electric light as a cure for irritability, nervous disorders, headaches and (my favorite) backward children.

The period between 1925 and 1940 witnessed a dramatic expansion of lighting design converging Colonial Revival, Arts and Crafts, Art Deco and Eclectic styles. Colonial Revival fixtures are simple, functional, unpretentious and quintessentially American. Victorian tend to be more ornate, and Arts and Crafts geometric. The 1925 Paris World Fair showcased many transitional designs, and in particular launched the Art Moderne style of sleek, machine-styled shapes which was later called Art Deco. Deco was popular through the mid-20th century and, though out of favor for decades, has recently been revived. Many fixtures and appliances from the 1930s through 1950s show Deco characteristics, representing America's yearning for a more aerodynamic future. One is left to wonder, however, about the technological benefits of an aerodynamic fridge.

Through history, light has been supplied by four primary sources: the sun, candles, combustible fuels and electricity. While candles and combustible fuels have been rightfully retired and candles will always remain popular for romantic evenings, sustainable building focuses on better utilizing natural light and making any artificial light efficient and targeted for specific uses.

Fig. 14.8:
Architectural Eras of US Historic Homes.

Victorian	1860-1910
Arts and Crafts (Craftsman)	1900-1930
Colonial Revival	1905-1935
Deco/Moderne	1925-1940
Modern	1950-

Fig. 14.9-11:
Original fixtures are a treasure to find. If they are present, be sure to keep and rehabilitate.

A *lighting fixture* consists of the device that creates the light plus an artistic housing that often specifies its architectural style and time period.

There are a variety of suppliers offering period fixtures. Rejuvenation breaks down their catalogues into periods, a layperson's tool for matching fixture style to era. With a few exceptions, you can match your house's construction date with their catalogue schedule and get great results. This approach works best with simple lighting, since fixtures that are fussy require more careful matching to architectural style.

Stylistically, it's difficult to pull off lighting fixtures inconsistent with the era of house. Craftsman lighting will never look right in a strictly Victorian house, no matter how beautiful the fixture. Many lights pawned off as contemporary are really modern fixtures trying to be something from a previous era. Selection of such fixtures gives a false sense of time and place and is generally discouraged as a violation of preservation ethic.

Light Sources

Since the aesthetic housing uses no energy itself, efficiency issues can be pinned to the light source: the bulb. Fixtures come in many shapes and sizes, each requiring a different number and type of bulbs. Considerations include bulb shape, generation method, energy usage and color temperature.

Many original fixtures feature an exposed bulb, but this is less common with modern fixtures. When the bulb is exposed, it can

Standard Incandescent Bulb (watts)	ENERGY STAR® Qualified CFL (approximate equivalent watts)	Minimum Light Output (lumens)
40	10	450
60	15	800
75	20	1100
100	29	1600
150	38	2600

NATURAL RESOURCES CANADA

Fig. 14.12: *Wattage Equivalency Guide.*

limit options for what type of bulb is aesthetically appropriate. Spiral compact fluorescent bulbs can make a gorgeous original fixture look rather tacky. Until recently, exposed-bulb fixtures offered little alternative to inefficient incandescent. In 2008, CFLs and LEDs began mass production in a variety of shapes, targeting this exposed-bulb market. It may take some digging and price comparison, but the existence of these appropriately shaped and efficient bulbs addresses the last and final objection to replacing an incandescent bulb.

Lighting consumes 22% of all electricity in the US and the same ratio worldwide, a number that could be cut in half with the simple retirement of incandescent bulbs. By 2025, when we get completely off incandescents, it is estimated that lighting efficiencies will negate the need for 130 new power stations. CFLs and specific LEDs are excellent options to replace incandescents.

Incandescent bulbs pass an electric current through a thin filament, burning it to the point where it creates light. The bulb is fundamentally the same as Thomas Edison's original design 130 years ago. Incandescent bulbs are cheap and widely available. Unfortunately, 90% of the bulb's energy is lost as heat, a major inefficiency for a device whose primary function is to provide light. Heat is merely a wasted by-product. In fact, incandescents produce so much heat that an extremely tight house can actually be heated on incandescents alone. In hot climates, the heat produced by incandescent bulbs works against air conditioners, causing equipment to work harder and longer.

Halogen lamps are types of incandescents that last four times longer than traditional incandescents. They generally have non-compatible ballasts, specific to fixtures that require halogen light such as track lighting. Halogens give off a more bluish-white light than other incandescents. They get hotter than incandescents and can pose fire and burn hazards. You can actually get a sunburn from a halogen light. *Heat lamps* are another incandescent bulb used for the primary purpose of emitting heat (typically a meter-spinning 250W) and are installed in bathrooms and covered by a red filter to minimize their extremely bright visible light. Heat lamps are so hot they will melt plastic and thus require ceramic sockets.

Compared with modern alternatives, incandescents are extremely inefficient not only in terms of wasted energy but in longevity. Incandescents average 750 hours of service life, a fraction of the life of more efficient cooler burning bulbs described below. They're still the norm in the United States, though most Western countries are gradually phasing them out. The European Union is committed to phase out by 2012. The United States Clean Energy Act of 2007 effectively banned common incandescents by 2014.

Compact fluorescents (CFLs) use electricity to excite a mercury vapor, emitting light. They consume $1/5$th the energy of incandescents. Their spiral shape is a modification of fluorescent bulbs long common in commercial applications. CFLs are widely available for a few bucks each, costs having come down considerably, becoming the preferred replacement bulb. Some states, notably California, now require CFL installation in new kitchens and bathrooms. There are some notable downsides to CFLs: there are issues with motion sensors and dimmers, where metallic ballasts can cause interference. Electronic solid state ballasts avoid this problem but are more expensive and harder to find. Because the mercury in them is poisonous, CFLs must be disposed of carefully via hazardous waste. They cannot be thrown away in the regular trash. Florescent flicker can be harmful to epileptics. Their life is shortened when they are turned on and off frequently so they should not be installed in areas like hallways. Lastly, bulky size prevents CFLs from being used in some applications. I've had trouble getting CFLs to work with many compact fan light housings. CFLs average 15,000 hours of service life.

A *light emitting diode* (LED) is a small semi-conductor diode that turns an electrical current directly into light in the direction the device is pointing. They produce almost no heat, so all energy can be directed to lighting. LEDs consume $1/10$th the energy of incandescents, and roughly half the energy of CFLs. They last up to 60,000 hours, on average 40 times as long as incandescents. There are some challenges with directional lighting, which engineers are working diligently to solve. LEDs offer a variety of customization options and have few of the limitation of CFLs. LED lighting has been prohibitively expensive until recently. As prices come down, experts predict LEDs will come to dominate the light source marketplace.

The life cycle savings of efficient bulbs are well documented.

Lights that last 60,000 hours might not need changing in several human lifetimes. If used four hours a day, a LED will last 41 years. This saves time, hassle, ladders going in and out of the house, fall risk and material waste.

A Brief History of Electrical Systems

In any older home you're going to run into remnants of old wiring. A timeline study of residential electrical can be fascinating, but the fact is it's useful to know what you're working with and important to understand old wiring's associated risks. As a bonus, sometimes old systems can give clues to past modifications to the home, such as where the original kitchen was located.

Thomas Edison played a fatherly role in the development of electricity. In 1879,

	60-Watt Incandescent	15-Watt CFL (ENERGY STAR)
Initial cost (a)	$0.50	$6.99
Light output (lumens)	800	800
Life (hours)	1000	9000
Replacement light bulbs (b)	8 x $0.50 = $4.00	-
Lifetime electricity cost (c)	9000 hours x 60 x $0.08/kWh = $43.20	9000 hours x 15 x $0.08/kWh = $10.80
Total lifetime cost (a + b + c)	$47.70	$17.79
Life Savings	-	$29.91

NATURAL RESOURCES CANADA

Fig. 14.13:
Life Cycle Cost Comparisons.

Edison refined the first incandescent bulb, which lasted 40 hours and was subsequently marketed commercially. He remarked, "We will make electricity so cheap that only the rich will burn candles."

Knob-and-tube became the first major wiring system, in use from 1880-1930s as the least expensive option, and eventually dominated the marketplace. Thomas Edison's design used three paper-and-cloth insulated conductors mounted on wooden cleats spaced four feet apart. Porcelain cleats quickly replaced wood. When the wire needed to change direction, early electricians wound it around a porcelain knob. When the electrician wanted to pass through a joist or stud he drilled a small hole, and inserted a porcelain tube for the wire to pass through. Branches were soldered together. Knob-and-tube provided reasonable protection by separating the hot wire (with constant live current) from the neutral.

Electricity dramatically improved quality of life, accelerating its implementation.

As more electrocutions and fires took place, electricity quickly became a concern for politicians and insurers. By the turn of the 20th century, safety was paramount. In 1897, insurance companies and fire marshals pressured for adoption of the first National Electrical Code, prior to which electricity had been unregulated, dangerous and somewhat experimental.

In the 1900s spiral-bound flexible armored cable conduit (named *Greenfield* after the inventor of the most successful brand) allowed wire to be snaked through walls. Otherwise known as BX after the GE product name, Greenfield was extremely popular from 1910s-1930s and existed for decades after. Some BX featured grounding; some did not. Professionals used to retrofit the

Color temperature is a measurement of light's color chromaticity, measured in Kelvin (K). Temperature can alter moods and setting, so it's an important consideration in lighting design. Temperatures around 5000K produce cool, blue green colors, while 2700K produces warm, yellow red colors. Cool is best for visual tasks in an office, kitchen or workshop. Warm light is best for living space and is considered more complimentary to skin tones. Most residential lighting falls in the 2700-3600K range.

Some find CFL light too harsh and office-like, though CFLs are now available in spectrums as low as 2700K. *Full Spectrum bulbs* produce light in the 5500K range, comparable to daylight. They are often prescribed by doctors to combat seasonal affective disorder, common in northern regions where there is minimal sunshine in the winter months. Phosphor formulas have been modified to lower the color temperature of soft white CFLs, making them better suited to replace cooler incandescents.

In a single room, it's best to use lighting with similar color temperatures. Poor lighting can cause stress; mixed temperature lighting drives me crazy. Also, paint can look wildly different under different color temperatures of light, so paint swatches should be tested under the proposed lighting of the room — typically paint suppliers offer a variety of artificial lights to conduct such a test.

Fig. 14.14

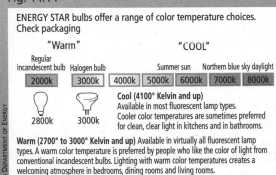

ENERGY STAR bulbs offer a range of color temperature choices. Check packaging

"Warm" "COOL"

Regular incandescent bulb / Halogen bulb / Summer sun / Northern blue sky daylight

| 2000k | 3000k | 4000k | 5000k | 6000k | 7000k | 8000k |

2800k 3000k

Cool (4100° Kelvin and up)
Available in most fluorescent lamp types.
Cooler color temperatures are sometimes preferred for clean, clear light in kitchens and in bathrooms.

Warm (2700° to 3000° Kelvin and up) Available in virtually all fluorescent lamp types. A warm color temperature is preferred by people who like the color of light from conventional incandescent bulbs. Lighting with warm color temperatures creates a welcoming atmosphere in bedrooms, dining rooms and living rooms.

US DEPARTMENT OF ENERGY

Fig. 14.15

Color Temperature	Source
1700 K	Match flame
1850 K	Candle flame
2800–3300 K	Incandescents
4100 K	Moonlight, xenon
5000 K	Horizon daylight
5500–6000 K	Typical daylight, electronic flash
6500 K	Daylight, overcast
9300 K	CRT screen

armor to serve as a ground, though the practice was recently made illegal due to electrocution hazard.

For the first two decades of the 20th century, service was supplied at 30A and 120V, plenty for lighting needs but not much more. By 1920, however, appliances had become commonplace, and wiring gauges were sized to fit different load demands.

In the 1930s, the US Rural Electrical Administration lit up rural America with massive government projects. Knob-and-tube was written off as too expensive to install. Some original electrical systems in service for decades had run their service life, creating the first upgrade and remodel work for electricians. Typical service expanded to 60A and 240V. *Raceways* — embedding wire into a chase within baseboard trim — became a popular exposed retrofit technique. They were soon banned because they caused wood to ignite, and safer metal raceways are on the market today.

Many early systems featured exposed wire, as electricity was mostly retrofitted into existing structures. Exposed systems had aesthetic and functional problems, but concealed wire also proved problematic too. Troubleshooting was difficult, and the lime in plaster ate insulation, causing shorts. Electricians started snaking wire in conduits, often reclaimed iron gas pipes. While protected, the moisture and rust ate away cloth and paper insulation, causing copper electrical wire to arc with its conduit.

Longevity continues to drive innovation. By the 1940s, vinyl wire insulation made

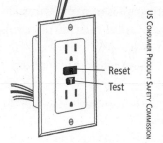

Fig. 14.16:
A GFCI receptacle always has a test and reset button.

Reset
Test

US CONSUMER PRODUCT SAFETY COMMISSION

conduits much more sensible. Grounding wires started surfacing in the 1950s, but still two more decades passed before they became commonplace. By 1965, the modern NM cable entered service, essentially the same product we use today. It's commonly called Romex after the Southwire Company product. Modern versions are able to withstand much higher temperatures — up to 194°F — than their old versions.

In recent years, electrical improvements have focused on limiting the risk of electrocution and fires. GFCI (Ground Fault Circuit Interrupter) receptacles are required where fatal electrocution risks were greatest; they were mandated near swimming pools and construction sites in 1971, on all outdoor circuits in 1973, in the bathroom in 1975, in the garage in 1978, near spas or hot tubs in 1981, in the kitchen since 1987 and in the crawl space/basement since 1990. In 1999, codes required hardwired electric smoke detectors, with battery backup capabilities, to be installed in every bedroom. Since 2002, bedroom circuits have required arc fault protections, which limits the risk of fires.

What You'll Find Wrong

The Hippocratic oath is of particular value in dealing with electrical: First, do no harm. Don't make a non-dangerous situation dangerous. Any situation offers three options.

1. Leave it alone.
2. Fix it.
3. Scrap the system and start fresh.

Each approach has its positive and negative qualities. The best solution depends on the scope of the work and on the condition of the existing wiring.

Before you buy an historic home or begin a major project, a general electrical inspection is imperative. As a homeowner or general contractor, you need to know what you are working with. Building inspectors cannot be relied on to check every issue with your electrical system to ensure it meets code, and this is particularly true when dealing with old wiring complications. It pays to have an electrician conduct a thorough examination.

Old wiring can be problematic. It can also be perfectly functional. A visual inspection can provide much of this information. When you open a receptacle, switch or *light box*, you can analyze the condition of wire sheathing and connections. Of course, such an inspection can also add stress to old wire, causing insulation to fray, bad connections to break and loose wires to arc. Old boxes tend to be small by modern standards and thus overcrowded. It's a particular problem with light boxes, which should generally be replaced when upgrading a fixture.

Old wire was often rated for temperatures up to 140°F, assuming its insulation is

Fig. 14.17-18: *Top, old wiring can be brittle, have deteriorated insulation or lack a ground. Any reason would be grounds for upgrade. Bottom, wiring for multiple switches can take up a lot of space, which old boxes might not have. New boxes are usually necessary for any significant remodeling.*

in the same state it was decades earlier. Many new fixtures require wire rated up to 194°F, so when tying new to old, be sure to read the fixture installation instructions and ensure compatibility with the wiring.

If you find a penny under a fuse, you can bet the circuit is damaged. The penny was used for overcurrent protection, preventing the fuse from breaking when it should, which creates a fire hazard. The presence of all 30A fuses indicates circuits being over-fused, since 30A currents are typically reserved for thirsty 240V appliance circuits. It's best to coordinate fuse size with wire gauge. You can also install S-type fuses, whose inserts prevent the installation of an oversized fuse.

Frayed knob-and-tube has lived its last days and must be replaced. But if the circuit is in good shape, is not being expanded and is not in an area being gutted, it's perfectly reasonable to keep knob-and-tube in good condition. Original splices should have a layer of friction tape, and any retrofit splicing should be confined to an accessible electrical box. Remember that insulation causes overheating, a particular problem with knob-and-tube. Do not insulate around or over active knob-and-tube, as the NEC prohibits it. Attic insulation over knob-and-tube increases the chance that someone will damage wire accidentally, causing an arc fire. Some local building code amendments still do allow insulating around knob-and-tube — notably California — as long as a sign is posted noting its presence. Still, check with your local official before pursu-

ing any insulation retrofit on top of old wiring.

Aluminum wire was in use from 1965 through 1973. It caused problems when connected to copper, caused oxide film buildup, increased resistance and caused significant fire risk. Aluminum wire has a silver hue, whereas copper looks more golden. The US Consumer Product Safety Commission offers prescriptive instruction on how to remediate problems associated with aluminum wiring. Options include repairing each outlet, switch and major appliance with a specialized connector or rewiring the entire home.

Many worry unnecessarily about *ungrounded electrical receptacles*. If the wiring is in good shape and there's no three pronged equipment on the circuit, there's limited reason to upgrade. Some circuits will never carry much current and may not need to be grounded. If the circuit will service larger loads, such as a refrigerator, an upgrade is warranted. Work with the designer, builder and electrician to plan out where heavy loads might be and run new wires to serve those sockets.

When planning a *ground retrofit*, no longer can the closest metallic pipe be used as a ground. Old systems often used this strategy, which can make your plumbing system live with current. This surprise then comes to light through a plumbing remodel, when the plumber's laborer cuts the grounding pipe, terminating access to ground and unbeknownst to him, makes the whole plumbing system live. Shocking, indeed.

New grounding wire can be run to an ungrounded socket, but it must follow the current-carrying wires and originate from the panel ground bus. At that point, you may as well run new Romex. Though it was common to retrofit a ground by tying a *cheater plug* to the receptacle's mounting screw, the practice is now considered illegal in most cases since the plugs create a false sense of security and shock hazard.

The simple fix is to install a GFCI on the ungrounded circuit. It still won't be grounded, but it will cut service if any fault occurs. The NEC requires a *No Equipment Ground* sticker on such a receptacle and any device on the load side of the receptacle.

Also, AFCI/GFCI breakers can be installed on ungrounded circuits such as knob-and-tube. The breaker will trip when an arc, often caused by melting insulation at loose terminals, occurs. A dual-listed AFCI/GFCI breaker allows you to replace two-wire receptacles with three-wire, and no grounding wire is required.

Amateur wiring is found in boxes, fixtures and electrical panels. One telltale sign is an excessive amount of exposed copper from the over removal of the wire's insulating sheathing. Professionals leave just enough wiring exposed — about half an inch — to tie circuits together with wire nuts. Too much exposure creates a fire hazard, particularly in an overcrowded box (also an amateur wiring clue). If the electrical panel looks particularly grim, it's best to have a professional sort it out.

A *circuit tester* can diagnose most possible problems. It indicates where current exists, where it does not and how much current is in a device. Note that current can

Electrical Design — Good

1. Install 12-gauge wire for receptacle and light circuits. Most electricians use 14-gauge to save cost, since the upgrade to 12-gauge might add $200-400 to the average house rewire. A 14-gauge circuit at 15A can have nine receptacles; a 12-gauge circuit at 20A can have 12 receptacles.
2. Install AFCIs for all bedrooms.
3. Install GFCIs in all wet areas, including kitchen counters, bathrooms and exterior sockets.
4. Hardwire interconnected battery backed-up smoke detectors outside each separate sleeping area. They must be interconnected so activation of one alarm will activate all alarms.
5. Install a receptacle on any wall longer than two feet, and ensure no part of a wall is more than six feet from an outlet.
6. Install kitchen receptacles separate from lighting circuits.
7. Install all appliances that require a ½-hp motor or greater — large refrigerators, dishwashers, pumps and air conditioners — on dedicated, separate circuits.
8. Install three-way switches at ends of hallways and at the bottom and top of stairs.
9. Install light switches on the wall adjacent to the latch side of the door.

travel in vessels other than wiring, and this is where it becomes particularly dangerous. HVAC ductwork can be live with 110V current. Absent ground fault protection, live ductwork can kill you. Most electrocution deaths occur from 110V residential

Electrical Design — Better

1. Mount fans in fan boxes because light boxes are not designed to bear a fan's weight and can create a fall hazard.
2. Retrofit watertight waterproof jackets for all exterior sockets.
3. Choose a large service panel, minimum 200A 40/40.
4. Do not extend or alter a non-code-compliant circuit, including to any ungrounded circuit such a knob-and-tube.
5. Install panel-mounted GFCIs, which have a longer service life than GFCI receptacles.
6. Conduct a walk through with your electrician or general contractor after framing inspection and mark placement for all electrical devices. Determine where furniture and electronics will go and adjust accordingly.

Electrical Design — Best

1. Wire bathroom light separate from the GFCI receptacle circuit; otherwise a trip might leave you in a dark room terrified after nearly getting electrocuted.
2. Specify the bottom of switches at 48 ½ inches AFF so sheetrockers only have to cut one board.
3. Keep the bath fan out of the shower and bath footprint where it can cause drafts.
4. Avoid fluorescents in the garage; they don't perform well in cold temperatures.
5. Do not mix wire types on a single circuit.
6. To make future upgrades easier, install fan boxes in bedrooms even if a fan is not being installed at present.

Fig. 14.19: *Group like wires together and color code the panel for quick referencing.*

7. Plan the electrical panel in advance, group like wires together, color code and legibly label the panel.
8. Place panel where it is easily accessible.
9. Install a whole house surge protector.

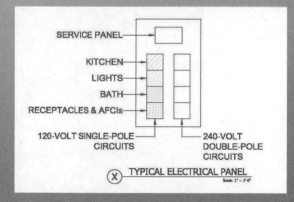

SERVICE PANEL

KITCHEN
LIGHTS
BATH
RECEPTACLES & AFCIs

120-VOLT SINGLE-POLE CIRCUITS

240-VOLT DOUBLE-POLE CIRCUITS

(X) TYPICAL ELECTRICAL PANEL
Scale: 1" = 1'-6"

wiring, not 220V, commercial or high-voltage situations.

If a system has been altered many times resulting in multiple panels and varying kinds of wires, and if the project includes significant remodeling or reconfiguration, it may be best to start over. The costs of straightening it all out can exceed a total rewire. I've turned back into single family homes a lot of Victorians that had been carved up into three or four apartments, and they almost always required a total rewire. Otherwise, the client would be stuck with multiple subpanels and a hodgepodge of excess wiring.

System grounding requirements have evolved significantly over the last 100 years. The system ground protects your house, wiring and equipment from high voltage surges such as lightning strikes. If rewiring, you'll probably have to add a ground rod to meet modern code.

Sustainability

When considering all the sustainability issues surrounding your electrical system,

Fig. 14.20-22: *Top, the porcelain knob and tube of the namesake wiring. Bottom left, a stud cavity has both knob and tube and BX armored cable. Bottom right, a gut job allows for easy rewiring with modern 14-2 Romex.*

it's imperative to understand the electricity's source, how it is transferred and how it is used. Each offers opportunity for energy savings, reduction of environmental footprint and longevity.

Source

Nearly all historic homes source their energy from the local utility. In 2006, over 91% of American electricity was produced via non-renewable coal, gas or nuclear power. Clean and renewable are increasingly desired, and there are a variety of ways to get energy from such sources. First, you can produce power on-site and either use it or sell it back to the power grid. Second, you can buy offsets which effectively replace whatever energy you use back onto the grid with clean power.

Photovoltaic power (PV/Solar) converts solar energy into electricity by exciting silicon cells. PV is long a fascination of the sustainable energy crowd and is often a primary symbol for sustainable building. The industry is roughly doubling production every two years, showing skyrocketing demand. PV/Solar is an expensive technology but one that can be worthwhile when considering the many benefits ranging from tax credits, early adoption of technologies, geopolitical forces, as well as setting an example for children.

PV generation capabilities are measured in kW, with a typical residential system being two to four kW and producing a portion of the home's use. The average home in the US uses 900kWh per month, 10,800kWh

Fig. 14.23: *This historic bungalow is one of the greenest old houses in my part of the US, featuring a range of technologies that take the home off the grid. The solar panels on the street façade, however, disqualified it from receiving tax credits. As this book went to press, this state's SHPO was reconsidering their position on roof panels, though even under the more lenient criteria being considered this particular design would still be considered too obtrusive to qualify.*

annually. A four-kW PV system would produce 4,000kWh per year, roughly 35% of the home's electricity. Most find that a PV system large enough to take a house *off the grid* is not cost-effective. So, particularly in urban settings where electricity supply is available 99.99% of the time, it's rare to see PV cover 100% of a structure's power needs.

As of 2008, pricing of around $8,000-10,000 a kW for PV/Solar was typical. Demand, a general fluctuation in silicon pricing, and the economy cause prices to fluctuate. Many manufacturers are working on lowering the cost of solar power, and in the next decade we should see a price drop, although for the last few years I've seen prices go up, somewhat counterintuitive to conventional wisdom.

Those who generate power on-site can either use all the electricity they produce or sell it back to the grid. While it is more exotic to use PV power directly on your home or to try to be off the grid, there are a few financial reasons against doing so. Many states offer superior returns for putting clean electricity onto the public grid. *Net metering* allows a single electrical meter to spin forwards and backwards, measuring the net electrical usage and production of the site. *Buy-all-energy/sell-all-energy agreements* allow a producer to sell all their clean energy to the grid at a premium, then buy it back at the regular electrical rate. In North Carolina, we can sell our clean energy at $.18 per kWh and buy it back at $.09, effectively buying electrons at half the price we sell them for.

Some choose not to sell to the grid, comforted by the knowledge that their PV energy is used directly in their structure. This is a bit silly; since electricity travels on the path of least resistance, any electricity produced from your PV panels and sold to the grid is most likely coming right back into the house to serve immediate demand.

There are massive tax credits available for solar installations. The US federal government offers 35% rebate on solar installations, capped at $2,000 a year, with overages moving forward to future years. States such as North Carolina offer an additional 30% energy efficiency credit.[1]

Interestingly, electrical upgrades are qualifying costs under historic tax credit guidelines, potentially offering an additional 30% credit. Each state varies in interpretation of what qualifies, and some may have exclusions disallowing a double tax credit claim for historic and energy efficiency rationales. There are some complexities involving depreciation, alternative minimum tax and recapture that are best reserved for a CPA, but where allowable 95% in potential credits can make quick work of return-on-investment math. Calculations typically yield a six to ten year payback using the energy credits. Depending on the state, historic tax credits can shrink solar paybacks to less than a single year.

Still, large roof panels on a historic home are generally frowned upon by historic districts. There is evidence this is changing, but any plan to install PV on an historic home warrants conversations with relevant authorities first. SHPOs tend to be supportive of solar panels as long as they are not viewable from the street. This limits installations to rear roof facades, which may not work on certain houses. South-facing houses may be nixed all together.

On the bright side, PV is a great long-term investment and revenue stream. As with many cost-saving technologies, payback periods and income generation can only start after a system is installed. As our installer says, "The best time to plant a tree is last year."

Renewable Offsets

Renewable energy certificates (RECs) are tradable environmental commodities that represent the benefits of renewable power over dirty production. They allow homeowners to upgrade to clean electricity without ever producing energy on their lot. Certificates verify that the electricity you use is replaced onto the grid with clean power. Renewable energy producers generate revenue from both the sale of electrons and RECs. The sale of the RECs helps make them cost competitive with dirtier producers. There are a variety of ways to buy RECs. Most utilities offer some form of clean power upgrade, often for $2-4 per 100-kWh block, averaging $15-20 per month extra. Be wary of this, however, as environmentalists quip that there is little value in supporting a *coal-for-less* utility's clean power program where any profits might go back into producing dirty power more cheaply. Some private companies offer the same service; you purchase RECs separate from your utility bill.[2]

Transfer

Demand management systems reduce usage during peak demand when energy production is strained. Peak power is the least sustainable because it is fueled by backup generators, which are the most inefficient and polluting. Demand management clients contract with utilities on time-of-use rates, which are higher during peak hours. Throughout the day, a computer monitors usage. The system lowers appliance loads during peak times by delaying tasks such as laundry and dishwashing until late in the day, when there is lower demand. The demand management system does not use less electricity, it just spreads it out more evenly. Settings are tweaked to minimize disturbance to occupants, and most occupants aren't even aware a system is in use.

Because such time-of-use rates are essentially commercial billing retrofitted to residential homes, such systems are best installed on large houses with large demands. Their installation costs are not worth it on smaller structures. Demand management systems are not available everywhere, but increasingly available in combination with *smart meters* that give homeowners real time data on specific electrical loads. Such information empowers occupants to turn off unnecessary loads and conserve energy. Xcel Energy of Colorado is now in the process of a massive smart meter installation. It's best to contact your local utility to see what options they offer.

Usage

At the end of the day, energy efficiency is much like water efficiency; it's ultimately left to the end user. LED lights left on all night still waste energy. Amory Lovins coined the term *negawatt* in 1989, outlining a plan to reduce electricity demand rather than increase production. Theoretically, negawatts grow supply by increasing efficiency of usage and spreading demand over a greater period of time. Measuring negawatts could create theoretical tradable units of saved energy. For example, shutting down air conditioners during peak demand means fewer power plants need to be built. It's the same concept used in today's demand management systems. Users can create negawatts by lowering peak loads and generally using electricity only when it is necessary.

The rest of sustainable electrical design is quite logical. Keep and rehabilitate old fixtures wherever possible. Don't demolish what you can keep. Use lights to illuminate spaces where needed, particularly work space, and avoid mood lighting or too much lighting in living spaces that do not require it.

Use and enhance natural light. Operable blinds, skylights, screen doors and windows all help use free natural forces to heat, cool and light your home. Any time you use natural forces, the electrical meter doesn't spin.

Strategies and Inspections

Electrical work should be done after plumbing and mechanical. Mechanical systems are big and bulky, but offer some flexibility in placement and duct routing. Plumbing systems, particularly waste lines, go where they have to go and offer little opportunity for alternative pathways. Electricians work with flexible wire, easily routed around obstructions. After electrical inspection comes framing inspection (to ensure that tradework penetrations did not impact the structural integrity of the home), followed by insulation.

There's no specific threshold of work that requires you to bring the whole structure to modern code. If you're altering something, that thing must be upgraded. You can change a receptacle or a light on the old wiring, but if you're reconstructing a wall, that wall needs to be upgraded to code. Due to their presence of water and daily use, kitchens and bathrooms should receive modern code-compliant circuits as part of any remodel effort.

Follow basic logic. New code is best, safest and most efficient. Where possible, upgrade to new code. Where it's not possible, at least understand the limitations of your system and don't make a bad problem worse or awaken a sleeping giant. After all, that giant may burn your house down.

Life and longevity are the two most overlooked aspects of sustainable electrical work. After all, there's nothing sustainable about death by electrocution. Nor is there any joy in watching all of the embodied energy in a home being celebrated in a blaze of glory. Do plan for the future. Use a large panel and stub lines for known future additions, remodels and reconfigurations so as to avoid unnecessary destruction a few decades on. Easily accessible chases are great ways to leave a blank slate for the future. Who knows what sort of wiring we'll be installing in another 20 years?

Conclusion

Old homes are green. Old home operations are not.

The way historic houses were built — with respect to quality, longevity and place — are all in synchronicity with sustainable principles of environmental footprint, recycling and resource efficiency. But the costs to operate such inefficient structures greatly hinders the aims of green building, and more notably, preservation. Improving these inefficiencies must be aggressively pursued to sustain the rebirth of our cities, the roots and engines of our society. The movement back to urban corridors can only be accelerated by doing so.

Old structures in the US are now being restored at perhaps their greatest rate in history. Yet it's a resettlement that often happens with little fanfare or press. Why? Perhaps because each structure is rehabilitated individually, organically, much like it was built in the first place. Such developments occur on an infinitesimal scale compared to the mass development that has dominated US construction for seven decades. Even so-called new urbanism, which aims to replicate all the benefits of old neighborhoods, in practice creates nothing more than planned communities, as artificial as their suburban counterparts. Though dense and urban, these developments still offer a minimal pool of floor plans and strikingly few customization options beyond color of the countertop. The nature of an old home, with its one-of-a-kind features, ownership chain and history, offers something such developments never can: American individualism.

We humans naturally gravitate toward the romance of rehabilitation. Is it because we want to be part of a legacy bigger than ourselves? Or is it because humans desire something that is uniquely theirs? Probably both. Custom new construction is undeniably unique and owned, but it fails to help us understand and develop a sense of place. Making an old home your own fosters your own individual identity while honoring past owners, occupants and tradespeople, too, making us one with our world and our past.

Perhaps the greatest benefit to society that historic preservation offers is its inherent role in a sustainable society. Rarely would one buy an old home solely because it's the green thing to do. But the mere purchase of an old home decreases traffic and fossil fuel use, increasing personal health and community. It decreases material load, increasing recycling. It rejects short-lived quantity in favor of longevity and quality. And it rejects new construction materials, while emphasizing use of already existing resources. As architect Michael Corbett quipped, "You know you're on the right path when the solution solves problems you weren't even working on."

But beyond the romance and individualism fostered by rehabilitating an old house, technical science must not be ignored. This is where proponents of both sustainability and preservation fail to meet and foster their goals. Conservation, the eventual goal of both movements, is not rocket science. But conservation takes understanding, effort and the constant desire to implement and improve.

You must arm yourself with the knowledge to make decisions in your own best interest, the best interest of the house, its community and all its future occupants. You've done this through your reading, but the breadth of information is so great that it requires you to seek out additional experts. In most regions, there are many to call on: general contractors, designers, architects, preservation consultants, restoration carpenters, masons, architectural salvage stores, preservation organizations, neighborhood associations, neighbors, listservs and books.

Finally, the axioms are simple. With respect to preservation, preserve. All of the tradework inputs into your home — from design through woodworking and windows — is special, unique and literally irreplaceable. With respect to sustainability, sustain. Your decisions today will ripple for centuries. You and your home's future occupants will be saving (or paying) incrementally for all the design and construction decisions you make today.

Constantly remind yourself that your home was here long before you, and will be here long after you are gone. There's no better way to honor an old home than to remind ourselves of that awesome responsibility and opportunity.

Appendix[1]:

Historic Rehabilitation Tax Credit Programs by State

Fig. A1

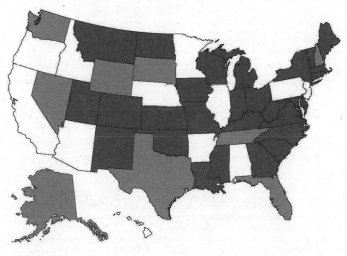

- States with income tax credits
- States that do not tax income
- States without rehab tax credits

Fig. A1-4: *National Trust for Historic Preservation,*
republished with permission.

Fig. A2

State	State Income Tax Credit	Contact
Colorado	20% credit for income-producing and homeowner properties. No aggregate statewide dollar cap, but per project cap of $50,000 per year. Minimum investment: $5,000. Carry forward: 10 years. DOI standards apply and work must be completed within 2 years of inception date of project. CLG can review and approve project. Sunset date for credit is 2009.	Colorado Historical Society 303-866-3395 http://www.coloradohistory-oahp.org/programareas/itc/taxcredits.htm
Connecticut	Commencing Jan. 1, 2008, 25% credit for mixed residential (includes owner-occupied and rental) and nonresidential uses where at least 33% of total square footage of rehab is for residential use. 5% add-on credit for affordable housing. Cap: $50 million over 3 years and $5 million per project. Carry forward: 5 years. Freely transferable either by direct sale or disproportionate allocation among partners of a syndication partnership. 25% credit for rehabilitating commercial or industrial buildings for "residential use." Cap: $2.7 million per project and $15 million annual aggregate. Carry forward: 5 years. Freely transferable either by direct sale or disproportionate allocation among partners of a syndication partnership. Minimum expenditure: 25% of assessed building value. 30% credit for eligible rehab of owner-occupied residence, including apartments up to 4 units. Eligible properties: National and/or State Register of Historic Places, must be located in areas targeted as distressed. Cap: $30,000/dwelling, $3 million statewide/year. Recapture period 5 years. Carry forward: 4 years. Minimum expenditure: $25,000.	Connecticut Historical Commission 860-566-3005 http://www.cultureandtourism.org
Delaware	20% credit for income-producing properties and a 30% homeowner credit. A 10% bonus credit applies for both rental and owner-occupied projects that qualify as low-income housing. Carry forward: 10 years. Homeowner credit cannot exceed $20,000. Credits are freely transferable either by direct transfer or disproportionate allocation. The credit to be claimed in annual progress-based installments with phased projects. Changes in 2005 increased the maximum amount of credits in any fiscal year to $5 million.	Delaware State Historic Preservation Office 302-739-5685 www.history.delaware.gov/preservation/taxcredit.shtml
Georgia	20% credit for eligible income-producing properties; 10% for owner-occupied properties in non-target area and 15% for owner-occupied properties in target area. Project limit of $5,000 in credits over 10 years. Transfer permitted by disproportionate allocation.	Georgia Historic Preservation Division 404-656-2840 www.dnr.state.ga.us/dnr/histpres
Indiana	20% of rehab costs up to $100,000 for qualifying commercial, rental housing, barns and farm buildings. Minimum investment $10,000. Per-project cap: $100,000. $450,000 annual statewide cap for commercial credits and $250,000 for owner-occupied residences. State register properties qualify. Carry forward: 15 years. Pre-approval of work required. No fees. DOI standards apply. Owner-occupied residential: 20% of rehab costs. Costs must exceed $10,000.	Indiana Department of Natural Resources 317-232-1646 http://www.state.in.us/dnr/historic/incentives.html
Iowa	25% credit for eligible commercial, income-producing and non-income-producing residential properties and barns built before 1937. Annual cap: $10 million State Fiscal Year 2008, $15 million SFY2009, and $20 million SFY2010 and each fiscal year thereafter. Cap: $100,000 per residential unit. Fully refundable with interest or may be credited for the following year. Minimum expenditure: 50% of the assessed value of the commercial property, excluding the land; $25,000 or 25% of the fair market value of the residential or barn property, excluding the land. Set asides: 10% of credits for small projects; 40% for projects located in Cultural and Entertainment Districts.	State Historical Society of Iowa Historic Preservation and Cultural and Entertainment District Tax Credit Program 515-281-4137 http://www.iowahistory.org/preservation/financial_assistance/state_tax_credit/ia_state_tax_credit.html
Kansas	25% income tax credit for commercial and residential properties. Carry forward: 10 years. $5,000 minimum on qualified expenditures necessary. Credit freely transferable either by direct transfer or disproportionate allocation. No annual program cap, and no per-project cap.	Kansas State Historical Society 785-272-8681 http://www.kshs.org/resource/statetax.htm
Kentucky	30% income tax credit for owner-occupied residential properties. A minimum investment of $20,000 is required, with the total credit not to exceed $60,000. 20% income tax credit for all other properties including properties owned by entities exempt from tax under Section 501(c)(3) of the Internal Revenue Code and state and local governments. Minimum investment of $20,000 or the adjusted basis, whichever is greater, subject to $400,000 per project cap. Credit is freely transferable. $3 million total program cap annually.	Kentucky Heritage Council 502-564-7005 http://www.heritage.ky.gov

Chart prepared by staff from Center for State and Local Policy.

Fig. A3

State	State Income Tax Credit	Contact
Louisiana	25% credit for income-producing properties in "downtown development districts." $5 million cap per taxpayer for structures within a downtown development district. No state-wide cap for commercial credits. Directly transferable. 5 year carry-forward for commercial credits. 25% rate for owner-occupied residences, adjusted down based on income. $1 million statewide cap for owner-occupied residences. Homeowner credit must be taken in five equal annual installments and is fully refundable. Minimum investment: $10,000 for income-producing properties; $20,000 for owner-occupied residences.	Louisiana Department of Culture, Recreation & Tourism 225-342-8160 http://www.crt.state.la.us/hp/ taxincentives.htm
Maine	20% credit for rehab of income-producing properties eligible for the federal tax credit. Minimum expenditures: same as federal tax credit. Cap: $100,000/year, per taxpayer; no annual statewide cap.	Maine Historic Preservation Commission 207-287-2132 http://www.maine.gov/mhpc
Maryland	20% credit for commercial and tax exempt entities under IRC 501(c)(3) and owner-occupied residences. Through FY2010, annual appropriation required for commercial credit; no annual cap for owner-occupied residences. Per-project cap: commercial – $3 million; Owner-occupied – $50,000. Competitive award process for commercial credits. No competition for credits for owner-occupied structures. No more than 75% of funds available in any year may go to any single jurisdiction. Minimum investment: $5,000 for homeowners and a rehab cost that exceeds the adjusted basis of the property for commercial applicants. Fully refundable.	Maryland Historical Trust 410-514-7628 http://www.marylandhistoricaltrust. net/taxcr.html
Massachusetts	20% credit for eligible income-producing properties. 25% credit for projects with affordable housing. $50 million annual statewide cap. Carry forward: 5 years. DOI standards apply. Permits direct transfer of credit or transfer by disproportionate allocation. Minimum investment: 25% of adjusted basis.	Massachusetts Historical Commission 617-727-8470 http://www.sec.state.ma.us/mhc/ mhctax/taxidx.htm
Michigan	25% credit for qualified rehab of historic commercial and owner-occupied residential buildings. Commercial credit reduces to 5% when federal 20% credit is claimed. Eligibility: National, state, or local designated properties. DOI standards apply. Minimum expenditures: 10% of State Equalized Value of the property. 5 year recapture period. Carry forward: 10 years. Commercial credit permits transfer by disproportionate allocation.	Michigan Historical Center 517-373-1630 http://www.michigan.gov/hpcredit
Mississippi	25% credit for commercial property and for owner-occupied residences. Upcapped credit with minimum investment of 50% of the total basis for commercial properties; $5,000 for owner-occupied residences. Carry forward: 10 years.	Division of Historic Preservation, Mississippi Department of Archives and History 601-576-6940 http://www.mdah.state.ms.us/hpres/ prestaxincent.html
Missouri	25% credit for commercial and owner-occupied residential properties listed in National Register or in a certified historic district. Minimum investment: 50% of adjusted basis of the structure. Rehab work must meet DOI standards. Carry back: 3 years. Carry forward: 10 years. No annual or per-project cap. Transfer permitted by direct transfer or disproportionate allocation.	Missouri Historic Preservation Program 573-751-7858 http://www.dnr.mo.gov/shpo/ TaxCrdts.htm
Montana	Income-producing certified historic properties automatically receive 5% state tax credit if the property qualifies for the 20% federal credit. Carry forward: 7 years.	Montana State Historic Office 406-444-7715 www.his.state.mt.us
New Mexico	50% of rehab costs for all properties listed in the State Register of Cultural Properties. Also applies to stabilization and protection of archeological sites listed in the State Register of Cultural Properties. No annual statewide cap. Per-project cap: $25,000 outside an Arts and Cultural District; $50,000 located within an Arts and Cultural District. DOI standards apply. Carry forward: 4 years. Pre-approval required.	New Mexico Historic Preservation Division 505-827-6320 http://www.nmhistoricpreservation. org/ PROGRAMS/creditsloans_ taxcredits.htm
New York	Credit equal to 30% credit of the federal credit value (approximately 6% of the rehab cost) for commercial properties receiving federal rehab credit. 20% credit for eligible residences listed on the State or National Register and located in federally-recognized distressed census tracts. Cap: $100,000 per commercial project; $25,000 per residential project with a minimum $5,000 investment. Carry forward: unlimited. Residential credit requires municipal authorization. Pre-approval and completed work certification required. New York State Historic Barns Tax Credit: 25% rehab credit for historic barns. Must be income-producing, built or placed in agricultural service before 1936 and rehab cannot "materially alter the historic appearance."	NYS Historic Preservation Office 518-237-8643 http://nysparks.state.ny.us/shpo/

Fig. A4

State	State Income Tax Credit	Contact
North Carolina	30% credit for historic homeowners and 20% for income-producing properties. Minimum investment for 30% credit: $25,000. Credit must be taken in 5 equal annual installments. Carry forward: 5 years. Minimum investment for commercial: same as federal credit. State tax credit of 30% or 40%, depending on location, for rehabilitating historic industrial buildings.	North Carolina Historic Preservation Office 919-733-4763 http://www.hpo.dcr.state.nc.us/tchome.htm
North Dakota	25% credit for eligible historic property that is part of a Renaissance Zone Project. Project cap of $250,000. Carry forward: 5 years.	State Historical Society of North Dakota 701-328-2666 http://www.state.nd.us/hist/RehabCredits.htm
Ohio	25% credit. No annual statewide or per-project dollar cap. Cap: 100 projects per year for two years through June 30, 2009. Applications accepted in the order filed; only projects that will result in a net gain in state and local taxes will be approved and ODOD must determine that the tax credit is a major factor in applicant's decision to rehabilitate the building or increase the level of investment in the building. Pre-approval of work required; DOI Standards for Rehabilitation apply. Fully refundable.	Ohio Historic Preservation Office 614-298-2000 www.ohiohistory.org/resource/histpres
Oklahoma	20% income tax credit for all eligible commercial and rental residential properties that qualify for the federal tax credit. Minimum investment: same as federal credit. No statewide or per-project caps. Carry forward: 10 years. Freely transferable for 5 years.	Oklahoma State Historic Preservation Office 405-522-4484 www.okhistory.org/shpo/shpom.htm
Rhode Island	30% credit for income-producing projects. Minimum investment must exceed 50% of adjusted basis of structure. No yearly cap, and no project cap. Freely transferable. Carry forward: 10 years. 20% credit for owner-occupied residential. Minimum investment: $2,000. Maximum credit allowable per-project per year: $2,000. Unused credits may be carried forward as long as property maintained. Interior work ineligible for owner-occupied residences. State register properties qualify.	Rhode Island Historical Preservation & Heritage Commission http://www.preservation.ri.gov/credits/
South Carolina	10% credit for commercial properties eligible for federal credit; 25% for other eligible properties. Minimum investment for non-commercial properties: $15,000. All credits must be taken in 5 equal annual installments. No statewide or per-project dollar caps. Pass-through entities (other than "S" corporations) may transfer credit by means of disproportionate allocation. Credits for owner-occupied residences limited to one per structure each 10 years. Pre-approval required.	South Carolina Department of Archives and History 803-896-6100 http://www.state.sc.us/scdah/hpfinancialinc.htm
Utah	20% credit for residential owner-occupied and non-owner-occupied. Cap: none. Minimum investment: $10,000 over 3 years. DOI standards apply. No fees.	Utah State Historical Society 801-533-3500 http://history.utah.gov/historic_preservation/financial_assistance/index.html
Vermont	All credits limited to commercial buildings located in designated downtowns or village centers. 10% credit for projects approved for federal credit. 25% credit for facade improvement projects, limited to $25,000 per project. 50% credit for certain code improvement projects, with maximum credit of $50,000. 9-year carry-forward. Credits may be transferred to bank in exchange for cash or interest rate reduction. Annual total program cap: $1.5 million.	Vermont Division for Historic Preservation 802-828-3211 http://www.historicvermont.org/financial/credits.html
Virginia	25% for commercial and owner-occupied residential properties. Reconstruction and improvements must amount to at least 25% of the assessed value for owner-occupied buildings and at least 50% for non-owner-occupied buildings. Carry forward: 10 years. National and state register properties eligible. DOI standards apply. No caps. Transfer by disproportionate allocation permitted.	Virginia Department of Historic Resources 804-367-2323 http://www.dhr.virginia.gov/tax_credits/tax_credit.htm
West Virginia	10% credit for buildings eligible for federal credit; 20% credit for eligible owner-occupied residences. Commercial buildings entitled to same carry-back and carry-forward provisions as are available for federal credit. Owner-occupied residences entitled to 5-year carry forward. Both commercial credits and homeowner credits may be directly transferred or transferred by disproportionate allocation. Minimum investment in homeownership projects: 20% of assessed value. No statewide or per project dollar caps.	West Virginia Historic Preservation Office 304-558-0220 http://www.wvculture.org/shpo/tcresoverview.html
Wisconsin	25% credit for owner-occupied residential properties. Per-project cap: $10,000. Minimum investment: $10,000 over 2 years; extendable to 5 years. 5% credit for commercial properties, not subject to statewide or per-project caps. Minimum investment: expenses equal to building's adjusted basis.	State Historical Society of Wisconsin 608-264-6490 http://www.wisconsinhistory.org/hp/architecture/index.asp

Endnotes

1 Sustainability

1. William McDonough and Michael Braungar. *Cradle to Cradle: Remaking the Way We Make Things.* North Point, 2002.
2. These guidelines are available free: REGREEN ASID & USGBC. *Residential Remodeling Guidelines,* 2nd ed. [online]. [cited June 1, 2009]. regreenprogram.org/docs/regreen_guidelines.pdf
3. These guidelines are available free: National Association of Home Builders. *Model Green Home Building Guidelines.* [online]. [cited June 1, 2009]. nahbgreen.org/content/pdf/nahb_ guidelines.pdf.
4. Alex Wilson. "Fixing our homes can help fix our country: an open letter to President Barack Obama." [online]. [cited June 1, 2009]. taunton.com/finehomebuilding/departments/taking-issue/open-letter-to-president-barack-obama.aspx.

2 Preservation

1. Stewart Brand. *How Buildings Learn: What Happens After They're Built.* Penguin, 1995, p. 88.
2. Robert E. Stipe, ed. *A Richer Heritage: Historic Preservation in the Twenty-First Century.*

University of North Carolina, 2003, p. xv.
3. Richard Moe. "Sustainability and Historic Preservation." Speech to the Los Angeles Conservancy, November 12, 2008. [online]. [cited July 28, 2009]. preservationnation.org/about-us/press-center.
4. See Appendix.
5. US National Park Service Technical Preservation Services. *The Secretary of the Interior's Standards for the Treatment of Historic Properties.* [online]. [cited June 2, 2009]. nps.gov/history/hps/tps/standards_guidelines.htm.
6. US National Park Service. *Illustrated Guidelines for Rehabilitating Historic Buildings.* [online]. [cited June 2, 2009]. nps.gov/history/hps/tps/ tax/rhb/.

3 Dollars and Sense

1. District of Columbia Office of Planning. *A Vision for Growing an Inclusive City: A Framework for the Washington, DC Comprehensive Plan Update.* July 2004. [online]. [cited June 4, 2009]. planning.dc.gov/ planning/cwp/view, a,1354,q,614757,planningnav,|32341|.asp.
2. See Appendix.

3. National Trust for Historic Preservation. *State Tax Credits for Historic Preservation: A State-by-State Summary.* [online]. [cited September 30, 2009]. preservationnation.org/resources/find-funding/additional-resources/taxincentives.pdf

4. Ibid.

5. Donovan Rypkema. *The Economics of Historic Preservaiton: A Community Leader's Guide,* 2nd ed. National Trust for Historic Preservation, 2005, p. 96.

6. "Getting the Right Insurance for your Historic Building." *Forum News,* Vol XV#4 (March/April 2009). For more information see also: National Trust Insurance Services website [online]. [cited June 9, 2009]. nationaltrust-insurance.org.

7. For simplicity's sake, I have used an interest-only loan in this example. If one chooses a traditional amortizing mortgage, the numbers will indeed change slightly, but the core points of this example do not. Principal payments are not deductible. When you pay down mortgage principal each month, you are simply paying yourself back. A principal payment lowers your checking account while lowering your loan balance by the same amount, a net-zero transaction to an owner's net worth.

8. Some states allow for mortgage interest deductibility on state income taxes as well, which would increase the savings.

9. While these credits are relatively easy to take (it is a simple line item in TurboTax), there are some complexities with the application, qualifying expenditures and length of time one can take the credits. You should discuss your situation with a preservation consultant and an accountant.

10. North Carolina Department of Revenue requires that credits to be taken over a minimum of five years and maximum of ten.

Unused balances carry forward each year, and begin to decrease in value in the sixth year.

11. The US Internal Revenue Service taxes rental income, and thus net rental income is more accurately calculated as $576 per month ($800-$224 tax). I have omitted rental income tax liability for the sake of simplicity.

5 Kitchens

1. US Environmental Protection Agency and US Department of Energy. Energy Star Recycle home page. [online]. [cited June 19, 2009]. energystar.gov/index.cfm?c=recycle.pr_recycle.

6 Living Spaces

1. This chapter focuses purely on the fireplace's aesthetic qualities. The structural and functional part of the fireplace and chimney are covered in the Exterior chapter.

2. Paint is covered further in the Exterior chapter.

7 Attics

1. US National Park Service. *The Secretary of the Interior's Standards for Rehabilitation.* [online]. [cited June 24, 2009]. nps.gov/history/hps/TPS/tax/rhb/stand.htm.

8 Exterior

1. Virginia and Lee McAlester. *A Field Guide to American Houses.* Knopf, 1984, p. 262.

2. John H. Myers, revised by Gary L. Hume. *Aluminum and Vinyl Siding on Historic Buildings: The Appropriateness of Substitute Materials for Resurfacing Historic Wood Frame Buildings.* US National Park Service, Technical Preservation Services, Preservation Brief #8. [online]. [cited June 26, 2008]. nps.gov/history/hps/tps/briefs/brief08.htm.

3. Washington, NC Historic Preservation Commission. Department of Planning and Development, Historic Preservation Design

Guidelines Section 8: Historic Preservation Commission Policy Statements. *Artificial Siding Policy Statement.* [online]. [cited October 11, 2009]. ci.washington.nc.us/client_resources/ planning/planning_historicartsidepol.htm.

4. US Environmental Protection Agency. *An Introduction to Indoor Air Quality: Pollutants and Sources of Indoor Air Pollution — Organic Gases (Volatile Organic Compounds — VOCs).* [online]. [cited June 27, 2009]. epa.gov/iaq/voc.html.

9 Structural

1. Nash, George. *"Renovating Old Houses: Bringing New Life to Vintage Homes.* Taunton, 2003. Chapter 3: Foundations."

2. The Sears Archive. *History of Sears Modern Homes.* [online]. [cited June 30, 2009]. searsarchives.com/homes/history.htm.

10 The Envelope

1. Chapter 11 describes these special windows in more detail.

2. Advanced Energy. *A Quick Reference on Closed Crawl Spaces,* p. 4. [online]. [cited September 25, 2009]. advancedenergy.org/buildings/ knowledge_library/crawl_spaces/pdfs/Closed% 20Crawl%20Spaces_Quick%20Reference.pdf.

3. International Code Council. *International Residential Code, 2006.* Section R806.4.

4. Cyrus Dastur and Bruce Davis. "Closed Crawlspaces Do Double Duty." *Home Energy Magazine* (2005 Special Issue). [online]. [cited July 3, 2009]. environmentalbuilding.net/docs/ cs%20article%20home%20energy%20mag.pdf.

5. Arnie Katz. *Survival of the Molds.* Advanced Energy website. [online]. [cited August 13, 2009]. advancedenergy.org/buildings/ knowledge_ library/indoor_air_quality/ survival_of_the_molds.html.

11 Windows

1. Daniel S. Morrison. "Get the Right Replacement Window." *Fine Homebuilding,* October/November 2004, p. 53.

2. Carl Elefante. "The Greenest Building Is... One That Is Already Built." National Trust for Historic Preservation. *Forum Journal,* Vol 21#4 (Summer 2007). [online]. [cited July 7, 2009]. vancouverheritagefoundation.org/Forum_ Journal_Summer2007_Elefante_ greenestbuilding.pdf.pdf.

3. John H. Myers. *The Repair of Historic Wooden Windows.* National Park Service Technical Preservation Services, Preservation Brief #9. [online]. [cited July 7, 2009]. nps.gov/history/hps/TPS/briefs/brief09.htm.

4. US Department of Energy. *Energy Savers — Storm Windows.* [online]. [cited September 3, 2009]. energysavers.gov/your_home/windows_ doors_skylights/index.cfm/mytopic=13490.

5. Joseph H. Klems. "Measured winter performance of storm windows." Lawrence Berkeley National Laboratory, Paper # LBNL-51453, 2002. [online]. [cited September 25, 2009]. repositories.cdlib.org/cgi/viewcontent. cgi?article=2373&context=lbnl; Baird M. Smith. *Conserving Energy in Historic Buildings.* National Park Service Technical Preservation Services, Preservation Brief #3. [online]. [cited July 7, 2009]. nps.gov/history/hps/ tps/briefs/ brief03.htm.

12 Plumbing

1. Water — Use It Wisely. *Water Conservation Tips, Facts and Resources.* [online]. [cited July 8, 2009]. wateruseitwisely.com.

2. International Code Council. *2009 International Plumbing Code.* ICC, 2009, p. 97.

3. International Code Council. *2009 International Plumbing Code.* ICC, 2009, unpaginated special definition.

13 HVAC

1. Matthew Teague. "Is Wood Heat the Answer?" *Fine Homebuilding* 198 (October/November 1988), p. 45.

14 Electrical

1. A comprehensive list of solar tax credits by state is available online: North Carolina Solar Center. *Database of State Incentives for Renewables and Efficiency.* [online]. [cited July 20, 2009]. dsireusa.org/.
2. For example: Renewable Choice Energy. [online]. [cited July 20, 2009]. renewablechoice.com; Sterling Planet. [online]. [cited July 20, 2009]. sterlingplanet.com; Green Mountain Energy Company. [online]. [cited July 20, 2009]. greenmountain.com.

Appendix

Harry K. Schwartz. "State Tax Credits for Historic Preservation." National Trust for Historic Preservation model public policies, October 2007. [online]. [cited September 10, 2009]. preservationnation.org/resources/public-policy/center-for-state-local-policy/additional-resources/MPP-State-Tax-Credits- 2007.pdf.

Glossary

ABS: acrylonitrile butadiene styrene.

accent lighting: a type of lighting that highlights plants, artwork or tables, typically using track lighting or adjustable recessed fixtures with a narrow, focused beam of light.

accessory dwelling: a second (or multiple) dwelling on a property with full amenities including private bathroom and kitchen.

ACH: air change per hour.

acrylic copolymer: a sticky, clear, flexible caulk, ideal for sealing dissimilar material such as wood to window sashes.

acrylic latex: a paintable all-purpose caulk that is easy to clean up but does not expand or move as well as others, so is inappropriate for caulking dissimilar material.

acrylonitrile butadiene styrene: pipe that is comparable to PVC, less toxic in retirement and offers more sound insulation than PVC.

actual cash value: a value, determined by an insurance adjuster, that values property loss by calculating comparable ("like kind") materials minus depreciation.

actual dimension lumber: framing lumber that is the actual dimensions of its name. i.e. a 2x4 actually measures 2 inches by 4 inches.

addition: any expansion of a home's existing building envelope.

air admittance valve: one-way mechanical vent that negates the need for a conventional vent through the roof.

air change per hour: the number of times per hour the entire volume of air in a house is replaced with fresh outdoor air.

air handler: the part of a central HVAC unit that conditions and circulates air, including a heating (and/or cooling) device and blower.

ambient lighting: a type of lighting that is soft, often dimmable, and designed to set moods for entertaining. It includes over or in-cabinet lighting, cove lighting above a soffit shelf, indirect pendants or wall sconces.

annual fuel utilization efficiency: an energy efficiency rating for fuel-fired heating systems which considers start up, cool down and other typical operating losses.

appraised home value: the market value of a property.

arc fault circuit interrupter: a circuit breaker which detects electrical arcs from high resistance, low current shorts, cutting power before a fire starts.

artificial siding: siding made from synthetics, including vinyl, aluminum, concrete or composites.

asbestos: a mineral fiber and known human carcinogen once extremely prevalent in building materials including insulation, fireproof siding, tile mastic, acoustic tiles and ductwork tape.

ashpit (aka ashdump): a place that receives ashes swept from the fire where they can be removed at a later time, through a cleanout door.

attached rental: a form of accessory dwelling.

backdraft: potentially hazardous combustion gases escaping into the house's living space instead of going up the chimney.

balloon framing: a stick-built house construction method that used manufactured dimensional lumber generated from production sawmills, that built the exterior envelope first (the balloon) followed by the interior floors and walls.

black water: the dirtiest wastewater, a term that is typically reserved for bacteria-filled toilet water but also includes waste from kitchen sinks.

blower door test: a test that determines a home's airtightness and primary leak points by placing a large fan in an exterior opening that pressurizes or depressurizes the structure.

boiler: a typically fuel-fired system used to heat water for hydronic heating. Boilers can also heat water for domestic uses through a tankless coil or indirectly, an application most efficient in cool climates.

British thermal unit: the amount of heat required to raise one pound of water (about a pint) 1°F. One Btu has roughly the heat content of a flaming match.

Btu: British thermal unit.

building envelope: the exterior components of a house that provide protection from outdoor elements. It is defined by the foundation, framed exterior walls, roof, insulation, penetrations and air-sealing materials.

butyl rubber: a sticky black caulk best used in sealing dissimilar materials, such as glazing to substrate.

buy-all-energy/sell-all-energy agreement: a contractual agreement between a micropower producer and an electric utility that allows the producer to sell clean energy to the grid at a premium rate, then buy it back at the regular electrical rate.

carry back: the ability to apply current tax credits against taxes due in previous years.

carry forward: the ability to apply current tax credits against taxes due in future years.

certified local government: a local government certified by the state historic preservation office with the capacity to administer historic preservation programs.

cast iron pipe: absorbs sound better than plastic pipe and is by far the most dimensionally stable pipe.

certified historic structure: a building which is a) listed individually on the National Register of Historic Places, b) located within a National Register Historic District and is certified as contributing to the district or c) located in, and contributing to, a local historic district that has been certified by the National Park Service.

certified rehabilitation: a rehabilitation which has been approved by the State Historic Preservation Office or the National Park Service.

CFL: compact fluorescent lamp, also known as compact florescent light.

cfm: cubic feet per minute.

chase: a structure built for the purpose of concealing systems, including electrical wire, ductwork and plumbing.

chimney cap: a protective detail installed at the top of a chimney to prevent water from draining into the chimney or animals from nesting inside.

circuit breaker: an electrical switch designed to automatically protect an electrical current from damage.

cistern: a container for storing water, typically part of a rainwater harvesting system.

clapboard: a wood siding installed in overlapping horizontal rows.

cloudy day effect: a lighting mood set (intentionally or accidentally) by the overuse of ambient lighting in lieu of all other lighting types. Such designs tend to make everything look bland, flat and without depth.

CMU: concrete masonry unit.

color temperature: a measurement of light's color chromaticity, measured in Kelvin (K).

compact fluorescent lamp: fluorescent lightbulb in the form of a tube that is twisted into a spiral.

composite trim: trim made from long lasting, dimensionally stable materials which match the look and feel of wood.

concrete masonry unit: a structural block made of concrete, commonly used for wall or pier construction.

condenser coil: the warm side of the heat pump/ refrigeration cycle, the outside unit of an air conditioning system.

conduction: the transfer of heat energy through matter, such as insulation.

convection: the transfer of heat in a gas or liquid by movement of fluid currents, such as the stack effect.

conventional (tanked) water heater: a mechanical device that heats and stores hot water for use when demanded.

cornice: an often ornate part of historic houses where the roof eave and gable rake meet.

cradle to cradle: a theory that human-made systems should follow natural cycles of essentially waste-free production so that all inputs into a system, process or consumer good can be recycled.

creosote: the buildup of carbon materials from the combustion of coal or wood tar.

cross-linked polyethylene: a plastic tubing commonly used for hot and cold water supply and radiant heating.

cubic feet per minute: the measure of a fluid through a stationary point in a one minute time period. The measurement is used by HVAC engineers when conducting a Manual D to properly size ductwork and fans.

damper: a mechanical device that opens and closes to regulate drafts.

dampproofing: a moisture management technique that keeps most water out of the foundation, but will likely allow water through in a torrential rain.

daylighting: the use of the sun for daytime lighting needs.

declining market: a mortgage underwriters' term for a decrease in housing prices throughout a geographic area.

dehumidifier: a device that takes moisture out of the air, intentionally making it dryer and lowering humidity.

demand management system: a computer control for electrical systems which monitors loads and automatically reduces usage during peak demand periods.

dewpoint: the temperature at which water vapor condenses into water or ice.

disproportionate allocation: the disproportionate splitting of a tax credit's value through a partnership, corporations' members or shareholders.

double hung window: a two-sash window where both sashes operate vertically. The dominant window type in residential construction.

double pane window: a window glass assembly where two panes of glass are separated by a sealed layer of gas that reduces heat transfer.

drip edge: an L-shaped flashing installed under the first course of shingles on the eave and at the rake.

dual-flush toilet: a toilet that provides two flush options: 1) a full-volume 1.6 gallon flush for solid wastes and 2) a reduced-volume flush when only liquid needs to be flushed.

duct blaster: a calibrated air-flow measurement system engineered to test the air tightness of forced-air ductwork.

ductwork: hollow units that carry tempered air into, through and out of a structure.

eave: part of the roof overhang that maintains a horizontal plane. Some definitions refer to the eave as any edge of a roof, including the rake.

efflorescence: a white substance on masonry, proof that moisture has pushed soluble salts in brick or CMU block to the surface.

electrical panel (aka main panel, circuitry panel, distribution board, panel board, fuse box or breaker box): the distribution component of an electrical system that divides a main power feed into smaller circuits.

electric-resistance heat (aka heat strip): the heat provided when high-resistance wires convert electric current directly into heat.

embodied energy: a value derived from the energy resources that have already been spent on a structure, including material, transport, labor, intellectual and financial capital.

EnergyGuide: a US Federal Trade Commission label that lists the predicted energy consumption of an appliance or HVAC system and compares the device's performance with other products in that category.

energy recovery ventilator: a warm-climate ventilator that captures outgoing cool air and transfers it to incoming fresh air through a heat exchanger.

Energy Star: a labeling system for the most energy-efficient products on the market.

EPS: expanded polystyrene, a foamboard insulation.

ERV: energy recovery ventilator.

evaporator coil: the cold side of the heat pump/ refrigeration cycle, the inside unit of an air conditioning system.

expanded polystyrene: a type of rigid foam insulation similar to styrofoam coffee cups.

extruded polystyrene: a type of rigid foam insulation often used in below grade exterior walls and underneath concrete slabs.

firebox: the chimney opening and planes directly adjacent to the combustion source.

fixed storm window: a non-operable storm window that is placed on the exterior of the primary window to reduce heat transfer.

flashing: a material, installed at transition points and usually made from sheet metal, rubber or plastics, which keeps rain and snow from entering a building.

floor refinishing: the process of renewing an existing floor by removing the top surfaces of the floor with progressively finer sand paper, then finishing with a sealer.

flow rate: the volume of a fluid that passes through a medium over a unit of time.

footing: the below-ground mass, generally made of concrete or brick, that supports the foundation wall and transfers the structure's load to earth.

forced-air heating: a heat distribution system where warm air is generated from a furnace or heat pump, then forced through a network of ducts.

Forest Stewardship Council: a nonprofit organization that promotes sustainable forestry practices.

formaldehyde: a harmful but widely-used chemical found in many building products.

foundation: a structure that transfers loads to earth.

framing: the process of forming a stick-built structure. Also the members that define separate rooms and carry floor, wall and roof loads to the foundation.

French drain: subsurface swale covered with perforated pipe and drainage gravel, allowing surface grading to remain natural.

fresh air intake: the supply pipe through which outside air is drawn into a building.

friable: tending to break down or disintegrate.

frosted glass: a decorative glass made by etching or sand blasting.

frost heave: an undesired situation where water freezes in poorly draining soil then expands, pushing the footing, foundation and house upward.

frost line: the depth at which groundwater is expected to freeze in a respective climate.

furnace: a gas-fired, oil-fired, wood-fired or electric system used to warm air for a forced-air heating system.

fuse: a circuit breaker featuring a thin wire that is designed to break when overheated.

geothermal: an HVAC system that uses the earth's constant ground temperature to heat and cool.

GFCI: ground fault circuit interrupter.

ghostmark: physical architectural evidence of a previously existing design that has since been removed or altered.

girder: a structural member that bears directly on the foundation.

glazing: the transparent or translucent layer of window or door that transmits light.

grading: the slope of earth, of particular importance around the foundation.

gray water: relatively clean water from plumbing sources such as baths, showers, laundry and bathroom sinks.

grille: the facing across a duct opening.

ground fault circuit interrupter: a circuit breaker which detects unbalanced currents from low-resistance, high-current shorts on failed circuitry and trips the breaker.

halogen lightbulb: an incandescent bulb that is generally specific to fixtures such as track lighting.

header: a structural member placed over a window or door void to distribute loads above around the opening.

heat exchanger: a device built to transfer heat from one material to another.

heat gain: the amount of cooling needed to maintain desired temperatures and humidity in controlled air.

heat loss: the amount of heating needed to maintain desired temperatures and humidity in controlled air.

heat pump: a heating and cooling system in which a refrigerant fluid is alternately evaporated and condensed by altering its pressure, moving heat from where it is not wanted to where it is.

heat recovery ventilator: a cold-climate recovery ventilator that captures outgoing hot air and transfers it to incoming fresh air through a heat exchanger.

HEPA filter: a very fine air filter that removes a minimum of 99.97% of airborne particles 0.3 micrometers (μm) in diameter.

HEPA: high efficiency particulate air.

HET: high-efficiency toilet.

high-efficiency toilet: a toilet that provides at least 20% water savings over the US federally mandated maximum of 1.6 gallons per flush.

historic district: a geographic area with a significant number of structures that share common features, history or associated architecture and contribute to an individual listing on a historic registry.

historic preservation: the movement that that seeks to preserve, conserve and protect buildings, neighborhoods and/or other items of historic significance.

historic replacement cost: an insurance term that allows for a property loss to be reconstructed in line with historic standards, including the restoration of original features.

home run plumbing system: a water supply piping system where individual plumbing lines run from a central manifold directly to each plumbing fixture without any additional joints.

house appreciation: the rise in an asset's value that the owner can realize through refinance or sale.

house deflation: a decline in a home's asset value.

HSPF rating: Heating Seasonal Performance Factor rating, the efficiency rating of a heat pump when operating in heating mode.

humidifier: a device that adds moisture into the air.

humidity: the measure of water vapor present in the air.

HVAC: heating, ventilating and air conditioning, also referred to as climate control or mechanical work.

hydrostatic pressure: the force that water presents against a foundation wall.

IAQ: indoor air quality.

incandescent lightbulb: a bulb that passes an electric current through a thin filament, burning it to the point where it creates light.

income-producing structure: a structure put into service for commercial, retail or rental use.

indoor air quality: quality of air in an interior environment, considering factors such as emissions of volatile organic compounds from paints and finishes, moisture presence, formaldehyde emissions from cabinets and mechanical ventilation.

infiltration: uncontrolled air leakage through cracks and transitions in the building envelope.

insulation: a material that has a resistance to transfer of energy - acoustic, electrical, thermal or otherwise.

interior storm: a non-operable storm window that is placed on the interior of the primary window to reduce heat transfer.

IRC: International Residential Code, the dominant building code for residential structures.

joist: a framing member that carries floor load and bears directly on girders.

KCMA: Kitchen Cabinet Manufacturers Association, creator of an environmental stewardship label for sustainable cabinetry.

KDAT: kiln dried after treatment, a desired process for pressure treated lumber.

kilowatt-hour: a measure of electricity consumption. One 100-watt lightbulb on for ten hours consumes one kWh.

knob-and-tube: an early electrical wiring system that used paper-and-cloth insulated conductors, porcelain knobs, tubes and cleats as wire guides.

kWh: kilowatt-hour.

laminated veneer lumber: an engineered structural wood product assembled from multiple layers of thin wood assembled with glue under high pressure.

laminate glass: a thin film placed between two panes of glass, used for security or soundproofing purposes.

latex paint: the dominant paint material in the market, widely available in low or no-VOC formulas that are better for the environment.

LCA: life cycle analysis.

lead: a toxic heavy metal common to paints made prior to 1978, and a near given in old homes.

LED: light emitting diode.

LEED for Homes: The USGBC's rating system for green home construction.

leverage (financial): the use of debt to enhance an investment such as a house. Home mortgages are typically leveraged 4:1, equaling an 80% loan to value.

life cycle analysis: evaluating a home's cradle-to-grave impact through raw material acquisitions, manufacturing, construction, maintenance and operation to demolition and retirement.

life cycle cost: the economic cost of a material over its expected life.

light emitting diode: a small semi-conductor diode that turns an electrical current directly into light in the direction the device is pointing.

load-bearing wall: a wall that transfers weight from a structure other than itself, such as floor or roof.

loan to value: a ratio expressed as the amount of mortgage debt relative to the appraised value of a home.

low-e: a microscopically thin layer of film on window glazing that helps reflect radiant heat.

low flow: describes water-saving plumbing fixtures such as toilets and faucets that use less than standard water flow.

LTV: loan to value.

LVL: laminated veneer lumber.

manifold plumbing system: an efficient water supply system that runs individual lines from a source manifold directly to each individual fixture.

mantle: a trim piece made to cover rough transitions between the plaster, floor, hearth and firebox.

Manual D: the prescriptive instruction for properly designed and sized residential ductwork.

Manual J: a prescriptive HVAC design checklist that addresses many variables such as local climate, insulation levels, the number of occupants and efficiency of major home appliances.

master suite: portion of the house where the adult owners sleep, get dressed and bathe, often consisting of master bedroom, master bath and closets.

MDF: medium-density fiberboard.

mechanical ventilation: a powered ventilation system that ensures adequate indoor air quality by using fans to exhaust stale indoor air.

medium-density fiberboard: a commonly used, engineered construction panel made from particles, wax or resin that is assembled under high pressure.

MERV: minimum efficient reporting value.

mid-span girder: a retrofit framing repair that installs a drop girder under overspanned floor joists, effectively cutting the span in half.

minimum efficient reporting value: the efficiency rating of a forced-air filter, ranging from 1-16.

mini split: a ductless forced-air HVAC system.

moisture: the presence of water, generally in trace amounts of liquid or gaseous state.

mold: microscopic fungi that are common in all households. Some molds are toxigenic and linked to *Sick Building Syndrome.*

museum effect: a lighting mood set (intentionally or accidentally) by the overuse of accent lighting in lieu of all other lighting types.

NAHB: the US National Association of Home Builders.

National Park Service: a US agency that regulates and manages parks, national monuments and historical properties.

National Register of Historic Places: the inventory of the US's most significant historical, architectural, engineered structures.

NEC: National Electrical Code, a US-based system of standards for safe installation of electrical wiring.

net metering: allows a single electrical meter to spin forwards and backwards, measuring the net electrical usage and production on a site.

NKBA: National Kitchen and Bath Association, an international trade association of kitchen and bath professionals.

nominal dimensional lumber: modern framing lumber that has actual dimensions smaller than its name: i.e. a 2x4 is actually 1.5 inches by 3.5 inches.

non-income-producing structure: a structure, such as a private home, that does not generate income.

non-vented crawl space: the incorporating of a crawl space into the conditioned thermal envelope, keeping moisture and exterior air from flowing under the home.

NPS: The US National Park Service.

oil paint: a longer lasting, thicker paint which offers a more historic feel. Oil is much higher in VOC/ppm, penetrates wood better, glues to objects, hides knots better and dries slowly, minimizing brush marks.

on center: a term used to describe framing spacing of joists, studs or rafters, typically 16 inches on center.

on-demand (tankless) water heater: a hot water heater that creates hot water only as it is needed. It has no tank and therefore no standby heat loss.

operating cost: the cost of operating an appliance, system or home, factoring energy usage, maintenance and repairs.

oriented strand board: a commonly used, engineered construction panel made from layered strands of wood bonded with wax or resin which is assembled under high pressure.

OSB: oriented strand board.

OSHA: Occupational Safety and Health Administration, part of the US Department of Labor which issues and enforces rules for workplace safety and health.

payback period: the length of time it takes for an investment to pay for itself.

PB: polybutylene.

PE: polyethylene.

PEX: cross-linked polyethylene.

photovoltaic: a system of panels and inverters that generates electricity from sunlight.

pier: a foundation assembly that supports girders and sill beams and rests on footings.

pier and curtain wall: a foundation wall assembly that features load-bearing piers separated by non-load-bearing curtain walls.

pier foundation: a building foundation made of piers instead of continuous walls.

platform framing: a stick-built house construction method where each story is built on its own platform.

PME: plumbing, mechanical and electrical, the three most common specialty-licensed subcontractors in construction. The letters sometimes appear in different order (i.e. MEP).

polybutylene: a rigid plastic pipe, prone to bursting, that is no longer installed in the US due to class action lawsuits.

polyethylene: a commonly used supply pipe used for water mains.

polyisocyanurate: a rigid foam insulation, typically with a foil facing on both sides, used in walls and roofs.

polyurethane expanding foam: closed cell foam insulation available in small pressurized cans used for weatherizing and insulating small crevices.

polyurethane foam: an insulation material made on-site by mixing polyol and isocyanate with an expanding blowing agent.

PVC: polyvinyl chloride, the most commonly found plastic in building construction, widely used as drainage piping, exterior decking and siding, window construction and electrical wire.

preservation: the movement that seeks to preserve, conserve and protect buildings, neighborhoods and/or other items of historic significance.

pressure-treated wood: wood that has been chemically treated to extend its life when exposed to outdoor elements.

programmable thermostat: an HVAC-controlling device that automates predefined temperature settings.

PV: photovoltaic.

radiant floor heating: a conductive heating system where hot water circulates through tubing embedded in the floor, creating a low-temperature radiator under foot.

radiation: the transfer of energy through electromagnetic waves, such as those produced by the sun.

rafter: a sloped structural member designed to support the roof deck.

rainwater: liquid precipitation from the sky, calculated as roof and surface runoff.

rake: the generally triangular edge of a roof on a gable end.

rebar: reinforcing bar.

REC: renewable energy certificate.

recirculating hot water: a system that delivers hot water with minimal delay, using a pump to circulate water to and from the water heater.

reconfiguration: a rearrangement of space or fixtures, typically determined during a space planning process.

reconstruction: recreating vanished or non-surviving portions of a property for interpretive purposes.

refrigerant: a compound used in refrigerators, air conditioners and heat pumps to transfer heat from one place to another.

rehabilitation: the repair of an historic property to meet continuing or changing uses while retaining the property's historic character.

reinforcing bar: a steel bar used to strengthen concrete and masonry structures.

relative humidity: the ratio of the amount of water vapor present relative to the maximum amount the air can hold at a given temperature.

renewable energy: thermal or electrical energy produced using solar, wind, hydropower, biomass or other renewable sources.

renewable energy certificate: a tradable environmental commodity that represents the benefits of renewable power over dirty production.

replacement cost value: an insurance term that stipulates that damaged items be replaced with items of *like kind and value,* a subjective method that may not be adequate for historic property.

replication: the accurate reproduction of a material, fixture or detail.

restoration: the depiction of a property at a particular period of time in its history, while removing evidence of other periods.

retrofit: the addition of new technology or features to older homes or systems.

RH: relative humidity.

R-value: a measure of resistance to heat flow. The higher the R-value, the lower the heat loss.

sealed combustion: a combustion system in which outside combustion air is fed directly into the combustion chamber and flue gases are exhausted directly outside.

Secretary of the Interior's Standards for Rehabilitation: The US federal standards that govern tax credit rehabilitation projects.

SEER: seasonal energy efficiency ratio, the energy performance rating of a central air conditioner or heat pump operating in cooling mode.

sheathing: sheet or strip material installed on the exterior of wall studs or rafters.

SHGC: solar heat gain coefficient.

SHPO: state historic preservation office.

silicone: the most flexible of all caulks, durable, longer lasting than latex, costing roughly two to three times as much.

sill beam: a structural member that is similar to a girder but rests on the exterior foundation wall instead of interior piers.

single hung window: a two-sash window where the top sash is fixed and the bottom sash operates vertically. A dominant window type in early US construction.

single pane window: a glass assembly where one pane of separates interior and exterior environments.

SISR: The US Secretary of the Interior's Standards for Rehabilitation.

sistering: the process of installing a additional framing member adjacent and parallel to a similar framing member.

skip sheathing: a roof or wall sheathing where gaps exist between the wood.

smart meter: an advanced electrical utility meter that records consumption in more precise detail, and more real time, than a conventional meter.

solar collector: a device for capturing solar energy and transferring heat to a medium that circulates through it, such as water, air or glycol.

solar heat gain coefficient: the measure of direct solar radiant heat that gets through a window. Lower SHCG values reduce cooling needs but limit passive solar heat gain in winter.

soldier course: an extra wide course of bricks at the bottom of the brick pier or foundation wall, a common footing design in old homes.

spray foam: see polyurethane foam.

square: a roofing term denoting 100 square feet of roofing, a 10x10 section; often the unitary method used in roof installations.

stack effect: a process caused by warm air's tendency to rise.

standby heat loss: wasted heat in a hot water supply that occurs even though no hot water valve is open.

state historic preservation office: the state level agency responsible for surveying historic properties, reviewing National Register nominations, reviewing the impact of development projects on historic properties (section 106 review) and supporting general private sector rehabilitations.

streetscape: the portion of the historic home viewable from the street, where architectural integrity of the exterior is most important.

strip sheathing: a roof or wall sheathing made from 1x lumber, generally installed in a diagonal pattern.

stud: the vertical structural member used for wall framing, typically 2x4 and 16 inches on center.

Studor vent: see air admittance valve.

subcontractor: an individual or business that performs part or all of the obligations of another's contract.

sub: subcontractor.

sump pump: a mechanism used to remove water accumulated in a sump pit, commonly placed at the low point in a basement, crawl space or exterior.

superinsulate: to insulate extremely well, either by exceeding recommended R-values or by minimizing insulation voids and thermal breaks.

supply system: the pressurized part of the plumbing system that supplies water to the home.

sustainability: the capacity to endure through a pursuit of longevity.

sustainable development: the ability of humans to produce a built environment for today's needs that does not compromise future generations' ability to do the same.

swale: a graded low point of ground used for drainage and management of stormwater.

syndication: the sale or transfer of credits from an owner with less tax liability to one with more tax liability, a common practice with income-producing federal credits.

task lighting: functional work light targeted at specific activity spaces, such as book reading or food preparation.

tempered glass: specialty glass that is processed to increase strength over normal glass.

thermal envelope: the heated and cooled area of a structure.

thermal mass: a heavy material such as concrete or stone that absorbs and holds a significant amount of heat.

TnG (aka T&G): tongue and groove.

tongue and groove flooring: typical wood flooring design where the floor is secured by nailing a tongue which is then concealed by the groove of the adjacent piece.

transferability: the ability to make an outright transfer or assignment of a tax credit to another person or entity.

triple bottom line: an expanded set of business values that aims to aspire, track and quantify the three bottom lines of financial, environmental and social success.

triple track storm: a modern storm window assembly that features screens and storms that can be easily swapped.

tuck pointing: the process of renewing a failing masonry mortar joint.

underground storage tank: a below-ground reservoir, generally used for fuel.

United States Green Building Council: a nonprofit, nongovernmental organization that provides sustainable building tools and benchmarks to the public and promotes and certifies green buildings.

USGBC: United States Green Building Council.

UST: underground storage tank.

vapor: airborne water in a gaseous state.

vapor diffusion: the movement of water vapor through a material.

vapor retarder: A material that restricts vapor diffusion.

variable air volume air handler: an HVAC return and blower fan system where the volume of air provided to conditioned space is varied to control comfort, energy usage and humidity.

VAV: variable air volume.

ventilation: the replacement of indoor air with outdoor air by way of mechanical fans or through building design elements such as ridge vents or windows.

vinyl: see polyvinyl chloride.

visible light transmittance: the measure of visible light that gets through a window.

VOC: volatile organic compound.

volatile organic compound: an organic compound that evaporates harmful gases into the atmosphere.

VT: visible light transmittance.

warm side: the side of the wall assembly that is warm.

waste management plan: a plan that formally addresses the organization and disposal of waste generated during construction.

waste system: the gravity and air pressure-based part of the plumbing system that removes waste from the home.

wastewater: water from toilets, showers, sinks, dishwashers and clothes washers that typically flows into a municipal sewer system.

waterproofing: a moisture management technique that keeps all water from entering the foundation.

WaterSense: a program developed by the US Environmental Protection Agency to promote water-efficient plumbing fixtures.

water table: where ground water pressure meets equilibrium with atmospheric pressure.

weatherstripping: a material designed to prevent heat transfer at transition points.

whole house fan: a large fan installed in a building's ceiling and designed to force cool air into the house and hot air into the attic by accelerating the stack effect.

wire gauge: a measurement of how large an electrical wire is, which determines the volume of electrical current the wire can carry with reasonable resistance.

work triangle: a tenet of kitchen design that states the range, sink and refrigerator should all be easily accessible to one another.

XPS: extruded polystyrene, a rigid foam board insulation.

References

Arnold, Rick. "Save Energy with Rigid-Foam Insulation." *Fine Homebuilding* 181 (2006), pp. 88-91.

"Bathroom Design: an Environmental View." Wasauna. [online]. [cited September 10, 2009]. wasauna.com/bathroom-design.html.

Berger, Diane. *The Bathroom*. Abbeville, 1996.

Bock, Gordon. "Past Perfect: Go With the Flow" *Old House Journal*. [online]. [cited September 10, 2009]. oldhousejournal.com/Past_Perfect/magazine/1388.

Bock, Gordon. "Plaster Repair Options." *Old House Journal*, November-December 2007, pp. 54-57. [online]. [cited September 10, 2009]. oldhousejournal.com/Plaster_Repair_Options/magazine/1467.

Bock, Gordon. "Stems, Seats, and Handles" *Old House Journal*. [online]. [cited September 10, 2009]. oldhousejournal.com/Stems_Seats_and_Handles/magazine/1418.

Bock, Gordon, and John Leeke. "Rehabbing Clapboards." *Old House Journal*, July-August 2007, pp. 31-32.

Brand, Stewart. *How Buildings Learn: What Happens After They're Built*. Penguin, 1995.

Buster, David. "Kitchen Design: Understanding the Work Triangle and Kitchen Layouts." Family Resource.com. [online]. [cited September 10, 2009]. familyresource.com/lifestyles/interior-design-and-decoration/kitchen-design-understanding-the-work-triangle-and-kitchen-layouts.

Cauldwell, Rex. *Plumbing*. Taunton, 2007.

Cauldwell, Rex. "Ten Common Wiring Problems" *Fine Homebuilding* 136 (2000/ 2001), pp. 114-119.

Cauldwell, Rex. *Wiring a House,* completely revised and updated edition. Taunton, 2008.

Chotiner, Michael. "Making Sense of Chimney Liners." *Old House Journal*, November-December 2007, pp. 36-41. [online]. [cited September 10, 2009]. oldhousejournal.com/Chimney_Liners/magazine/1465.

Davis, John Michael. "Exterior Trim Details that Last." *Fine Homebuilding* 141 (2001), pp. 60-65.

Davis, John Michael. "New Life for Old Double-Hung Windows." *Fine Homebuilding* 192 (2007), pp. 76-79.

DeWolf, Anne. "'Plunging' into the History of Your Bathroom: Trends in Bath Design Before World War II." *Northwest Renovation*. [online]. [cited September 10, 2009]. nwrenovation.com/13bathhistory.html.

Elefante, Carl. "The Greenest Building Is…One That Is Already Built." National Trust for Historic Preservation. *Forum Journal,* Vol 21#4

(Summer 2007). [online]. [cited July 7, 2009]. www.vancouverheritagefoundation.org/ Forum_Journal_Summer2007_Elefante_ greenestbuilding. pdf.pdf.

Elkington, John. *Cannibals with Forks: The Triple Bottom Line of 21st Century Business.* New Society, 1998.

Fisher, Charles K. and Hugh C. Miller, eds. *Caring for Your Historic House.* Abrams, 1998.

Fisher, Kathleen. "We Sing the Eclectic Electric." *Old House Journal.* [online]. [cited September 10, 2009]. oldhousejournal.com/we_sing_ the_eclectic_electric/magazine/1435.

"Floor Repair Pointers." *Old House Journal,* March-April 2008, pp. 60-63.

Freeman, John Crosby. "Let There Be Light for Everyone." *Old House Journal.* [online]. [cited September 10, 2009]. oldhousejournal.com/Let_ There_Be_Light_for_Everyone/magazine/1368.

Gaulkin, Zachary. "Has Latex Won the Paint Wars?" *Fine Homebuilding* 121 (1999), pp. 63-67.

Gibson, Scott. "Why Pay More for Paint?" *Fine Homebuilding* 198 (2008), pp. 63-67.

Gugelmann, Alice. *The Use of Spray Polyurethane Foam in Historic Buildings.* Unpublished UNC Master's intern paper.

Heesen, Jerry. "Wiring Your House for Today — and Tomorrow." *Fine Homebuilding* 145 (2002), pp. 92-97.

Historic Chicago Bungalow Initiative. "Bungalow Design Guidelines." [online]. [cited September 10, 2009]. chicagobungalow.org/filebin/pdf/B- LOW%20DESIGN%20Guidelines.pdf.

Howard, J. Myrick. *Buying Time for Heritage: How to Save an Endangered Historic Property.* University of North Carolina, 2007.

"Illuminating Choices." *Old House Journal,* January-February 2009, pp. 60-63.

International Code Council. *International Plumbing Code,* 2006 and 2009 editions. ICC, 2006 and 2009, chapter 12 and appendix C.

Johnston, David R. and Kim Master. *Green Remodeling: Changing the World One Room at a Time.* New Society, 2004.

Katz, Arnie. *Survival of the Molds.* Advanced Energy website. [online]. [cited August 13, 2009]. advancedenergy.org/buildings/knowledge_ library/indoor_air_quality/survival_of_the_ molds.html.

"Kitchen Confidential." *Old House Journal,* March- April 2009, pp. 59-63.

Kitchen, Judith L. Caring for Your *Old House: A Guide for Owners and Residents.* Wiley, 1991.

"Kitchen Lighting Fixture Types." Kitchen Remodel Ideas. [online]. [cited September 10, 2009]. kitchenremodelideas.com/let-the-light-in/ lighting-option/.

"Lighting: A brilliant new approach." *The Economist,* March 19, 2009. [online]. [cited September 10, 2009]. economist.com/sciencetechnology/ displayStory.cfm?story_id=13315818. (only available to Economist subscribers)

Lord, Peter and Noelle. "A Clearer View of Floor Finishes." *Old House Journal.* [online]. [cited September 15, 2009]. oldhousejournal.com/A_ Clearer_View/ magazine/1040.

Lord, Peter and Noelle. "Repairing Plaster Cracks." *Old House Journal.* [online]. [cited September 15, 2009]. oldhousejournal.com/Repairing_ Plaster_Cracks/magazine/1072.

Lotz, Bill. "A brief history of Thermal Insulation." *RSI,* February 1, 2006. [online]. [cited September 15, 2009]. rsimag.com/rsi/article/ articleDetail.jsp?id=312975.

Macneil, Gregory. "Getting Under Second Skins." *Old House Journal,* July-August 2007, pp. 48- 53. [online]. [cited September 15, 2009]. oldhousejournal.com/GettingUnder SecondSkins/magazine/ 1445.

Martin, Clare. "The Glass Menagerie." *Old House Journal,* May-June 2008, pp. 60-65. [online].

[cited September 15, 2009]. oldhousejournal.com/magazine/1506

May, Jeffrey C. *My House is Killing Me!: The Home Guide for Families with Allergies and Asthma.* Johns Hopkins, 2001.

McAlester, Virginia and Lee. *A Field Guide to American Houses.* Knopf, 1984.

McCluskey, Eileen. "Retrofitting Radiant Heating." *This Old House,* December 2007, pp. 51-53. [online]. [cited September 15, 2009]. thisoldhouse.com/toh/article/ 0,,20163505,00.html

McKee, Harley J. *Introduction to Early American Masonry.* Preservation, 1973.

Minnesota Blue Flame Gas Association. "Humidity and the Indoor Environment." [online]. [cited September 10, 2009]. blue-flame.org/datasheets/humidity.html.

Myers, John H. *The Repair of Historic Wooden Windows.* National Park Service Technical Preservation Services, Preservation Brief #9. [online]. [cited July 7, 2009]. nps.gov/history/hps/TPS/briefs/brief09.htm.

Nash, George. *Renovating Old Houses: Bringing New Life to Vintage Homes.* Taunton, 2003.

National Association of Home Builders. *Model Green Home Building Guidelines.* [online]. [cited June 1, 2009]. nahbgreen.org/ content/pdf/nahb_ guidelines.pdf.

Natural Resources Canada. *Energy Efficiency.* [online]. [cited September 29, 2009]. nrcan.gc.ca/eneene/effeff/resintro-eng.php.

OHJ Editorial Staff. "35 Tips for Restoring Old Houses" *Old House Journal.* [online]. [cited September 10, 2009]. oldhousejournal.com/35_tips_for_restoring_ old_houses/magazine/1545.

Pettit, Betsy. "Remodeling for Energy Efficiency." *Fine Homebuilding* 194 (2008), pp. 51-57.

Popejoy, Clifford A. "Is Your Old Wiring Safe?" *Fine Homebuilding* 169 (2005), pp. 74-77.

Powell, Jane, and Linda Svendsen. *Bungalow Kitchens.* Gibbs-Smith, 2000.

"Preservation Goes Green." *Old House Journal,* March-April 2008, p. 14.

Primoli, Mark. "Tax Aspects of the Historic Preservation Tax Incentives — Frequently Asked Questions." National Park Service, Historic Preservation Tax Incentives Program. [online]. [cited September 10, 2009]. nps.gov/history/hps/tps/tax/download/IRS_ FAQs.pdf.

REGREEN ASID & USGBC. *Residential Remodeling Guidelines,* 2nd ed. [online]. [cited June 1, 2009]. regreenprogram.org/docs/regreen_ guidelines.pdf.

Roberts, Jennifer. *Good Green Homes.* Gibbs Smith, 2003.

Rodda, John and Lucio Ubertini, eds. *The Basis of Civilization — Water Science?* International Association of Hydrological Sciences, 2004. [online]. [cited September 15, 2009]. books.google.com/books?id= JI65-MygMm0C&printsec= frontcover.

Rodriguez, Mario. "A New Way to Repair Old Plaster." *Fine Homebuilding* 103 (1996), pp. 90-93.

Rypkema, Donovan. "Culture, Historic Preservation and Economic Development in the 21st Century." Leadership Conference on Conservancy and Development, September 1999. [online]. [cited September 15, 2009]. columbia.edu/cu/ china/DRPAP.html.

Rypkema, Donovan. *The Economics of Historic Preservation: A Community Leader's Guide.* National Trust for Historic Preservation, 2005.

Schmickle, William E. *The Politics of Historic Districts: A Primer for Grassroots Preservation.* AltaMira, 2006.

Schwartz, Harry K. "State Tax Credits for Historic Preservation." National Trust for Historic Preservation model public policies, October

2007. [online]. [cited September 10, 2009]. preservationnation.org/resources/public-policy/center-for-state-local-policy/additional-resources/MPP-State-Tax-Credits-2007.pdf.

Schwartz, Max, and Hamid Azizi. *Builder's Guide to Drainage & Retaining Walls*. Builder's, 2007.

Sedovic, Walter, and Jill H. Gotthelf. "What Replacement Windows Can't Replace: The Real Cost of Removing Historic Windows." *Journal of Preservation Technology*, Vol. 36#4 (2005), pp. 25-29.

Shapiro, David E. "Working With Old Wiring." *Fine Homebuilding* 120 (1998/ 1999), pp. 112-115.

Sherman, Max H. "Houses Need to Breathe… Right?" *Fine Homebuilding*, April-May 2006. [online]. [cited September 15, 2009]. taunton.com/finehomebuilding/PDF/Free/021178064.pdf.

Sinick, Debra. "How Many Trees Does it Take to Build a 2000 Square Foot Home and Other Amazing Facts." Eastside Real Estate Buzz, July 26, 2007. [online]. [cited September 10, 2009]. eastsiderealestatebuzz.com/2007/07/26/how-many-trees-does-it-take-to-build-a-2000-square-foot-home-and-other-amazing- facts/.

Siskos, Catherine. "The State of Old-House Real Estate." *Old House Journal*, November-December 2006, pp. 62-65. [online]. [cited September 15, 2009]. oldhousejournal.com/magazine/2006/dec/state-of-old-house.shtml.

Skaates, George. "Roughing in Drain Lines." *Fine Homebuilding* 39 (1987), pp. 33-37.

Sommer, Robin Langley. *The Old House Book*. Barnes and Noble, 1999.

South, David B. "'R' Fairy Tale: The Myth of Insulation Values." Monolithic Dome Institute. [online]. [cited September 22, 2009]. static.monolithic.com/plan-design/rfairy/index.html.

Stephen, George. *New Life for Old Houses: A Guide to Restoration and Repair*. Preservation Press, 1989.

Stipe, Robert E., ed. *A Richer Heritage: Historic Preservation in the Twenty-First Century*. University of North Carolina, 2003.

Susanka, Sarah. *The Not So Big House: A Blueprint for the Way We Really Live*. Taunton, 2001.

Susanka, Sarah. *Not So Big Remodeling: Tailoring Your Home for the Way You Really Live*. Taunton, 2009.

"Taking the Mystery Out of Kitchen Design." ServiceMagic.com. [online]. [cited September 10, 2009]. docs.hdpi.com/ PE-Links/articles/kitchen-mystery.html.

Teague, Matthew. "Is Wood Heat the Answer?" *Fine Homebuilding* 198 (October/ November 1988), pp. 40-45.

Teague, Matthew. "Kitchen Lighting Design." *Fine Homebuilding* 199 (Kitchens & Baths), pp. 67-73.

Tschoepe, Ray. "The Short Course on Historic Mortar." *Old House Journal*, January-February 2008, pp. 56-57.

Tschoepe, Ray. "To Build a Better Porch." *Old House Journal*, July-August 2007, pp. 54-55.

Tschoepe, Ray. "Weatherstripping 101: Prepare Your House for Winter." *Old House Journal*, November-December 2008, pp. 68-71.

US Department of Energy. *Energy Efficiency and Renewable Energy*. [online]. [cited September 29, 2009] eere.energy.gov.

US Department of Housing and Urban Development. *Lead Paint Safety: A Field Guide for Painting, Home Maintenance, and Renovation Work*. [online]. [cited September 10, 2009]. hud.gov/offices/lead/training/ LBPguide.pdf

US Energy Information Administration. "Residential Energy Consumption Survey." [online]. [cited September 10, 2009]. eia.doe.gov/emeu/recs/contents.html.

Venolia, Carol and Kelly Lerner. *Natural Remodeling for the Not-So-Green House: Bringing Your Home into Harmony with Nature.* Lark, 2006.

Wheeler, Elizabeth J. "Saving Structural Brickwork." *Old House Journal.* [online]. [cited September 22, 2009]. oldhousejournal.com/saving_brickwork/magazine/1454.

Whitehead, Randall. "Designing Balanced Lighting." *Journal of Light Construction,* November 2001. [online]. [cited September 22, 2009]. jlconline.com. Archive. Go to November 2001.

Wolfe, Sarah. *Historic Windows and Energy Efficiency.* Unpublished UNC Master's intern paper.

Young, Robert A. *Historic Preservation Technology: A Primer.* Wiley, 2008.

Zukowski, Karen. "Sparkle & Glow." *Old House Journal.* [online]. [cited September 22, 2009]. oldhousejournal.com/sparkle_glow/magazine/1481.

Index

Page numbers in **bold** indicate photographs and figures.

About the Author

Aaron Lubeck is president at Trinity Design/Build, a restoration contractor and preservation consultancy specializing in retrofitting sustainable building practices into old houses. As a member of the United States Green Building Council and the National Trust for Historic Preservation, Aaron prides himself on approaching general contracting and preservation from an academic angle, with an emphasis on environmental impact and building science. He's a specialist in using historic tax credit incentives to fund green building features. In addition to receiving numerous preservation awards under his leadership, Trinity designed and restored some of the first historic buildings to be featured on North Carolina Sustainable Energy Association's green building tour, including the company's 1927 headquarters which achieved USGBC's highest rating of LEED platinum.

Aaron has authored trade articles and lectured on topics related to sustainability and historic preservation, including building redevelopment, tax credit policy, green marketing, insulation retrofits, window rehabilitation and old urbanism. He is a member of the Business Accelerator for Sustainable Entrepreneurship (BASE) program at the University of North Carolina's Kenan-Flagler Business School.

Aaron Lubeck lives in Durham, North Carolina with his wife and two children.

If you have enjoyed *Green Restorations* you might also enjoy other

BOOKS TO BUILD A NEW SOCIETY

Our books provide positive solutions for people who want to
make a difference. We specialize in:

Sustainable Living • Green Building • Peak Oil • Renewable Energy
Environment & Economy • Natural Building & Appropriate Technology
Progressive Leadership • Resistance and Community
Educational and Parenting Resources

New Society Publishers

ENVIRONMENTAL BENEFITS STATEMENT

New Society Publishers has chosen to produce this book on Enviro 100, recycled paper
made with **100% post consumer waste**, processed chlorine free, and old growth
free.

For every 5,000 books printed, New Society saves the following resources:[1]

36	Trees
3,255	Pounds of Solid Waste
3,581	Gallons of Water
4,671	Kilowatt Hours of Electricity
5,917	Pounds of Greenhouse Gases
25	Pounds of HAPs, VOCs, and AOX Combined
9	Cubic Yards of Landfill Space

[1]Environmental benefits are calculated based on research done by the Environmental Defense Fund and
other members of the Paper Task Force who study the environmental impacts of the paper industry.

For a full list of NSP's titles, please call **1-800-567-6772** *or check out our website at:*

www.newsociety.com

NEW SOCIETY PUBLISHERS